The END of DEATH

The deeper teachings of A Course in Miracles

NOUK SANCHEZ

VOLUME ONE:
THE DEVELOPMENT OF TRUST

*With additional text on embodiment
and a guided embodiment meditation audio
by Stacy Sully
(meditation audio is downloadable from www.EndOfDeath.com)*

gentle
joyous
INDUSTRIES

ISBN 10: 0-9838421-0-8
ISBN 13: 978-0-9838421-0-1
Library of Congress Control Number: 2013955886
Printed in the United States of America and in the UK

Cover painting created by: Luis Tillus
Edited by: Carrie Triffet

Published by: Gentle Joyous Industries
Ventura, CA 93003
www.gentlejoyous.com

ABSOLUTE CERTAINTY The DEATH of DEATH

"Your newborn purpose is nursed by angels, cherished by the Holy Spirit and protected by God Himself. It needs not your protection; it is [yours.] For it is deathless, and within it lies the end of death."
T-19.IV.C.9:4-6

ACKNOWLEDGEMENTS

Thanks to: Tomas Vieira, Rikki Vieira, Nick Sanchez, Sparo Arika Vigil, Stacy Sully, Dr. Norma Clarke, Michele Longo O'Donnell, and to Annelies Ekeler for the inspiration of the ego-egg symbol that appears on the cover. Thanks to Carrie Triffet for her gifts of faith and patience in editing this book; to Steve Wood for his divinely inspired composition of the Aramaic Lord's Prayer (found in the audiobook, which he also produced), and to Sparo Vigil for her devotion and trust in learning to sing this powerful prayer. Thanks also to Connie Salles for the AWAKENS acronym.

I'd also like to thank the following people for their generous financial support. Their donations made all three versions (hard copy, e-book and audio book) of this book possible: Phill Palmer, Nina Martins, Anne Reynolds, Joan Coghlan, Sonja Spahn, Joel Brass, Ray Dudenbostel, Sandie Rooke, Sally Patton, Lisa Kriedman, Jacalyn Hunt, Sue Edgecombe and Chris, Robert Deery, Deborah Malaga, Eric Pearson, Rev. Myron Jones, Calico Hickey, Elisabeth Light, Maho Hayashi, Sandra Newell, Warren Cotton, Eric Pearson and Mary Ann Keena.

This book contains diagrams, exercises, Atonement Process text and meditations that are available in printable format from the *End of Death* website. A guided (audio) embodiment meditation by Stacy Sully, and audio versions of the meditations included within the text of this book are also available at this same link: *www.EndOfDeath.com*

CONTENTS

CHAPTER FOUR

CHAPTER FIVE

CHAPTER EIGHT

CHAPTER NINE

CHAPTER TEN

CHAPTER ELEVEN

WARNING!

The End of Death will pry open the deepest, most sacred hidden idol cherished by the ego thought system. This book exposes our greatest, most powerful unconscious motivator for separation and suffering since the beginning of time. Death is this secret motivator, and our unconscious attraction to it runs extremely deep.

The End of Death, presents a radically new understanding of the life-changing teachings gifted us through *A Course in Miracles*. The *Course* is an unparalleled, multi-dimensional spiritual teaching. In *The End of Death*, the holographic and immensely powerful message of the *Course* is clearly decoded for all to see and experience firsthand.

The explanations and exercises found within this book invite the reader to experience profound transformation. This transformation heralds a complete reality reversal from a life of fear to one of exuberant Love and joy.

Death is the underpinning of the ego's world. Without death, there could be no ego, no fear, no sickness, suffering or lack. Everything found in our world appears to be given life because of our rock-solid belief in death.

Death is the concept at the very core of the ego thought system, as the *Course* tells us. We are asked by the *Course* to look closely and realize the very notion of death is an epic ego hoax. *The End of Death* pierces through our dense layers of ego resistance to recognize this truth for our self, thereby unmasking the hoax once and for all.

PROLOGUE: NOUK AND TOMAS

"No matter what and no matter who might seem to come between us, let us never abandon each other."

After twenty years of studying and living *A Course in Miracles* principles, my soul buddy and teaching partner Tomas Vieira and I had reached a particularly miraculous state of union in our relationship. Having transformed a highly dysfunctional special relationship into a totally forgiven Holy Relationship, we finally enjoyed a remarkable level of Love that had eluded us previously. This kind of Love (with a capital "L") could never be threatened by anyone or anything. Not even by death.

As this amazingly conscious and indestructible Love grew, we discovered it transferred to all our relationships including everyone and everything from our past. The catalysts for these miraculous transformations were the abundant and consistent forgiveness opportunities we offered to each other!

If you are familiar with *A Course in Miracles*, you know it is a path to awaken from suffering that rests exclusively on a practice of forgiveness. This is not regular forgiveness, but a quantum form of forgiveness—one with the ability to completely eradicate all forms of suffering. While forgiveness is the means by which we awaken from all forms of adversity, the Holy Relationship is the key conduit through which we miraculously zip past eons of unnecessary pain. All we need is one completely forgiven relationship (or at least the willingness to accomplish it). And this is how we learn real Love is, indeed, indestructible and eternal. At the same time we recognize special love, (the kind of love the world accepts as real, spelled here with a small "l"), as the counterfeit variety.

There is an easy way to tell which is which. If you experience a love that can change, that can be threatened by another, or by a situation, this is not Love. It might pass for human love, however it's at the other end of the real Love scale. Therefore no matter how it masquerades as real love, it's actually hate in disguise. This kind of special, conditional love is what keeps the world endlessly cycling from birth to death. Special love is the kind of love that leads to heartbreak, destruction and separation.

Miraculous healing comes from our commitment to un-learn the ego's brand of special love, and embrace the Holy Relationship's goal of forgiveness. Take heart! It's our degree of commitment that is important, not how many times we seem to fail in achievement of this goal. Forgiveness is an ongoing process. And the consistent truth is there is only *one* to forgive: Our own self, for imagining there could exist anything other than perfect Love.

Tomas and I were determined to discover the nature of perfect Love. Our relationship was born on a balmy night in 1984. As we lay on the warm sand of a tropical Australian beach, we were inspired to express our deeply cherished intent to experience real, indestructible Love—an authentic, divinely eternal Love, a Love that could never be threatened. A Love that went beyond the personal. And somewhere deep down, we seemed to know this process of un-learning special love would indeed take us to the eternally changeless Love within.

On that miraculous night with God as Witness, we were inspired to commit to a profound and life-changing promise— one that we continue to remain faithful to even after seeming death. The vow we exchanged was this: "No matter what and no matter who might seem to come between us, let us never abandon each other." And as we spoke these words in unison, we felt our powerful commitment reverberate throughout the universe.

Tomas and I learned much about the ego's obsession with form instead of content. *A Course in Miracles* is a pathway that exposes all the hidden places where the ego obscures real Love by focusing on form to the exclusion of content. For instance, we may love another for what they do (form) rather than for who they are (content). So if they stop doing what we want, or start doing something we don't like, we withdraw our love. Special love is based on this unspoken assumption: *I will love you while you meet my ego needs. And if you love me, then you will do what I want.*

The problem is it's the ego that sets these conditions and makes these demands, not the Holy Self. This is not real Love, but the ego's foundationless pseudo-love. And it is actually a form of destruction, and therefore separation.

During our twenty-six years together, Tomas and I grew closer than we could possibly have imagined. To transform our relationship, we were guided to let go of our marriage (form) in order to save our relationship (content). This was deeply inspired guidance specific to both of us at the time, although this decision is certainly not necessary for most people. Through continuous trust in the Holy Spirit, we released the original form and roles of our relationship, yet kept and nourished the content, which allowed our Love to grow exponentially. In December of 2009, we renewed our original vow from 1984: *"No matter what and no matter who might seem to come between us, let us never abandon each other."*

Tomas developed cancer and passed one year later, in December of 2010. Miraculously, although his body is no longer present, our communication remains unbroken. While this may sound strange, Tomas and I continue to work together to this day, and our work is far more efficient and powerful now that he's free of the unrelenting distractions of a body.

I have a body and he now does not, so his passing presented us the opportunity to undergo yet another change in the form of our relationship. We both knew Tomas' illusory change in form would not threaten our commitment to jointly explore Jesus' deeper teachings in *A Course in Miracles*. In fact, we knew this change in form was the grandest of all opportunities we had encountered so far, as it would provide us the necessary catalyst to miraculously deepen our understanding of the *Course*'s teachings on how to become a miracle worker.

The fundamental message of these deeper teachings is this: *There is no death, therefore there is no separation.* Nor is there truly any kind of adversity, disease, scarcity, conflict or suffering. All of these arise from our belief in them. As we have discovered, these beliefs actually stem from both a deep unconscious fear of Love, and an equally deep love of fear.

There could be no suffering of any kind unless we profoundly feared God's Love. This fear is very deeply hidden in the unconscious, yet it drives all our beliefs, motivations and values, as well as our worldly experiences. Since Tomas' passing, I have received a great gift of clarity and understanding. I now see how to recognize and exhume our deeply hidden fear of God, so we can relinquish it once and for all. Only then can we wholeheartedly trust in God's Love, enjoying a deep and unshakeable sense of divine security and Love.

For Tomas and me, it took twenty years to recognize and exhume our unconscious fear of God's Love. But it needn't take you that long! If you have truly had enough suffering and are willing to take this pathway, your experience can be much quicker and more joyous than ours was.

Jesus' message of transformation heralds a universal shift of mammoth proportions. It's the complete reversal of the world's thought system, beliefs, laws and values. Ultimately this reversal and transformation of suffering into joy and Love rests upon our willing abdication of the ego's most cherished idol. There is one central dream at the ego's core, and it's the very foundation responsible for feeding and upholding the entire ego's reign: The illusion of death itself.

As long as our attraction to death remains unconscious, death in all its numerous forms will still be feared and believed to be true. But simply put, if death is true, there is no God. If we believe in death in any form, we unconsciously choose to fear God—which means we fear Love. Death and God are mutually exclusive. Death *and* God cannot coexist. I have come to realize pain, sickness, scarcity and conflict are also illusory forms of death. While these remain in our perception as external threats to be defended against, we cannot know God's Love. And while we hang onto these beliefs, we will deny our self the joy of learning that we are the living expression of God's mighty and all-Loving Will here on Earth.

"Death is indeed the death of God, if He is Love." M-27.5:5
"If death is real for anything, there is no life. Death denies life. But if there is reality in life, death is denied. No compromise in this is possible." M-27.4.2-5

This book is not about immortality of the body. Only the ego would be obsessed with the idea of clinging to the form of a limited body forever. This teaching is about reclaiming our union in God's Love, thereby recognizing and embodying our one Holy Self. We are called to follow Jesus' message, not *after* death (as the ego teaches), but right here and now while experiencing life in a body. In the Bible, Jesus promises us this: *"Verily, verily, I say unto you, He that believeth on me, the works that I do shall he do also; and greater works than these shall he do; because I go unto my Father."* (King James Bible, Cambridge Version)

After many years of living the principles of forgiveness as taught by the *Course*, I finally perceive the holographic nature and limitless depth of Jesus' message. We might read the *Course* many times and each time see in it something we didn't notice or understand before. For me, the message has been received gradually. Its many deeper layers have revealed themselves in direct proportion to the degree of trust I have been willing to place in Love, while learning to relinquish fear. It has been an ongoing process, and continues still.

Sixteen years before writing this book, Tomas and I read many passages in the *Course* about the unreality of sickness and death. These passages were consistent. But back then we simply could not grasp this concept, because these afflictions still seemed very real to us. As a result, we were unable to comprehensively integrate these teachings in a practical way. To us, deprivation, suffering, sickness and death were at least as real as God was. We tried to straddle these two opposing realities, as everyone does. We attempted to justify the many ungodly occurrences in our lives by convincing ourselves God was in charge and bringing us lessons as learning opportunities.

We didn't believe we were worthy enough to accept the real truth: That God (our Holy Self) doesn't *do* suffering—never did and never will. All encompassing Love is just that, all encompassing with no opposite. It brings copious expressions of absolute joy and peace. For Tomas and me, the belief we must learn through suffering had to be questioned in depth, because God's Will never

xvi

brings suffering; only the ego does. Suffering has nothing to do with God's Love. It has everything to do with the ego's projection of god (with a small "g"). Jesus sums up how Tomas and I felt before we experienced a comprehensive shift into trust:

> *"Listen to what the ego says, and see what it directs you see, and it is sure that you will see yourself as tiny, vulnerable and afraid. You will experience depression, a sense of worthlessness, and feelings of impermanence and unreality. You will believe that you are helpless prey to forces far beyond your own control, and far more powerful than you. And you will think the world you made directs your destiny." T-21.V.2:3-6*

Slowly, as the ego belief system fell away for us, we began to appreciate that all suffering was brought about by our mistaken identity, our identification with the personal self. This self is wholly an ego fabrication, a will that is entirely independent from Love.

We (the Holy Self) are as powerful as the Christ, because we are expressions of God's Will. The Holy Self *is* the Christ. We share in this magnificent and limitless grace. I could never have accepted this truth until relatively recently, because I was far too fearful to relinquish the ego's interpretation of self as victim. Releasing this image of my small self would mean giving up the world as I knew it. Little did I realize the only thing we ever lose when relinquishing ego is the ability to suffer. Yet the "cost" of becoming a miracle worker seemed a price too great to pay back then.

Due to our extreme unconscious fear of God's Love, we don't dare seriously entertain the possibility that our minds hold limitless power. Our minds are so powerful, in fact, that we can and will undo all the suffering we have ever made, as soon as we choose to. Every seemingly real ego law (such as disease, conflict, deprivation and death) we learn to question will eventually fizzle in response to our embodied power in Christ's Love. This can never be achieved by intellectual study alone, but through the meticulous review and undoing of everything in which we previously placed our faith. This undoing is forgiveness in action.

Since his passing, I've been in almost constant communication with Tomas. I have learned that any form of sadness or grief cuts communication because it makes the idea of death as separation a reality. The miracles, joy and peace that have permeated my life as a result are testimony that there is no death. Tomas and I signed up to help bring this profound paradigm shift from death to Life into being. It is the overturning of a depraved dream of death, and the heralding of an epic dream of Life, healing and Love. This is what Jesus calls the Real World, also referred to as the Happy Dream. We will all come to it, eventually.

Tomas Awakened

Tomas awakened quite some time before he left the body. By the time of his passing, there was no individual, personal Tomas left. How did this manifest in form? He was consistently open, loving and joyous, regardless of the appearance or seeming condition of the body. It was not *his* body after all, and he knew this.

He had decided to use the illusion of cancer as a catalyst to awaken quickly. He chose to prioritize peace above all else, in every situation. He invited the Holy Spirit to help him reinterpret everything the ego made, including disease, as a means to awaken within the dream. He didn't try to save his life out of fear. After all, what was there to save his life *from*, if God's Love is all there is?

While this seems an extreme lesson, his choice to see past all appearances contrary to Love was an invitation to instant awakening. Many of us say we want to awaken from suffering, but we don't prioritize peace consistently. A multitude of earthly priorities top our list of goals, and mindfully choosing to perceive peace is usually a last ditch attempt at problem solving. We'd much rather see change take place outside our mind, whether in our body, in a situation or another's behavior. Tomas used his illness as a means to awaken. And he did so by consistently choosing only peace in each moment, even when appearances tempted him to believe he was a fragile body and not an eternal being.

Hours before Tomas passed, his body slid into rapid decline as it quickly shut down. He was entirely lucid during this final phase, but I, Nouk, experienced a meltdown. I saw the body falling away and I wept in frustration and confusion. How could he leave me? Why hadn't his cancer been miraculously healed? Tomas was not able to speak, so he motioned to me for pen and paper. And while I sat beside him sobbing, he scrawled out the following note to me: *"Noukie, look beyond appearances…we turn every doubt, fear and appearance over to Christ. We trust in His plan for our salvation—one moment at a time. Then we witness that we are still here. But more than that, we witness the stillness and peace, and we know that it can only be Him who is achieving this goal…we must be on track."*

The discipline he chose was to uncompromisingly surrender all concern for the body to the Holy Spirit. It is my belief one cannot do this and *not* awaken quickly. After all, the body is our greatest distraction and obstacle to remembering we are one in God.

Our daughter Rikki and I returned to our home in New Mexico after Tomas passed. It was then I experienced the darkest possible night of the soul. My dilemma was not so much that Tomas had left his body; our Holy Love was such that I knew the absence of his body could not threaten our consistent communication.

I found I could not stand the pain and confusion of trying to hold two irreconcilable beliefs. Would I choose fear or Love? Death or Life? It was clear I couldn't hang onto both. As far as I understood at the time, Jesus teaches that even here in the dream, after the mind has fully healed and we embody the knowledge that we are under no laws but God's, the ego's laws are reversed. God's laws prevail. Simply put, according to the *Course*, when one lives out from the Christ within, he can heal the sick and raise the dead (Miracle principle number twenty-four in *ACIM*).

While taking care of Tomas in those last few months, I had unknowingly developed a major ego attachment, secretly believing Tomas would completely recover from illness as a living witness to these deeper teaching of Jesus. I didn't know at the time that neither of us had fully grasped these teachings *experientially*. Therefore his passing by means of disease was especially challenging for me.

I saw that Tomas did not suffer, was joyful and in a state of great peace. But I couldn't reconcile these questions: *"Why did*

Tomas leave through disease? Why didn't he awaken in a healthy body?" His priority had been simple. He intended to awaken now, not later. The means for this awakening took the form of disease, a perfect vehicle through which he could unflinchingly challenge every temptation to perceive the reality of fear, pain and death. Tomas chose cancer, which offered him an extreme opportunity requiring vigilant discipline to choose *only* Love.

He prioritized peace and consistently chose it. In doing so, he traveled at warp speed along a one-way street, which unerringly led him to awaken—unlike most of us, who choose to meander along many two-way streets for lifetimes. But if he truly awakened, as it certainly seemed he had, why had he passed in the way that he did?

In my understanding, to live out from the Christ meant the body would no longer be used to demonstrate attack. It would no longer be a weapon of ego, but the temple of the Holy Spirit, its only purpose to extend God's Love and healing. Sickness and death would be non-issues to the Christed Self, having already been seen through and overcome.

Instead of death as we know it, Jesus tells us when the time comes to leave the body once and for all, the event will be peaceful and joyous, as the body's job here would be complete. Its death would not be brought about by the ravages of disease, aging and pain. Jesus teaches that the body, once surrendered completely to Spirit, becomes the most important vehicle through which we learn to overcome the ego world. More importantly, it teaches us to overcome the ego's central dream of physical death itself, just as Jesus Himself did.

It took me quite awhile to recognize that Tomas did awaken *in* the ego dream, however he did not awaken *from* the ego's dream of death as Jesus teaches in the *Course*. There is a fundamental difference between these two awakenings, and this subject is covered well in *The End of Death*.

I have come to realize Jesus is calling for us not merely to awaken in the dream as Tomas did, but to awaken from the ego dream of sickness and death altogether; to break the cycle of birth and death entirely. This requires us to embody and live out from the invulnerable Holy Self, through forgiveness and the full acceptance of Atonement—the complete undoing of fear and guilt. The outcome of these actions is the total reversal of the ego's dream. It is the overcoming and undoing of everything we originally made to attack our self and to separate from God. This reunion with the Holy Self is the glorious state Jesus calls the Real World or Happy Dream.

My Dark Night of the Soul

When I arrived back home in New Mexico after Tomas had passed, I slipped into a state of terrible confusion and grief. Our daughter Rikki helped me to remember that *only* Love is real. How could separation be real as well? How could Tomas be anywhere but here and now? After all, he hadn't gone anywhere. If there was grief, then there must also be a belief in separation— that Tomas had indeed died and gone away, and that we could no longer communicate.

On the night of my darkest experience, hell made itself known in my mind. All my trust in Holy Spirit appeared to fall away. Perhaps a godless hell was all that really existed. Maybe all else was fantasy. Then I realized I must be hallucinating. Either this godlessness was really the truth, or I was delirious and insane. My desperate desire to understand exactly what happened to Tomas had overshadowed my trust in Holy Spirit. The result was an unbearable sense of separation. I cried out for help.

I heard Tomas' voice in my mind ask me this question: *Do you want to understand, or do you want peace?* I got it. The need to understand was an ego ploy. Choosing to *accept* the situation without understanding would bring me back to peace, and open me up to communication with both Spirit and Tomas.

I pulled an *ACIM* quotation card, which read: "*...if you want peace, you must give up the idea of conflict entirely and for all time.*" *T-7.VI.8:9* And that was that! From that moment, I let everything *not of God* simply fall away. Any thought, emotion or manifestation of pain that arose was released. I knew they were all just appearances, and I had chosen to look past all appearances and onto the face of Christ instead.

The most astounding part of this miraculous shift has been my lack of grief. I've discovered in each moment I consciously choose joy and peace, inhabiting the now moment without judgment or belief in stories of pain or loss, then Tomas is here too. It's impossible to be separated as long as we refuse to enter the personal mind, dredging up past memories of sentimental special love.

These ego projections of past love have nothing to do with the real Love we share. How can I miss Tomas if I have been blessed with the awareness that he is *still here* and more accessible to me than ever before? Sure, it's a bit weird not to have him around in a body, but this is yet another lesson that proves the illusory and temporary nature of form. The *content*, thank God, is eternal and unchanging!

I will not let this change of form cause me to doubt. Contrary to what the ego teaches, I am learning it is safe to surrender the form (in this case, Tomas' body) in order to keep the content of the Love we share.

When we were guided to end our marriage to save the relationship, it had been a real test of faith. As we accomplished this shift, we discovered a profound Love that could never be threatened—not by anyone or anything, not even by death.

Now I feel I'm being asked to embrace an upgrade of the earlier test of our relationship. Accepting there is no break in communication with Tomas now seems to pose a larger challenge than the one we underwent earlier when we ended the marriage to save the relationship. However I choose to remember what Jesus says in the *Course*: There is no hierarchy of illusions and there is no order of difficulty in miracles. I can sustain this wonderful perception as long as I stay vigilant, consistently choosing to look past all appearances that are contrary to Truth, Love and changeless Reality.

Tomas said this to us: "I am not going anywhere. And I pledge to expose the lie that death is! Stay tuned…"

We believe he will make good on his promise to help expose the lie of death. Jesus says the following:

"In the holy instant the condition of love is met, for minds are joined without the body's interference, and where there is communication there is peace. The Prince of Peace was born to re-establish the condition of love by teaching that communication remains unbroken even if the body is destroyed, provided that you see not the body as the necessary means of communication. And if you understand this lesson, you will realize that to sacrifice the body is to sacrifice nothing, and communication, which must be of the mind, cannot be sacrificed. T-15.XI.7.1-4

I continue to learn, allowing all blocks to my awareness of Love's presence to fall away. I now recognize what our greatest power is, here in the dream. *It is the power to choose in every single instant.* This means in any moment our buttons are pushed, we can choose to look past all ego appearances and onto the face of Truth. If God's Love is all there is in reality, then we must learn to deny anything not of Love any power to hurt us. This is true forgiveness. It's a discipline. And we don't really make this consistent choice for peace until we have had enough suffering. Jesus talks about making this choice:

"I have already told you that you can be as vigilant against the ego as for it. This lesson teaches not only that you can be, but that you [must] be. It does not concern itself with order of difficulty, but with clear-cut priority for vigilance. This lesson is unequivocal in that it teaches there must be no exceptions, although it does not deny that the temptation to make exceptions will occur. Here, then, your consistency is called on despite chaos. Yet chaos and consistency cannot coexist for long, since they are mutually exclusive. As long as you must be vigilant against anything, however, you are not recognizing this mutual exclusiveness, and still believe that you can choose either one. By teaching [what] to choose, the Holy Spirit will ultimately teach you that you need not choose at all. This will finally liberate your mind from choice, and direct it towards creation within the Kingdom." T-6.V.C.4:2-10

Tomas leaves me with one great lesson now. If I can vigilantly hold to his magnificent demonstration of faith and trust, this one lesson will indeed take me to Truth, to the one Love we all are. I hope—no, I trust—that you too will join me on this journey in remembering to choose *only* Love, and *only* peace, regardless of so-called appearances.

~ Nouk Sanchez, October 2013

CHAPTER ONE

THE EGO: A BRIEF OVERVIEW

From my current vantage point, after more than two decades of walking the path of *A Course in Miracles*, I see clearly that the ego is nothing more than the will to suffer. It's also an unconscious desire to be alone and separate.

Yet who in his right mind would ever consciously choose to suffer all alone for eons in the illusion of time? No one would—if he was truly *in* his right mind. Clearly, the ego thought system is the *wrong* mind. Life as we know it, as lived through the unconscious ego, is chock full of all kinds of suffering.

The ego is only a mental construct, an illusory personal identity-self. It's a separate will through which we made a world apart from God's Love. This self is not real and is ultimately unsustainable. Yet, from the eternal, unchangeable Will of all-encompassing Love, came a mad little thought. And the thought was to experience "not God."

Included in the experience of "not God" are all the laws of the world we believe are natural and immutable, such as time, nature, birth and death. Rejecting our original, incorruptible state of all-encompassing Love (which has no opposite), we chose instead to experience Love's opposite as the state of fear. We've used this lens of fear to perceive ourselves, others and the world. Thankfully this fearful perception, convincing as it seems to us, is really just a dream state. The eternal truth of our Holy perfection remains unaffected by this dream.

Ungodly side effects are part of the ego's fearful projection, including horrendously distorted phenomena such as sickness, emotional and physical pain, accidents, conflicts, scarcity, and (the final icing on the ego's cake), physical death. All these are our own unconscious projections we've chosen to experience. We use them as a distraction, insuring we will never have to wake up from this dream of fear.

Our fearful projections seem to us very real external threats against which we must defend our self. In our perception they are independent of us, possessing magical power to hurt us. This is what Jesus says about how the ego mind uses the body's eyes (and its other senses) to interpret what it wants us to perceive:

> *It is the mind that interprets the eyes' messages and gives them "meaning." And this meaning does not exist in the world outside at all. What is seen as "reality" is simply what the mind prefers. Its hierarchy of values is projected outward, and it sends the body's eyes to find it." M-8.3:4-7*

> *"You have become at odds with the world as you perceive it, because you think it is antagonistic to you. This is a necessary consequence of what you have done... you must realize that your hatred is in your mind and not outside it before you can get rid of it; and why you must get rid of it before you can perceive the world as it really is." T-12. III.7:7-10.*

WHY DO WE PERSIST IN SUFFERING?

Why would we prefer the illusion of fear and threat over consistent Love, safety and joy? What is the payoff? Our deeply buried fear of God is the burning fury that fuels our unconscious will to suffer. This secret catalyst keeps us identified with the personal self and its insane will to remain separate from God. Guilt motivates our ongoing desire to run away from God. This is our deepest, darkest defense against God's Love. Our guilt is caused by the imaginary belief we killed God—because we seemingly abandoned Love. We unconsciously believe we committed an unforgivable crime, forever darkening the universe. We believe we've sinned on an epic scale. And according to the ego, sin cannot be erased.

This deep-seated, unconscious belief in our own eternal guilt is of an unbearable magnitude, so it was buried, denied and forgotten. When something too shocking and traumatic occurs, we dissociate and go into denial. And when denial occurs, as psychology informs us, projection of the denied experience will result. So we no longer perceive the one cause of all fear as originating within our own mind; we now see the source of our terror, the guilt we have denied, as *outside* us in the form of others, or inside our own bodies, or in the world at large.

Sin, guilt and fear make up the vicious cycle of the ego. We believe we've sinned, so we carry deep guilt, which is projected externally. The natural result of this projection is that its effects appear to return and attack us, often in a form that seems unrelated and random. So we teach our self that our bodies, other people and the world are to be feared and controlled.

The ego's survival depends on keeping our attention turned outward! As long as we still buy into the misperception that everyone and everything including sickness, scarcity and death are independent phenomena that exist outside us, we continue to attract suffering.

By keeping us convinced of our victimhood, distracted by the never-ending pursuit of pleasure, love, abundance and health—while simultaneously attempting to avoid pain, loss, scarcity and death, the ego effectively has us turned inside out. Or more accurately, turned against our Holy Self. This is the Self that clearly recognizes all suffering has but one source, regardless of what outer appearances may look like. And that one source is the ego, found nowhere but within our own mind.

As long as we choose to harbor the unconscious guilt, keeping it safe in the dark, never daring to look at it, we will continue to believe the source of our suffering is found in others, in the past, in situations and in our own bodies. When we finally decide we have had enough of the ego's frantically fruitless external search for the causes of both suffering and salvation, only then are we ready to start the journey of undoing the ego.

KNOW THYSELF: THE HOLY SELF

Our true Holy Self is deeply buried under the ego's false image of the self. While this false ego identity remains desired and intact, it obscures the infinite majesty and unassailable security of our Holy Self. We must choose one self-identity or the other, as the two are mutually exclusive. They are diametrically opposed in every way, and cannot coexist.

To find our True Self we need the help of others, as it's impossible to find the Holy Self alone. Other people serve as flawless mirrors of our own repressed and unrecognized judgments, beliefs and values. Everyone we encounter in our lives acts as a screen upon which we project all our denied guilt. They show us just where our emotional triggers are. And we need these triggering experiences so we can initiate the process of identifying and forgiving the true cause of our suffering, which is always in our own mind. It's never outside of us in the past, the body, or in the behavior of others.

Before we dive directly into the search for our one Holy Self, however, we must be committed to undoing the false self; this is a process that involves the reversal of all our beliefs and values. The journey of undoing the ego means we dare to look within, to find the hidden split in our mind. This split remains invisible to us until we choose to shed light on it. The ego survives by keeping itself shrouded in darkness. This darkness is necessary to maintain its cycle of fear, keeping our guilt projections hidden from us so we never discover them. As long as the hidden guilt goes undetected, the ego can project it outward to seemingly attack us from the outside, in as many forms as possible.

Its closed-circuit system is deliberately intended to keep us in permanent fear, ensuring we return always to the ego itself, consulting it for solutions to the very problems *it* projects. Yet lasting solutions will never be offered by the ego, for its consistent mantra is *seek but do not find*.

IDENTIFYING THE INTERNAL SPLIT

"The miracle is possible when cause and consequence are brought together, not kept separate." T-26.VII.14:1-2

"Sickness and sin are seen as consequence and cause, in a relationship kept hidden from awareness that it may be carefully preserved from reason's light." T-26.VII.2:4

The internal split that feeds the illusion of separation is kept alive by our reluctance to look within. We all fear the effects of looking deeply inward, as we are unconsciously convinced we will be struck dead with horror as a result. In addition, based on my own experience and that of others I've worked with, I've concluded we all seem to share a very deep belief, whether consciously or unconsciously, in our own extreme worthlessness.

This sense of unworthiness is baseless, of course, even though it seems so real to us. It is just a mask that hides the guilt we are terrified to look upon. Deep shame or unworthiness, painful and destructive as their effects might be, are just convenient disguises for what lies underneath. Guilt is the treasure the ego never wants us to discover within, because once we do, we can easily let it go. And when we release the guilt, the ego and its attraction to suffering must disappear with it.

The guilt beneath our unworthiness is our shared unconscious conviction that we separated from God, and that He is therefore out to get us. Although we assume there are thousands of things we are guilty of in our lives, and millions of things to judge and fear, actually only one deeply unconscious belief spawns them all: Our unconscious fear of God.

All feelings of guilt, and every trigger for fear and anger are projections of this one deep source of guilt. When we realize this, we can begin to heal an entire range of problems in our lives that appear to be unrelated to this issue, such as sickness, relationship problems, scarcity, addiction, depression, obsessions, procrastination, loneliness and more.

As long as our core fear of God is kept underground, and we allow the ego to fracture and project it outward daily in so many seemingly unrelated ways, we will remain in suffering.

Until we willingly exhume all that lies hidden within, we cannot know firsthand our perfect immunity, safety and security. We must gather the courage to look within, doing radical self -inquiry each time we feel our emotions triggered by others or by situations. What is the true cause and nature of this problem? Where does its source really lie?

Within every mind exist two opposing thought systems: The ego and God—or more specifically, fear and Love. Only Love is real. The ego is kept alive only by our choice to hold these opposing thought systems separate from one other. When brought together, it immediately becomes clear only one can be embraced. When we exhume our deepest core beliefs, what we are doing is bringing the ego thought system to light, setting it next to the thought system of God, which ensures the ego's demise.

I'll give you one small example of bringing the ego's agenda to light: I may feel a cold coming on. I'm well aware I have an important project to complete, yet the uninvestigated ego chooses this moment to attack with a cold. Its aim? To thwart my plan, make me miserable and convince me I'm at the mercy of my body. Clearly then, as I reach for my tenth tissue, this is proof I must be a body and not God's perfect Child.

The ego secretly informs me I am separate from God's Love; it tells me I am powerless over the body, even though I share the infinite power of God's Will. If I were to choose this opportunity to look within and open to Spirit's thought system, I would realize only the mind can command the body—the body could never betray me without my own consent. I would recognize *I* assign all meaning and power to everything in my world, including sickness. This cold has no meaning apart from what I give it, and cannot affect me unless I choose so in my mind. Armed with this empowering truth, I would question the ego consistently in this instance and every other that arose. In this continuing process of shedding light on its darkness, eventually the ego would have no choice but to disappear.

When we question the ego, we always do it by going inward for guidance from our Holy Self. We uncover what is untrue by exposing it to the light of Spirit. In my example of the cold, once realizing *I* must have decided for the cold, then I can, with Spirit, reverse this decision through forgiveness.

Upon radical self-inquiry, I may also find I invited the cold because of my fear of completing the project, or because I needed a "legitimate excuse" for a day off from work. No matter what I find within, if I want the cause of all suffering to be undone, I apply forgiveness. And forgiveness cannot occur until I'm willing to look within at the ego's projected lie, together with the light of Spirit's Love interpreting it correctly for me.

This process will feel counterintuitive. The ego believes our safety comes from *not* looking within, especially not looking at our darkest fears. But the truth is, whatever lies hidden in our unconscious will be projected outward. And it does so by manifesting as random attack coming from outside us. Our fears and judgments are the secret magnets that draw these experiences, working to attract the very things we try so desperately to avoid.

Jesus assures us our fears and the resulting attacks will always yield to Love, if they are brought to the light of awareness and not kept hidden:

> " *There is no darkness that the light of love will not dispel, unless it is concealed from love's beneficence. What is kept apart from love cannot share its healing power, because it has been separated off and kept in darkness.* " *T-14.VI.2:3-4*

Until we bring the light of awareness within, we will mistakenly presume the ego is who we are, not realizing another distinctly different internal thought system holds our True Identity. And as long as we believe in the reality of our ego-self, we will confuse our values and the beliefs we hold with who we are.

If someone criticizes something we do, or if they disagree with a particularly strong opinion we have, for example, we will take offense personally, as if our very identity has been threatened. We won't realize our actual identity cannot be threatened by any challenge to a coveted belief, opinion, or judgment we hold. We are not our values and beliefs, which are all changeable as the wind. Who we really are, beneath the illusory ego self, is changeless. We can't hope to know this in our firsthand experience until we begin to undo the false ego self-image we hold, recognizing it as the impostor it is.

This false self is made up of millions of unrecognized judgments, beliefs, values and opinions. None of them make up our True Identity. Instead, they fabricate who we are *not*. Yet we will not know who we are until these erroneous shreds of identity have been seen and willingly released.

> "*The search for truth is but the honest searching out of everything that interferes with truth.*" *T-14.VII.2:1*

By looking within with Spirit, holding no self-judgment, we will be surprised to find in every instance that only Love remains once we've taken an honest look inside. And it's the looking *without* judgment that is key to dispelling the darkness we once feared so greatly.

The ego's terror rises when we start to unearth our fears and realize they are ungrounded. As we unravel all the beliefs that have kept the wheel of suffering in motion, we begin to see the light. Gradually a decision is made to withdraw our dependence on the ego's authority. We turn more and more to the Spirit within, awaiting guidance through Love, rather than allowing ourselves to be manipulated through fear any longer.

A profound shift occurs when we recognize we can no longer maintain our belief in both opposing thought systems. And it's at this point that a sincere commitment must be made to only one of them. True and consistent peace comes only when we make this decision to be vigilantly mindful *for* God, and against the ego within our mind. Until then, the ego has a foothold in our perception and we will fall victim to its fear-based projections in all their many forms.

> *"Dissociation is a distorted process of thinking whereby two systems of belief which cannot coexist are both maintained. If they are brought together, their joint acceptance becomes impossible. But if one is kept in darkness from the other, their separation seems to keep them both alive and equal in their reality. Their joining thus becomes the source of fear, for if they meet, acceptance must be withdrawn from one of them. You cannot have them both, for each denies the other."* T-14.VII.4:3-7

The Holy Spirit lives within as our Holy Self, and is available to us in any instant we desire sanity and peace. But we must desire to look within at our fears and judgments with Him. While we hoard our concerns and fears, keeping them locked away, Spirit cannot help.

> *"The Holy Spirit asks of you but this; bring to Him every secret you have locked away from Him. Open every door to*

Him, and bid Him enter the darkness and lighten it away.
At your request He enters gladly... He sees for you, and
unless you look with Him He cannot see." T-14.VII.6:1-6

THE ICEBERG OF UNCONSCIOUS GUILT AND FEAR

Roughly ten percent of what occurs in our lives happens through conscious intention, while the remaining ninety percent is unconsciously driven by the ego's secret wish to be unfairly treated. This buried "iceberg" mass that drives our life seeks self-punishment by harboring our hidden unconscious beliefs, judgments, fears and defenses.

Remember that whatever we fear, resist, deny or defend against ends up being projected outward and manifested in our worldly experience. Until we unearth our hidden guilt and fear that reside within this buried mass, agreeing to release them (along with their manifested effects) through the forgiveness/ Atonement process, these unconscious fears will continue to materialize in our lives.

Within this dark, hidden mass of the ego can also be found all our unquestioned investment in the ego's laws—those laws that appear to sustain us, and also those that appear to attack us. What are these laws? There are many. We are convinced food, drink, money and medicine are vitally needed to sustain us; wouldn't we die of starvation, thirst, poverty or disease without them?

Conversely, we believe just as strongly that disease, pain, scarcity and death are laws that attack us, as these are seemingly laws we have no control over. All of these "laws" (and many others) are beliefs only, and each one must be reviewed and questioned deeply with Spirit.

We are not asked to give them up, but we do need to offer them to Spirit for reinterpretation.

As long as any of these laws are believed to cause either danger or healing, taking precedence over the limitless power of God, they will act as blocks to the awareness of Love's presence. All cause originates in the mind, and as long as we continue to falsely endow the ego's laws with the power to "cause" anything, we inadvertently reject the undoing of the real and *only* cause of all our suffering: Our deeply buried unconscious guilt.

In the very core of the iceberg's unconscious mass resides the cherished central dream of the ego. This is the concept of death, upon which all else is structured.

This core is our most compelling secret attraction. Collectively and individually, we have placed this foundational core of death upon our innermost altar—shoving all notions of God aside in order to do so. Death occupies the central space of holiest worship in the unconscious thought system of the ego. All other misplaced beliefs and assorted blocks to Love orbit around this central core.

CONSCIOUS EGO WILL:
Conscious beliefs and fears

EGO ICEBERG

UNCONSCIOUS GUILT
(unconscious self-hatred = self attack)
EGO BELIEFS
(Fears, defenses, values, judgments & secret expectations)
EGO'S LAWS
(Laws that sustain/attack us)
SEEKING COMPLETION
(Fulfillment through the ego)

EGO'S CENTRAL DREAM

DEATH as fear of God

UNCONSCIOUS EGO WILL:
Unconscious wish to be unfairly treated

Diagram #1
The Ego Iceberg

EGO'S UNCONSCIOUS WISH
TO BE UNFAIRLY TREATED

Defenses: The ego believes we have sinned monstrously and it finds us guilty. Therefore, in its view, we should expect punishment! Hence it constantly causes us to defend our self from threat. Yet all threats exist in the mind. They are not external dangers, as the ego would have us believe.

The cause of all sense of threat, as stated earlier, is unconscious guilt. Therefore this single cause is the only threat we need to heal. In Truth, all that exists is God's Love. As we work to undo the ego, we discover we have actually spent our lives defending and protecting our self *from* God's Love, by harboring our secret attraction to suffering, punishment and death.*

*Recommended reading: Lesson 135 in the *Course* - "*If I defend myself, I am attacked.*"

Ego laws that attack and sustain us: Everything we perceive in the world is projected outward by the ego thought system within our mind. The ego projects only what it wants us to see and believe. It wants us to remain solely reliant on *its* guidance, because its own survival would be threatened if we sought wiser counsel elsewhere.

The ego wants us to believe the body/world is more powerful than our own mind, and more powerful than God's Will. The last thing it wants is for us to recognize that all power resides in the mind. If we were to fully discover the power inherent in our right mind, we would drop the ego immediately.

As long as we go on mistakenly placing our faith in the body and world to sustain us and keep us safe, we will never know our power in God. Nor will we know the relief, joy and sense of profound safety that comes of discovering that *only* the Love of God truly sustains us. If we don't learn to trust in this Truth about our own nature, we will remain victims of the world we see.

Seeking fulfillment through the ego: When we seek fulfillment, control or to complete our self through the ego's means, what we're really doing is strengthening guilt. Whenever we try to fulfill or complete our self apart from Spirit, we reinforce our belief in the body's reality. We don't realize this incurs the ego's punishment. *Everything* we do with the ego attracts guilt.

All body appetites (over-eating, improving body image, dieting, nutrition, sex), money, career advancement, special relationships, desire for external approval, etc., are motivated by a drive for ego fulfillment. And ego fulfillment brings guilt. It's not that any of these behaviors are bad in themselves; they are simply neutral. The guilt comes in when we listen to the ego's counsel, attempting to seek or use these things to feel better about our self without asking for any input from Spirit.

> *"Whenever you attempt to reach a goal in which the body's betterment is cast as major beneficiary, you try to bring about your death...Seek not outside yourself. The search implies you are not whole within and fear to look upon your devastation, but prefer to seek outside yourself for what you are." T-29.VII.4:1:5-6*

Death, the ego's central dream: Death is at the very heart of our unconscious desires. While this attraction to death remains a deeply closeted secret, we continue unknowingly to follow its seductive siren song. The ego's intention is to kill the physical body before we awaken to our complete invulnerability in God's Love as our Holy Self. However, the ego continues to pursue us even after death.

> *"The ego wants [you] dead, but not itself. The outcome of its strange religion must therefore be the conviction that it can pursue you beyond the grave." T-15.I.3:3-4*

Yet the ego need not prevail in this goal. The entire thought system of the ego is kept afloat by only one cause: Our ongoing choice to believe and trust in it. All suffering comes from this unquestioned trust we place in whatever the ego testifies to. Most of us blindly trust in the ego, gullibly believing what our bodies' senses tell us is real.

As young children, we are raised by parents and educated in schools. However their main and misguided effort is directed toward helping us build bigger egos. With big strong egos we emerge into society. There we eagerly perceive scarcity, danger and conflict all around us, even as we simultaneously search endlessly for external fulfillment and happiness. This search is the individual and collective motivator for the entire world of ego desire. Yet the ego's hidden mantra is *seek but do not find.*

Television and mass media contribute greatly to feeding the fearful and unsatisfied ego, playing a major role in keeping us asleep in the ego dream. Many of us don't fully realize the damaging influence these subliminal ego messages have on our sense of self.

The journey of the development of trust that Jesus urges us to embark upon is a living process. It's a transfer of trust. Our trust is gradually withdrawn from the ego and its many worldly guises, through consistent self-inquiry and forgiveness. Only then can it be transferred to its rightful place, the Holy Self. This process is the systematic exhuming of all our beliefs, values and cultural conditioning, so all can be examined and brought to the light of Spirit's reinterpretation.

Make no mistake, the ego belief system is total. *Every* belief we have, whether conscious or unconscious, must be wholly reinterpreted. This means each and every one of the ego's beliefs is totally opposite to God's all-encompassing Love. If we believe in just one, we must accept the entire ego thought system. And that is why it's so important to question everything we believe, and to learn to forgive everything that triggers us. If it's not joyful and Loving, it is not real. Period. Anything that is not real is to be forgiven. And with forgiveness, the ego loses its death grip upon us.

"To learn this course requires willingness to question every value that you hold ...No belief is neutral." T-24.in.2:1-8

CHAPTER TWO

MIRACLES–ARE THEY LITERAL OR METAPHOR?

Is the miracle as taught by Jesus in *A Course in Miracles* meant purely as metaphor—or is it supposed to be taken literally? In other words, can a healed mind truly bring about a healed body? Or for that matter, a healed world?

Throughout my first two decades of *Course* study, I took much of Jesus' very clear teaching as metaphor. After all, I thought, we are not the body, and the body itself is an illusion. So what purpose would physical miracles serve? Wouldn't they make the body appear even more real to us? Why bother to heal the body, if it isn't real?

It was not until my own unconscious fear of God's Love had dissipated somewhat that I began to experience many indisputable miracles for myself, and this experience of firsthand miracles answered my question once and for all. I now realize miracles *must* be experienced as real occurrences, in order to fully believe the truth of these teachings.

A Course in Miracles is not a metaphorical teaching, nor is it meant to be perceived that way. I experience literal miracles, and because of this my trust and faith in the Holy Spirit have grown exponentially. This confidence, trust and faith are requirements for anyone who wishes to unlock the true message of the *Course* for themselves, because without this personal experience it would be impossible to believe all that Jesus is teaching us.

Simply put, miracles are a choice for God. The one unified Mind in God holds all power. Nothing else wields any power at all in Truth. The body itself is completely neutral, as is the world. The body, which is only a projection of the mind, has no ability of its own to change in appearance. This means it cannot age, sicken or heal, no matter what appearances may suggest to the contrary.

The biological laws we use to govern the body are not the laws of God. They are the ego's laws, and because these laws are not real in Truth, they can therefore quite easily be transformed.

All seeming changes the body displays arise from our choice of inner teacher. Where have we placed the power of our belief? Are we listening to the ego, in other words, or to Spirit? To fear or Love?

There can be no middle ground; it's always one or the other. All sickness, guilt, pain, decomposition and, ultimately, death come from the ego, and never from God's Love. All joy, Love, innocence, healing and life come from God, and never from the ego.

Death is the fiendishly clever shell game upon which this entire ego paradigm rests. If death is real, there is no God. If God is real, there is no death.

"Death is indeed the death of God, if He is Love." M-27.5:5
"And the last to be overcome will be death." Of course!
Without the idea of death there is no world. M-27.6:1-3
"All forms of sickness, even unto death, are physical expressions of the fear of awakening" T-8.IX.3:2

Death is the ego's escape hatch that keeps us from remembering God's Love as the True nature of our Holy Self. It is our most unconsciously compelling and compulsive method for evading liberation from the ego's dream of suffering. Yet an honest examination of death in the clear light of divine Spirit reveals its structure makes no sense.

Death, pain and sickness seek to prove the body is far more powerful than the one Mind unified in God's Will. All these forms of adversity are attempts to prove 1: That the body is more powerful than the mind. 2: That effect is cause. 3: That the body is indeed real and autonomous.

We will not truly recognize the body is an illusion, until we first discover the power of the mind. And we cannot know the power of the mind until we undo all the false beliefs we have bestowed upon the body and the world.

This means we must exhume and release our false dependence on, and defenses against, phenomena appearing to be outside the mind, including the body itself. As long as we remain victims of the body by believing it has the power to sicken or heal of its own, we will never truly know the power of the healed mind. And we will remain forever attracted to physical death as the ego's primary defense against awakening to the invulnerable Christ within.

Example 1): The body is believed to be sick, unhealed, broken or dying. In this demonstration, the ego seeks to prove the body is real and more powerful than God's Will, which always chooses perfect health and life. The ego seeks to prove physical matter holds dominion over the mind; it tells us cause and effect are reversed, with the effect (the body) more powerful than the mind that made it.

Sickness results when we unconsciously abdicate the body's purpose to the ego, allowing it to be used for attack via pursuit of pleasure and pain—which only lead to more sin, guilt, fear and death. True health is a direct result of turning the body's purpose over to Spirit completely. The idols of pleasure and pain are gladly exchanged for Love, guiltlessness and joy.

> *"One thing is sure; God, Who created neither sin nor death, wills not that you be bound by them. The shrouded figures in the funeral procession march not in honor of their Creator, Whose Will it is they live. They are not following His Will; they are opposing it."* T-19.IV.C.3:3-6

A broken body seeks to prove the mind is powerless over the body, that cause is powerless over effect. As long as the body is believed to be at cause and not simply an effect, it will seem to be at the mercy of ego laws such as disease, aging and pain. To believe we are at the body's mercy means we are firmly convinced there must be a hierarchy of illusions. It is a belief there indeed exists an order of difficulty in miracles.

Some things in life are easy to heal, in other words, yet others can never be changed. A body that can order a mind to dance to its tune must be powerful indeed, taking the place of God as the one who holds dominion. A sick body that chose to remain so against the mind's will, if it were possible to accomplish in Truth, would actually prove salvation is impossible!

> *"The idea that a body can be sick is a central concept in the ego's thought system. This thought gives the body autonomy, separates it from the mind, and keeps the idea of attack inviolate. If the body could be sick Atonement would be impossible...The body has become lord of the mind.*
> *M-22.3:2-5*

In this example the body has been given reality. How? In its demonstration of sickness, pain and death, we have unknowingly assigned it special power, making it immune to miracles. But why should form (which, after all, is inseparable from the mind that made it) be immune to the infinite healing that occurs in a miracle? Miracles are limitless in their power. And therefore there is no order of difficulty in accomplishing them.

As I recognize now, a sick body falls within the same order of illusion as a petty grievance. There is no fundamental difference in the ego's hierarchy of illusions. A sick, broken body and a grievance are both forms of attack, and are therefore equally healed by the miracle of forgiveness. The miracle is total. It works instantly to heal everything. *Everything.*

Unless, of course, we believe otherwise and decree the miracle is powerless to heal form—in which case it is! Because that's where we've chosen to invest the power of our belief. We have separated form from Spirit, and have thereby excluded it from healing. This means the ego has made form an idol separate from God. We unknowingly split cause from effect whenever we choose to divide form from Spirit. It can't be done in Truth, of course.

Form resides within our mind, and cannot be separate from it. Therefore, the issue is never about the form itself. The form is neutral! *Which* teacher are we calling upon to see and interpret this for us? Where are we investing our belief? In the ego, or in God's Love? If I'm choosing God I would affirm this: "God is in everything I see, because God is in my mind. *And what God sees through my mind is therefore healed.*" In other words, if I choose to see with Spirit, then what I see with Spirit is healed. It cannot be otherwise.

This choice can just as easily be affirmed through the ego: "Ego is in everything I see, because ego is in my mind. And what ego sees through my mind is therefore sick."

THE PHYSICAL MIRACLE

Example 2): The mind is healed through total forgiveness, which in the *Course* is called the Atonement, or the miracle. The mind is healed first, which then prompts the body to heal. The healed *cause* results in healed *effect*.

When experienced firsthand, this miracle of healing proves to us unquestionably that we are *not* a body. The sick body is powerless over the healed mind. The healed mind, being the cause, heals the body as its natural effect. Heal the cause and the effect must inevitably follow.

"A broken body shows the mind has not been healed. A miracle of healing proves that separation is without effect."
T-27.II.5:1-2

Here there is no hierarchy of illusions, and no order of difficulty in miracles. We recognize, embody and demonstrate, just as Jesus did, that we are under no laws but God's. Our Holiness literally reverses all the laws of the world. The Christ within takes dominion over everything the ego made to separate from God's Love. The healed mind causes all the laws of this world to be reversed, and in doing so, unveils the wondrous joy of the Real World.

> "Being sane, the mind heals the body because [it] has been healed. The sane mind cannot conceive of illness because it cannot conceive of attacking anyone or anything." T-5.V.5:2-3
>
> "There is no surer proof idolatry is what you wish than a belief there are some forms of sickness and of joylessness forgiveness cannot heal." T-30.VI.6:1

All forms of sickness testify against the Truth of God, because they claim we are merely a body. A weak, fragile and defenseless body—not the unassailable being we really are in Truth.

> "Pain demonstrates the body must be real. It is a loud, obscuring voice whose shrieks would silence what the Holy Spirit says, and keep His words from your awareness." T-27.VI.1:1-2
>
> "As fear is witness unto death, so is the miracle the witness unto life. The dying live, the dead arise, and pain has vanished." T-27.VI.5:7-9
>
> "[You] are a miracle, capable of creating in the likeness of your Creator. Everything else is your own nightmare, and does not exist. Only the creations of light are real." T-1.1.24:2-4
> Sickness is a defense against the truth. W-136.

Nowadays as I study the *Course*, I can see why I used to be so terrified to take these messages literally. If total spontaneous healings were to occur as a direct result of forgiveness, then the fearfully illusory foundation of this ego world would disintegrate virtually overnight.

The idols cherished by this world (idols of both pleasure and pain), would turn to dust as we remembered our irresistible longing to join once again in beloved oneness with God. The risen Christ within would indeed claim dominion over everything the ego made, abruptly reversing its deadly laws. To an ego mind, this would seem a terrible form of chaos indeed.

> *"The resurrection is the denial of death, being the assertion of life. Thus is all the thinking of the world reversed entirely."* M-28.2:1-2

Life comes from God and is therefore incorruptible. Life cannot be terminated by death, for this would mean God could be terminated by the ego, which is impossible!

> *"I raised the dead by knowing that life is an eternal attribute of everything that the living God created... I do not believe that there is an order of difficulty in miracles; you do."* T-4.IV.11:7-12

> *"The cost of the belief there must be some appearances beyond the hope of change is that the miracle cannot come forth from you consistently. For you have asked it be withheld from power to heal all dreams. There is no miracle you cannot have when you desire healing."* T-30.VIII.4.

If physical healing results from the employment of "magic," as the *Course* calls all forms of worldly medicine, and not from true forgiveness, then it would simply be a shift between illusions. We've merely moved from the illusion of sickness to the illusion of health. This is false healing, because the single cause of all sickness (unconscious guilt in the mind) has not been addressed. Therefore the sickness has no choice but to return again in another form.

Why should we want to run away from our own ability to call forth magnificent miracles in our lives? This great fear of physical miracles makes sense when we recognize our greatest fear is not death, but Life lived fully in the infinite power of God. This is Life given perfect expression, lived as and through our Holy Self.

If one's mind is truly healed as a result of accepting Atonement, it would be capable of causing spontaneous physical healing as one of its effects, much as Jesus accomplished during His time on Earth. This would indeed be a convincing demonstration of the astonishing power of forgiveness and Atonement.

What could serve as more compelling testimony than this to a sleeping world? The guilt that causes all sickness, once removed, cannot return again in different form. Jesus teaches the purpose of the miracle is to demonstrate that the separation is completely without effects or symptoms. And he asks you to join him in demonstrating this to the world.

OVERCOMING SCARCITY
ONCE AND FOR ALL

As we begin to undo the ego's fear of God, we are met with an exhilarating surprise. We start to recognize and release our unconscious devotion to the ego's god of suffering and scarcity, and as we do, a remarkable shift occurs almost immediately.*

*To unearth your unconscious projections of God, read the following excerpt: *"Are you fearful of God? An exercise,"* on page 93.

We discover pain, suffering and scarcity are purely fabrications concocted by the ego. They are not real, and they certainly cannot threaten us, once we recognize and forgive the beliefs that invite scarcity into our experience. Lack in any form is not part of God's all-encompassing Love. Nor are sickness, pain or suffering. Through the ego, we use scarcity to try to prove our separation from God's infinite supply is a real occurrence that actually happened. Yet we *are* God's Will, and we are His eternal Loving extensions, whether we are conscious of this Truth or not. There is no lack in God; therefore there can be no lack in us—unless we choose to invest our belief in the ego, which says scarcity is real.

Seen through Love's vision, we can't experience lack in Truth, because we *have* everything and we *are* everything. But we won't know this as our own living experience, until we begin to undo our blocks to the awareness of Love's presence. Scarcity, like sickness, pain and conflict, is an illusory belief that something exists other than God's all-encompassing Love, and that this other thing has power and dominion over God's Loving Will.

Our un-relinquished guilt forms our blocks to Love. Guilt spawns fear, and un-forgiven fear manifests in the world as our seeming reality. As long as we choose not to question our fears and beliefs, the ego's god will continue to cause us confusion and suffering. Miracles enable us to give to others what we know we already have. But if we're still hypnotized by the ego's scarcity spell, we will erroneously believe we have nothing to give. Don't you think the Holy Spirit's desire is for you to have everything, because He knows you are everything? It makes no sense to believe Spirit would ask us to give, yet delight in withholding abundant miracles from us.

"You have no problems that He cannot solve by offering you a miracle. Miracles are for you. And every fear or pain or trial you have has been undone." T-14.XI.9:2-4

WHAT DO YOU UNCONSCIOUSLY BELIEVE YOU DESERVE?

Scarcity is born from a mistaken belief about the nature of the self. I am referring here to the ego-self, of course, and not our True Identity as the Holy Self. As long as we believe in this false image of a self, mistaking it for who we really are, we willingly place our self under its harsh and erroneous laws. Deprivation is, after all, the basis of the ego thought system.

Everything the ego believes testifies to the unconscious conviction that you are fundamentally lacking. Hence the seemingly bottomless pit of unworthiness that always appears to sabotage your best intent. This pit of unworthiness arises from the deeply unconscious ego belief you have committed the most unforgivable sin imaginable: You abandoned God and made a false self (and world) in which to hide from Him.

Yet this fixed belief in your own unforgivably sinful nature is entirely mistaken. God cannot be betrayed or abandoned, and neither can we. (And by "we," I mean our Holy Self, of course.) Love can neither abandon, nor can it be abandoned. Only the ego's pseudo-love can whisper dark dreams of betrayal.

If we did not unconsciously believe we betrayed God, we would not secretly expect to be punished. We would not be capable of feeling guilt or fear. In fact, we could not suffer in any way. Only our unknowing commitment to guilt and fear as self-attack makes suffering possible. Yes, we seem to experience scarcity and suffering, but only because we truly believe, way deep down, that we deserve it.

When we collude with the ego, it administers our own self-punishment. Deprivation is the theme of the ego dream, and we spend all our days trying to defend our self against it. But the ego hides this important point from our awareness: Whatever we try to defend against, we actually *attract* into our experience. Our defense against it makes it real in our perception. Once it's real and we have made it an opponent, then it must attack us. That's the ego's law. This is why forgiveness is crucial to undoing suffering. We must look at all our defense attempts, together with Spirit, in order to perceive correctly and begin to undo suffering.

Through the ego, we seem to experience limitations in love, health, finances and every other area of life. If one area seems currently abundant, we scramble to protect it, fearing its loss. Everything we do is unconsciously based on this rigid frame of limitation. We our self made the frame. The frame is secured by the ego's belief that you, at heart, are destitute and must depend upon the ego's harsh instructions and restrictions in order to survive.

To *have*, in the ego world, demands that you must *get*. But to get means someone else will be deprived. The more you get, the less others will have. And the more they get, the less you will have. This is the ego's law. It operates based on a finite supply of love, health, happiness and money. It ensures you remain thoroughly distracted in your attempts to shift the proverbial deckchairs on a quickly sinking Titanic. All the while, unknown to you, it seeks your death.

GOD'S LAW OF ENDLESS SUPPLY

The Holy Spirit's laws are the total opposite of the ego's. Beneath the ego's shabby illusions of scarcity lay God's immutable laws, shining in their eternal perfection. Here, we recognize that giving *is* receiving; that in fact, giving is the way to keep whatever we value. Giving wholeheartedly ensures I never lose the thing I desire to experience. This is the Law of endless supply.

If I project judgment onto another, I am actually keeping and reinforcing the very guilt I tried to offload onto another. The same principle applies when I give Love, or any form of Love. The Love or forgiveness I give, I always give to myself. And this is most true if I give without conditions or secret expectation of approval.

Giving Love, joined with the Holy Self, insures that Love is what is also received by me. If I give love (small "l") with any sort of strings attached, to the degree I have offered this I have not actually given, but have taken. What I have really given is separation and attack. Clearly I must have separated from my Holy Self first, in expecting to gain approval or any form of advantage from outside.

When we begin to consciously question these ego laws and practice the forgiveness/Atonement process with them, a miraculous shift takes place. We learn it's safe to trust in our Holy

Self. And once the blocks to Love start falling away, we discover a wealth of abundance within. It is from this bountiful and eternal Self that real abundance is recognized—and once recognized, it is free to naturally extend outward into our experience.

As we willingly release our erroneous beliefs and judgments, we discover we're not alone: Spirit, as our Holy Self, is present always. We begin to realize our job is not to try to control our body, relationships, finances or the behavior of others, but to release all the judgments, beliefs and limitations we previously believed protected us. They never protected us. Their only purpose was to safeguard the ego, while simultaneously blocking us from accessing the true Source of eternal Love and abundance within.

Whenever we worry or attempt to control anything, we abandon our Self. We have chosen to vacate the seat of Holiness, and now no one is home. As a result, we will feel confused, fearful and lost. The presence of fear is a sure sign we have rejected God's Love, as fear is Love's opposite in our ego belief system. This sense of fearful isolation and abandonment will then be projected outward onto others, the body or finances in the form of scarcity. We could not experience scarcity unless we first abandoned our Self in some way. All attack is always self-attack.

It's helpful to do some radical self-inquiry on all the areas where you are dishonest with yourself. These would include beliefs and behaviors toward the body, image, health, finances, relationships, career, and so on. These are areas where you sacrifice, compromise yourself, settle for less, or sell out because you fear loss or change. As long as these fears remain secretly protected and hidden by the ego, they will return again and again as loss or scarcity in some form, no matter how much you try to exercise control through the ego. Look honestly at each of these areas, sharing them openly with Spirit. True healing begins with this small step.

No matter the form of suffering, there is always only one cause: Our sense of separation from God as our Holy Self. If we truly knew our Self, we could never *be* betrayed or abandoned. And we could never abandon our Self—or anyone else—because we would recognize we all share the one Holy Self. In this Truth, we could never suffer scarcity.

All abundance comes from within, but in order to claim it we must first show up, being present for our self as mindfully as possible. There can be no real abundance until we willingly release our unexamined belief in the ego's lies, and wholeheartedly embrace the one Love we seek within. And yes, that Love is found within, and never "out there." The perfection of God's Love cannot be held separate in our awareness, excluding our self from its innocence and perfection.

When we begin to unearth the ego's false beliefs and realize how thoroughly we have betrayed our self in the name of fear, it can be quite disturbing. As we withdraw blame and judgment from outside, the ego often turns it within as self-judgment. Yet there is no difference between judging others and judging the self.

All judgment is attack, and all judgment accrues guilt. The remedy is to stay mindfully present, paying attention whenever you notice you want to beat up on yourself, or to "check out" mentally or emotionally. Make it your goal to stay present without self-judgment, and ask Spirit to help you Lovingly witness the areas you wish to heal. Spirit, your Holy Self, is always here with you in any instant you withdraw judgment and resolve to stay present in the now moment.

There may be nothing you can do right now in your 3-D experience to change anything. That is not the point. Authentic change occurs when erroneous beliefs are shifted; change at the level of form follows very naturally afterward. Even if you cannot seem to shift things at a physical, tangible level, just stay mindfully present with Spirit while you express your new priority. Your intention is to invite Spirit in to heal your perception of scarcity. Do the forgiveness/Atonement process with those areas you wish to heal, and keep going until you've allowed Spirit to shift and heal the beliefs that are standing in your way. The Atonement Process can be found on page 297.

This is the most powerful action you could ever take, because it is healing at the level of cause. Once accomplished, the effect at the 3-D world level will effortlessly take care of itself. Nothing "healed" at the effect level is ever truly healed at all. We must always go to the source.

CLAIMING YOUR ABUNDANCE IN SPIRIT

Our team is deeply inspired to present an upcoming *Power of Power~Know ThySelf* retreat in Israel, to be held during Easter 2014. We sense this will be a hugely transformational retreat for many who attend. A five-day intensive retreat workshop will be combined with an extended tour of sacred sites, together comprising an unforgettable twelve-day experience of the Holy Land.

Many people throughout the world feel strongly called to join with us on this trip to Israel. Some appear to have the funds to come, while others appear to suffer from lack of funds. On this topic, I will share what I have learned about claiming our authenticity, and thus our abundance in Spirit.

In the past, when a learning opportunity of a lifetime, like this Israel trip appeared, as a would-be participant I would experience two simultaneous and distinctly opposite reactions. The first would be genuine delight and a deeply felt inner confirmation that I was divinely called to participate in the activity. The second would be the ego's immediate censoring or rejection of my enthusiasm. I would be bombarded with seemingly practical reasons why I couldn't possibly go: *You don't have the money! What about your responsibilities? Your partner? Your kids? The pets? You are so selfish even to consider this!*

This inner conflict would continue until I resigned myself to accept the ego's narrow limitations, rules and shameful verdict. To contest this verdict seemed too painful, so each time this situation arose I simply agreed to place my Self on hold instead. I believed what the ego told me. I did this even though I seethed with resentment, along with feelings of victimization and envy—especially when I witnessed others who appeared to be casually following their bliss. It wasn't until the pain became unbearable that I turned to Spirit within to heal the fundamental cause of all suffering. That fundamental cause is the ego thought system itself. It's my deep belief in unworthiness, and the consequent expectation of deprivation.

I wasn't alone in that behavior. This is what we do in the ego dream. Until the pain of separation becomes too much to bear, we continue to let the ego dictate what it believes we deserve. The degree of un-relinquished guilt we hoard determines the extent to which we'll feel a sense of scarcity. And the amount of guilt we hang onto determines the degree to which we'll place ourselves under the ego's reign of deprivation.

The point of the ego's thought system is to separate us from our Holy Self and from Spirit's endless supply. It's convinced of our guilt, and therefore does its best to restrict our joy and severely limit abundance. At the same time it compulsively acts to inhibit, regulate, curb and withhold our natural inner guidance and flow.

In short, to allow free reign to the ego is the opposite of trusting in our own deeply felt inner guidance. Of course! God forbid if we threw caution and Self-doubt to the wind, and decided to trust the small, still Voice within. All Heaven would break loose—quite literally!

MIRACLES ARE OUR INHERITANCE

True abundance is accessed when we choose to listen only to our inner Voice, the Holy Self. But for many, this Self has been covered over by a heavy blanket of fears, rules, laws, roles, obligations, expectations and Self-doubt. How in the world can we expect to receive clear guidance, as long as we keep choosing to listen to the ego's voice instead of Spirit's? In trusting Spirit, we free our self from the need to believe in the ego's rules, laws and limitations, all of which are based on fear and deprivation. Instead, we hold our inner vision as priority and we trust in it implicitly.

If inner guidance tells you to go to Israel (as one example), or to achieve whatever your real heart's desire is, then Heaven and Earth will move to accommodate God's Will. And this happens because your Holy Self *is* God's Will! Belief in scarcity is the ego's defense against God's Will. So if you side with scarcity, you place it as your priority above God's Will of endless supply. Scarcity will manifest as your reality, *because you have asked it to.*

As long as we choose the ego's will, it is every bit as powerful as God's Will here in the dream. God's Will is powerless over the ego, as long as we choose to place ourselves under the ego's reign. This is because we have been given free will to choose. God cannot override our free will choice to suffer. As long as we place our faith in the ego instead of the Holy Self, God's Will cannot be made manifest.

Do you honestly believe the ego's fantasy projection of lack of funds could possibly be more powerful than God's Will, if your divine inner guidance has indicated this thing you desire is for your highest good? The miracle is nothing more than a shift of perception; a shift from fear into Love. We can break the ego's cycle of scarcity once and for all by daring to look, with Spirit, at all the ways we have unknowingly chosen to be a victim of it.

If you truly desire to open to Spirit's abundance, you must examine some key misperceptions. Where have you mistakenly placed the cause of your scarcity? Do you perceive your scarcity as being caused by another? Do you believe its source is found in your financial obligations, or your family, your job, your income stream, the government, or the economy?

As long as these pseudo-causes are believed, you cannot access and therefore heal the real cause, which is your own unconscious guilt. All those pseudo-causes are actually the *effects* of your belief in scarcity. They are not the cause, despite their very real-seeming appearances. The real and only cause is always unconscious guilt disguised as deprivation. Once you accept this, and give the real cause (your erroneous perception of guilt or feelings of unworthiness) to Spirit, then your experience of scarcity is free to be healed by the miracle.

> *"The power of God, and not of you, engenders miracles. The miracle itself is but the witness that you have the power of God in you.... The power of God is limitless. And being always maximal, it offers everything to every call from anyone. There is no order of difficulty here. A call for help is given help." T-14.X.6:9-10, 12-15*

The miracle heals all. When we are willing to exhume and release our hierarchy of illusions, guess what? Suddenly a space opens inside us, one that is now vast enough to accept and receive Spirit's endless supply of abundance.

When we truly open to receive this magnificent abundance, we mirror our guiltlessness and Love to the world. For we have truly seen for our self there is no order of difficulty in miracles. We show the world that guilt, fear and scarcity are not a part of God. Therefore, none of these things are real. We become a beacon of light demonstrating to all that only Love is real, and that they, too, are Love.

> *"The miracle is the one thing you can do that transcends order, being based not on differences but on equality." T-14.X.2:7*

> *"Miracles are not in competition, and the number of them that you can do is limitless. They can be simultaneous and*

legion. This is not difficult to understand, once you conceive of them as possible at all. What is more difficult to grasp is the lack of order of difficulty that stamps the miracle as something that must come from elsewhere, not from here. From the world's viewpoint, this is impossible." T-14.X.3.

Through the ego we believe we know the specific forms we think will make us feel happy, loved, secure and healthy. Yet the truth is when we, apart from Spirit, decide the particular form our desire should take, we lose the understanding of its purpose. We have only one need: To heal our sense of separation from the incorruptible and eternal Love that we are. When we commit to healing this single necessity as our priority, everything we need will be given to us. This is God's Will.

The ego wishes. But the Holy Self Wills with God. If we seek to fulfill our needs from a sense of scarcity, we join in wishing with ego. And the outcome *must* be sabotage. Yet when we consciously Will with God, every need we have will be met effortlessly.

The ego's sense of lack stems from fear and guilt. Its underlying intent is self-punishment. Therefore when we attempt to meet our own needs through the ego, we are guaranteed to attract suffering in some form.

When scarcity tempts you to scheme with the ego, go deeper. Ask yourself, "Does this desire arise from a sense of scarcity (fear and guilt)? Or does it come from a sense of gratitude and abundance, a knowing of perfect certainty that all my needs are always met?"

God's Will is infinitely abundant. There is no lack in God, therefore there is no lack in you. You *are* God's Will and His Kingdom. The only seeming lack is that you have forgotten who you are. You don't need to get your needs met. This is the ego wishing with fear. You just need to surrender your fear wholeheartedly and open to accept and receive your inheritance. This is Willing with God. Thy will be done. And so it is.

"Instead of "Seek ye first the Kingdom of Heaven" say, "[Will] ye first the Kingdom of Heaven," and you have said, "I know what I am and I accept my own inheritance."
T-3.VII.11:8

Write your concerns in the scarcity pie chart.
Assign each a number from 0 to 10. 0 is no fear, 10 is extreme fear/concern.

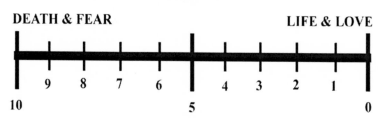

The degree of fear, 0-10, corresponds to your degree of resistance
to Love/God, and your unconscious attraction to death/suffering.

Diagram #2
Scarcity Chart with Fear Gauge

SCARCITY EXERCISE

Using pen and paper, let's do some sincere self-inquiry to discover where the ego holds you back from God's infinite source of supply. This exercise exhumes some of the ego's favorite storage areas for unconscious guilt. Chief among these is unconscious self-sabotage. Please be as present and honest as possible while answering the following questions.

1) On the scarcity pie chart diagram, identify the significant areas of scarcity in your own life. (You may add areas that are not specified if you wish.) Typical areas might be scarcity in finances, romance, sex, body/self image, health or emotional wellbeing, children, job, career or others.

2) What have you believed to be the cause of each one these? For example, you may believe *"the cause of financial scarcity is due to the present economy."* Or, *"the cause of my physical pain is due to a specific illness or condition."* Write them all down.

3) With each area of lack, write down your usual response to the perceived threat. For example, my usual response to financial scarcity might be this: *"I blame the economy, and then I look for alternative ways to improve my situation. I limit my spending, and barely make ends meet by taking on two jobs instead of one."*

4) With each area of lack, indicate your level of concern, anxiety and need to control. This reveals where your fears appear to manifest most strongly. From 0 - 10 with 0 representing no concern, anxiety or need to control, and 10 representing great concern, anxiety and need to control, rate each of your scarcity areas.

5) With radical self-honesty which one of the following two desires have you made your priority?
a) For the problem as you see it to improve or be solved? Or...
b) For your perception of the problem to be healed?

The ego is a master at diversion. Its commitment is to consistently divert our attention away from the real cause of all our problems. Our deep self-hatred is fueled by unconscious guilt, and this single issue lies at the root of our suffering. The resulting belief in our own extreme unworthiness is the secret motivator that drives all our fears.

As long as the real cause of all adversity remains unrecognized, it continues to be freely projected outward onto the world; it is then returned to us in the form of random chaos. We stay so busy attempting to remedy the symptoms or effects of these ego attacks that we rarely go within to ask for healing of their one true cause. And as we remain busily distracted by attempts to solve our problems independently from Spirit, the actual cause, the unconscious guilt, is left unhealed.

We cannot conceive of the infinitely Loving nature of God's Will for us. If we could, we would never dream of bothering to defend our self from scarcity, danger, loss or attack in any form. If we trusted in our Holy Self, we would know we cannot *be* attacked. If we really knew God's Will, we would also experience and accept the unlimited Love that is our inheritance.

As long as we prefer to trust in the ego's lies instead of God's Love as expressed through our Holy Self, we will unconsciously limit the expression of God's Love in our life. And this self-imposed limitation will manifest in our body through sickness, pain and aging, or through financial scarcity, depression, relationship conflict or other destructive forms.

REVIEWING YOUR ANSWERS

Which areas of your life do you use to hide, or separate from God's Love as your Holy Self? Go back and look at your answers to Question One: These areas of your life are some of the ways you choose to separate from God. The ego perceives lack in each of these areas. If you believe these challenges are real, you cannot forgive them.

Go to your answers for Question Two: These are the ego's interpretation of the causes of scarcity. Is the cause "out there" in the body, in another, in the world, or in the past? If you think it is, you are separating the problem from its real and only cause. As long as you exclude the real cause of unconscious guilt, it cannot be healed.

Go to your answers for Question Three: These are your usual ego fear responses to the areas of scarcity. And these areas of fear also represent your expectations. These are ways you habitually limit yourself and also divine abundance. They are your unconscious self-imposed restrictions on God's Love. God's Love is always endless supply, health, joy, oneness, Love and peace.

The ego attracts scarcity to us. This is a primary way to distract us from discovering *it* is the one cause of all adversity. If we really knew this, we would choose against the ego at every opportunity. But past experience colors our perception of challenges we seemingly face today. We believe the past is real, but what we don't recognize is that everything we ever learned has come from the ego's past—not from the eternal present of our Holy Self.

This means everything we thought we learned has actually been learned from the ego's projection. And what the ego learns is always used for attack. All the laws of the world operate from the ego's past script of prior experience. And they are all founded in fear.

You remain stuck and limited only because you must still be choosing to value what the past has taught you. You trust in your own experience and in the world as your teacher. Holy Spirit's miracles cannot touch the past or the future, as long as you insist on valuing these limitations. You anticipate the future based on your past ego experience, and then you plan for it accordingly. This is merely a continuation of the ego's prescription for unconscious self-attack.

By projecting the past onto the future you set up a defense against Love, which is found only in the present moment. The present is the only instant in which miracles can occur. Jesus teaches that your defenses are always against God as your Holy

Self. You defend against God every time you make decisions alone, or attempt to solve problems independently from Spirit. Through your defense, you give the illusory problem reality and thereby assign it power over you. Whatever you defend against, you must expect. Expectation is attraction, and what you attract must indeed manifest. It is vitally important to exhume all your unconscious fears so you can release them, in exchange for miracles.

"You would anticipate the future on the basis of your past experience, and plan for it accordingly. Yet by doing so you are aligning past and future, and not allowing the miracle, which could intervene between them, to free you to be born again." T-13.VI.4:7-8

Now review your answers to Question Four: You rated each of your areas of concern from 0 - 10, indicating your level of concern, anxiety and need for control. High ratings reflect your fear of God's Love in that particular area. If the level of fear is high, you clearly must still believe the ego's persistent sense of threat. Take note of the higher-rated areas, and be willing to take these issues to Spirit for healing. Ask to see the real cause of these issues, instead of your perception of them.

Lastly, review your answers to Question Five: Which do you desire more, to have the problem resolved or to have your perception of the problem healed? As long as you believe the problem requires resolution more than you believe your perception of separation and scarcity needs healing, the true cause of the problem *cannot be healed.* The cause will remain intact, continuing to sabotage various areas of your life.

I suggest you take all the areas you're now willing to heal through the forgiveness/Atonement process, found on page 297.

PROBLEMS NEVER LEAVE THEIR SOURCE

The person, the past, the sickness, the situation or the problem as we see it always occurs in our mind and nowhere else. When we displace the problem by perceiving it as outside us—as seeming to be caused by another, the body, the past, or elsewhere—we are acting faithlessly. If you did not doubt you are entirely worthy of being forgiven the cause of the problem in your own mind (to be healed of it, in other words), it would be removed. But your decision to doubt is born of your independent will not to allow the cause of the problem to be solved.

> *"Ideas leave not their source, and their effects but seem to be apart from them. Ideas are of the mind. What is projected out, and seems to be external to the mind, is not outside at all, but an effect of what is in, and has not left its source."*
> T-26.VII.4:7-9

The one cause of all problems is un-forgiveness of guilt in your mind. If you believe the cause of your suffering is found in any other place than your own mind, you have made the problem unsolvable. As Jesus teaches, cause (mind) and effect (form) can never be separated, except in delusions. Both the guilty cause of the problem and the problem itself are found only in our mind. The problem only appears to be outside us. This is nothing but an ego trick designed to convince us the cause of suffering lies someplace else. It's meant to keep us from ever discovering the real cause and source, which is the ego within our mind.

There is no problem or situation that faith will not undo and heal. There is nothing at the level of effect (meaning form or behavior) that cannot be healed. But to allow healing, your faith must be placed exclusively in the knowing that the cause is within your own mind—and not anywhere outside it, despite appearances.

If you go on pursuing the problem's resolution outside, trying to fix things at the effect level independent of Spirit's guidance, you will make the real solution impossible. If you wish to maintain that the problem's source is someone or something in the past or outside your own mind (including your own body), then the real meaning of the seeming problem along with its solution will be lost to you. The cause is always unforgiven self-hatred and guilt harbored within your mind, and self-forgiveness is always the solution. Failure to recognize this means the true cause of all problems will not have been healed, and will reappear again and again, albeit perhaps in different form.

All problems have already been solved. They all have only one source, which is in our mind. The solution for all problems is the Atonement, the divine correction of error, the undoing of fear. You need not earn it, because it is already your inheritance. But in order to claim this gift of correction, you must be willing to accept it. Are you ready? Or is the ego's obsessive desire for false humility and unworthiness far more valuable to you? — KEY

Drop it. You possess the power to drop this deep sense of unworthiness, and when you do, you set everyone free along with yourself. But as long as you choose to hang onto your sense of unworthiness, you will demand this same degree of worthlessness from others. And you will attack them for it.

Jesus was able to perform countless miracles. He facilitated healing at all levels, by undoing guilt in the minds of others. He undid the fear that blocked them from receiving the perfect healing that is everyone's inheritance. This profound healing of mind was received, allowing the miracle to transfer to the physical level as well. Physical miracles took the form of healing the body, control of weather and raising of the dead, to name but a few. The principle for each healing remained the same: Cause and effect are united in the mind, so when a mind is healed, physical healings follow.

Every healing He effected was total, and took no time to accomplish. He knew with certainty the source of all suffering occurred in one place only. No matter the appearance, the affliction or the seeming severity of the problem, Jesus knew all problems are equally illusory, therefore there could be no hierarchy among them. One source of suffering could not be more difficult to heal than another. And in His total faith, He was able to consistently call upon the miracle to heal them all.

Seeing no hierarchy among illusions, Jesus was perfectly able to recognize there is no order of difficulty in miracles.

> "It must be true the miracle can heal all forms of sickness, or it cannot heal. Its purpose cannot be to judge which forms are real, and which appearances are true. If one appearance must remain apart from healing, one illusion must be part of truth. And you could not escape all guilt, but only some of it." T-30.VI.7:1-4

Jesus adamantly states there is no ego appearance that cannot be overlooked and forgiven; no form of suffering that cannot be exchanged for the miracle of healing. If there were a hierarchy of sickness, for instance, where some illnesses were beyond the power of the miracle to heal, he says this would mean some "sins" must stand forever beyond forgiveness. It would mean one ego mistake actually could hold the power to undo creation itself and destroy the Will of God. Only if this impossible idea were possible, he says, could some appearances withstand the miracle and not be healed by it.

> "There can be no appearance that can not be overlooked. For if there were, it would be necessary first there be some sin that stands beyond forgiveness. There would be an error that is more than a mistake; a special form of error that remains unchangeable, eternal, and beyond correction or escape. There would be one mistake that had the power to undo creation, and to make a world that could replace it and destroy the Will of God. Only if this were possible could there be some appearances that could withstand the miracle, and not be healed by it." T-30.VI.5:4-8

Through the message of *A Course in Miracles*, Jesus calls to us to demonstrate our total invulnerability to all the ego made, just as He did. Truly, there is nothing else to do but wake from our dream of victimhood, suffering and death. The first step involves sorting out illusions from Truth. The Happy Dream is one where we no longer choose to attack our self through our own distorted projections. We plainly recognize no matter how convincing outer appearances may seem to be, they are unreal. We commit to looking beyond them, asking for corrected perception instead. This is forgiveness in process.

GIVING IS RECEIVING

I studied the *Course* for many years before I began to understand one of its central teachings: Giving is receiving. In our ego perception, when we give something away we appear to lose it; when we share something, we appear to have less for our self as a consequence. The ego's world is based on its law of deprivation, which is built upon a foundation of scarcity in all things. This is a warped, upside down perception, opposite to God's law of extension as abundance and infinite supply. Both these diametrically opposed thought systems are held in our mind simultaneously, but in order to see truly, we must first *un*-learn the ego's perception.

Because our mind is split, we don't see the Real World, which is a reflection of Heaven in our healed mind. Here, fear and guilt have already been undone. We don't seem able to access it consistently, because we value the ego's idols and world more. In the ego world, we are taught to perceive our self as separate from all we see; we are taught everything we perceive is outside our mind and independent of it. We are taught we are at the mercy of independent forces: Time and matter are believed to have power over us. The body is believed to be more powerful than the mind. We believe nature's laws both sustain and kill us. Our belief in the concept of physical death, together with the ego's overwhelming evidence in support of death, prove the "validity" of this point over and over.

In the ego's paradigm, cause and effect are reversed. We think the world, independent from our mind, is a cause in itself and we are but its effect. In this thought system, it is blasphemous to regard our mind as the only cause of all that appears to exist. It is regarded as ludicrous that the world cannot be a cause, but merely an effect of our mind.

But once the ego is dismissed, the mind returns to its divine purpose of extending Love. No longer does it project the ego's guilt and fear. Yet we have to choose this divine purpose willingly for ourselves.

Cause exists in our mind, and effect is the body/world, which appears to be outside us. Both cause and effect remain together in the mind and never leave it, so when we make a judgment against another or hold a grievance, we perpetuate an illusion about them. This illusion blocks all Truth. And because giving *is* receiving, the judgment we cast upon another is always an unseen judgment that we make about our self.

"You cannot perpetuate an illusion about another without perpetuating it about yourself." T-7.VIII.4:1

The ego's intention is to preserve conflict. It superficially attempts to diminish conflict on our behalf, so we don't realize its true intent. Its goal is to convince us to rely on it for all problem solving, persuasively promising us that doing so will free us from conflict. If we saw through the ego's false promises, it is well aware we might drop it and free our self instead.

"The ego always tries to preserve conflict. It is very ingenious in devising ways that seem to diminish conflict, because it does not want you to find conflict so intolerable that you will insist on giving it up. The ego therefore tries to persuade you that [it] can free you of conflict, lest you give the ego up and free yourself." T-7.VIII.2:2-4

By encouraging us to see our problems outside our self, caused by others, the body and the world, the ego compels us to keep miscreating through projection. We can't help but project judgment and blame, as long as we perceive the cause of problems outside our own mind. These actions are intertwined. The mind is all-powerful and its divine purpose is only to extend Love. The ego's aim is to portray the mind as impotent. It has misused the mind to project conflict outside us, in an effort to distract us from the real cause of conflict and suffering, which is the ego thought system itself.

> " Using its own warped version of the laws of God, the ego utilizes the power of the mind only to defeat the mind's real purpose. It projects conflict from your mind to other minds, in an attempt to persuade you that you have gotten rid of the problem." T-7.VIII.2:5-6

The ego believes it can offload its own dark thoughts and fears by projecting them onto others or the body. But casting judgment outward is the way to ensure we keep it for our self. It upholds and strengthens the underlying guilt that feeds our fears, defenses and need to control.

> "Giving it is how you [keep] it. The belief that by seeing it outside you have excluded it from within is a complete distortion of the power of extension. That is why those who project are vigilant for their own safety. They are afraid that their projections will return and hurt them. Believing they have blotted their projections from their own minds, they also believe their projections are trying to creep back in. Since the projections have not left their minds, they are forced to engage in constant activity in order not to recognize this." T-7.VIII.3:7-11

Despite the temptation to perceive attack and respond by judging or blaming another, we must remember all judgment is self-attack. We will unknowingly reinforce our own guilt, our own sense of self-hatred and self-attack, by believing we have been unfairly treated by someone or something out there in the world.

" [Do not be afraid of the ego.] It depends on your mind, and as you made it by believing in it, so you can dispel it by withdrawing belief from it. Do not project the responsibility for your belief in it onto anyone else, or you will preserve the belief. When you are willing to accept sole responsibility for the ego's existence you will have laid aside all anger and all attack, because they come from an attempt to project responsibility for your own errors. But having accepted the errors as yours, do not keep them. Give them over quickly to the Holy Spirit to be undone completely, so that all their effects will vanish from your mind and from the Sonship as a whole." T-7.VIII.5.

CHAPTER THREE

DOES GOD KNOW ABOUT THE WORLD?

Technically, God cannot know of something that masquerades as His opposite. God is all-encompassing Love *without* opposite. Nothing exists apart from this. All we perceive that seems to be Love's opposite exists merely as illusion within our wrong-minded perception.

Two dreams are occurring simultaneously in our mind: The ego's dream of the body/world, and the right-minded dream of the Real World. This right-minded dream can only be perceived through Spirit in our mind. Of these two dreams, the one we will see and experience is the one we currently believe and value. For most of us, it will be the ego's dream of body and world as existing outside and separate from the mind. Of course, cause and effect remain together in our mind no matter which dream we choose, and can never be separate.

The cause of the ego dream is our choice to believe in illusory sin, guilt and fear. Its effects within our mind are conflict, scarcity, pain, disease, loss and physical death. But once we change our mind through forgiveness, we change the cause in our mind. As the cause is healed of fear and returned to Love, the effects are free to be returned to Love as well.

We can apply advanced forgiveness to everything that threatens our peace. In doing so, we remember there is no one and no-thing out there to forgive. The following prayer was gifted me by Spirit, and invokes miraculous results when intended with heart-felt sincerity:

"Spirit, please help me forgive myself for using ___(person, situation, judgment, sickness, pain, self-judgment, sadness, anger, addiction, excess weight, depression, financial scarcity, etc)___ to attack myself and separate from Your Love as my Holy Self. Amen."

Everything that upsets us is a call for Love. It's a fresh opportunity to look mindfully with Spirit (and without self-judgment) at all we have unknowingly projected outside for the purpose of self-attack. Until we fully recognize that all attack is self-attack, we will continue to project and attract much suffering. Forgiveness gives us the opportunity to exhume and release our unconscious guilt and desire for punishment.

God does not know of our miscreations with the ego. A vast ocean is not aware of the nature of the tiny ripple that resists it, nor is the sun aware of a stray sunbeam. God sent the Holy Spirit into our mind to call us back to the Truth of our majestic Identity in God's Love.

Our single-minded choice to see only Love provides the cause for the healed Real World dream, or Happy Dream, within our mind. With corrected perception, no scarcity, conflict, disease or death can occur. In this dream, our trust has been transferred completely from the ego to our Holy Self. We have overcome fear and guilt, and we know who we are as infinite expressions of God's Love.

The Real World is not a place we go to. It is a state of mind that already exists, as it patiently waits for us to surrender all guilt, judgment and attack. In the Real World dream, we recognize we are the Kingdom of Heaven. Here there is no lack. We know we have everything because we *are* everything—for we recognize having and being are the same. The end of the world is not its fiery destruction, but its reinterpretation into Heaven. Spirit has the power to change the whole foundation of the world we see, thereby transforming it from the ego's dream into a dream without conflict, sickness, pain, loss or death.

"The end of the world is not its destruction, but its translation into Heaven." T-11.VIII.1:8

"The Holy Spirit has the power to change the whole foundation of the world you see to something else; a basis not insane, on which a sane perception can be based, another world perceived. And one in which nothing is contradicted that would lead the Son of God to sanity and joy. Nothing attests to death and cruelty; to separation and to differences. For here is everything perceived as one, and no one loses that each one may gain." T-25.VII.5.

This awakening, or transfer process from fear to Love, is what Jesus calls the development of trust (*Manual for Teachers, ACIM*). This transfer process is accomplished through forgiveness, which causes us to undergo a radical reversal of thoughts, beliefs and values. The Real World is *not* accomplished though death. It is realized only through knowing, without doubt, that only one power exists—and that power is God's Love as our one cherished, Holy Self.

God does not know the false self, the self we made up. This is why we feel so alone and vulnerable as we believe the ego's perception. But as the ego falls away, our Holy Self is revealed in our own awareness and experience. The Holy Self is embodied and embraced by us, so the infinite Love and security we previously craved now become known in our own experience, as our Self.

"The real world was given you by God in loving exchange for the world you made and the world you see. Only take it from the hand of Christ and look upon it. Its reality will make everything else invisible, for beholding it is total perception. And as you look upon it you will remember that it was always so. Nothingness will become invisible, for you will at last have seen truly." T-12.VIII.8:1-5

WHICH WORLD WILL I EXPERIENCE:
THE EGO'S, OR GOD'S?

We, the eternally guiltless extensions of God, fell asleep and dreamed we are separate from our Source. We willingly hallucinated an entire thought system of fear, along with a world based on separation and death. But the mind that did this is now awakening to recognize it has been split—and it desires to heal this separation and undo the ego thought system. This split mind has two simultaneous dreams running side by side, like two separate movies playing together on the same screen. One movie is the ego's world of fear and attack; the other is the Real World of endless Love, healing and joy. We see and experience the movie of our choice, whichever one we believe and therefore value. Both can't be seen at the same time. We always choose one or the other.

> *"The world you see must be denied, for sight of it is costing you a different kind of vision. [You cannot see both worlds,] for each of them involves a different kind of seeing, and depends on what you cherish. The sight of one is possible because you have denied the other." T-13.VII.2:1-3*

Everything we seem to see and experience in either movie has no intrinsic value or reality of its own. We give everything all the meaning it has for us. Everything, including the body/world, is inherently neutral. We either choose to look upon it with fear, or with Love. As we awaken, we realize the single cause of everything we perceive lies in our mind. As we undo our belief that outside cause can affect us, we simultaneously recognize all cause is within our mind. This means we are genuinely forgiving it. And as we do this, something quite profound occurs.

We begin to recognize for our self that nothing external, including the body, is separate from us. If we sense something in the body or the world, we know it's in our own mind and not something occurring externally. We realize firsthand that everything we seem to witness lives inside our mind. And although everything is inherently neutral, we clearly recognize its meaning is derived from our relationship with it.

Are we relating to it from the ego's fear, or from God's Love? It is our relationship with it that makes any given object or event part of a dream of death and separation, or part of a dream of awakening, life and oneness. Both dream movies are playing simultaneously. We can choose in any now moment, to decide which of these movies we wish to be in relationship with. The two movies are described here:

1) Through the Ego in my mind, I Make the World

While I perceive through the ego, there is indeed a body and a world "out there." I may recognize intellectually that both the body and world are in my mind. Yet while I remain entrenched in this world, still valuing its laws of sickness, pain, medicine, economics, nutrition, diet, aging, and death (to name only a few), I will not trust, know or demonstrate the power of the risen Christ within. I will not yet trust Love completely, because the central dream of death is still a cherished reality within my experience.

I still place the majority of my trust in the ego's domain, continuing to abide by its laws, independent from Spirit. Here, I may seem to espouse Jesus' teachings, but I am not yet willing to shift my allegiance entirely to trust in only God's laws. I do not yet know and demonstrate that there is no order of difficulty in miracles, because I still believe in a hierarchy of illusions. Here, I have placed my feet in two separate canoes, so to speak. One foot is in Spirit's canoe, and the other one in the ego's. I have not made an unequivocal choice to live out from the Christ within.

From this split-minded perception, I will still unconsciously believe God did create this world of guilt, fear, suffering and death. I still won't realize *I AM* God. I will see God as outside myself, and not abiding within me, as me—and as everyone else. Instead, I will continue to trust in what the ego informs my body's senses about the body and world.

In my body and the world, I will seem to suffer from the effects of separation between God and what appears to be *not* God—because I do not yet realize through firsthand experience that both God and ego are in my own mind. I won't know completely that both these diametrically opposed thought systems are in my mind, and that everything they each made or created is still in my mind, having never left its source. And that in each moment I can choose to perceive either one according to which I value.

I will still separate the body/world from my mind. I will not know the body/world exists purely as relationship in my mind. I will not realize it is never the body or world that are the problem, because I won't recognize body and world are neutral. I won't know the source of suffering or healing always lies in my relationship with it in my mind.

I will not recognize that all my special relationships with any aspects of the body/world must be transformed into Holy Relationships before true transcendence of form can occur. And because I don't yet accept this, I will believe and thus witness to the ego's belief that the world is departed by death, not transcended by Truth.

2) Through God in my Mind, I Co-create the World

As I awaken to the Christ as the one power within, I see this: The body/world the ego made to attack God's Love, and that which God created are both in my mind. All exists within my mind, therefore as my mind is healed, my relationship with all will be Holy, and will emanate from this Love. Here I will witness the effects of having healed the one true cause of all suffering. The symptoms, the body/world, are also healed as a result.

Now is the ego dream of suffering and death transformed into Spirit's dream of joy and Life. This is the Real World, the Happy Dream. Through forgiveness, we switch from one dream movie to the other. The ego's central dream of death is the foundation of the cycle of birth and death, which perpetuates the illusion of time. But how could there possibly exist an opposite or end to God's all-encompassing Love and Life? As

I overcome my unconscious devotion to guilt and death, what then could I possibly fear?

As I come to recognize and truly embody my own guiltlessness through deep acceptance, I no longer expect punishment and no longer need defense. I have accepted God's Identity as my own. As I embrace and embody this Love within, I allow the Christ to live through me as my True Identity. And as the breath of Christ heals through me, I am filled with the knowing I cannot be attacked. Love is living me now. And God's perfect innocence witnesses to my invulnerability. I cannot be affected by anything the illusory ego made as an attack on Love.

As I courageously exhume the ego's belief system and exchange it for miracles of forgiveness, my mind is healed. Recognizing that everything I seem to see is in my mind, I wholeheartedly offer my miscreations to Spirit, in exchange for healed perception. The result is that all I seem to see is healed as well. God is in my mind, and everything God in my mind sees, is healed.

Healing of the cause in my mind must extend to healing the effects as well, because ideas leave not their source. I recognize everything including the body/world are neither outside nor separate from me, but are merely relationships that live in my mind. And I choose to heal these relationships with everyone, with the body, the past, and the world. They can only be healed where they exist together as one—in my mind.

I learn to look past that which my body's eyes seem to see, and in doing so my inner vision is strengthened. I gradually withdraw allegiance from all the ego's laws I once believed in so completely.

If I am still too fearful to trust only in God's Laws, then I consciously invite Spirit to heal my perception...*while* I take medication, eat, balance my financial affairs, and attend to all other matters of life in 3-D perception. I do this without guilt, trusting that by inviting Spirit into these activities I will receive the miracle.

I recognize whenever I perceive the ego's movie, it stems from fear in my mind. And when I perceive the Real World movie, it is born from Love in my mind. I recognize the ego's world *and* Spirit's Real World are both in my mind. As Jesus tells us, He already overcame the ego's world on our behalf, through his resurrection. He undid the central dream of death for us all. All that's required of me is to fully accept this for myself.

From this perception it is clear the ego movie in my mind is certainly not of God. Unlike the Happy Dream, the ego's movie is not a dream I dream with God. This is a dream without God, which makes it a nightmare of separation and death. But as I look upon the glory of the Real World dream, I know God did indeed create this magnificent dream of healing. God in my mind created the Real World dream of grace-filled joy and Love. And it is a perfect reflection of the Love of God that *I AM*, and that we all are.

IS THE SCRIPT ALREADY WRITTEN?

Students of *A Course in Miracles* often refer to the *Course*'s teaching that the script is already written. In the past I thought this meant fate had already been set in stone, and it didn't matter what I did or didn't do. But now I realize it means *God Is*, regardless of the illusions we seem to perceive here in the dream. The right-minded part of us is constant, sure and eternal. It is changeless. It always has been and always will be, even while we think we are lost in the ego. In the ego's mindless state, we are simply asleep and unaware of the real script, in which we are consciously and continuously united with God's Will.

We are gifted with free will. We will use it to choose either the ego or Spirit in any given moment. But if we choose ego, it does not make the ego real. The script is already written in God's Loving perfection, and it is full of exuberant joy. This remains true whether or not we choose to believe in a dream of suffering and death instead. The sooner we choose against the ego's dream, then, the quicker we can claim conscious awareness of the all-encompassing Love that has forever been, and always will be the essence of our Holy Self.

Through Jesus' resurrection and the Atonement, the ego's dream was already undone long ago. But we have free will to choose, so we exercise it by hanging out a little longer in the illusory ego's hell state, instead of choosing to dwell in Heaven's state. Therefore, in our perception it seems to take time to free our self. Yet the instant we commit our self wholly and irrevocably to choose only Love, peace and joy, that is the very moment only Love, peace and joy become what we perceive.

We can only perceive what we value. If we value fear, we perceive suffering. If we value only Love, we perceive and experience only Love. Until our unconscious blocks to Love have been exhumed and exchanged for miracles, we will continue to see a body/world of suffering. This is what the Atonement is for. Once we choose to accept forgiveness in every circumstance and every moment, the Real World will be restored to our awareness. This will occur when we decide to value only Love.

"When you want only love you will see nothing else." T-12. VII.8:1

The ego's paradigm has no script, because its dream exists apart from God. And anything apart from God simply does not exist. So how, in Truth, could it ever have a script? The ego's illusory script does have a consistent and repetitive goal, however, which is to kill our body before we awaken to the recognition that we share God's power, and thus also share in His invulnerability.

Beware the mistaken belief that Spirit brings us suffering in the form of lessons. Spirit is Love, and Love can only bring Love, peace, happiness and joy. Any lessons we learn through suffering are not brought to us by Spirit. There is no script requiring us to learn in this way. These hard lessons are choices we make, a path we ourselves freely choose to take. In Truth, all errors or pain can be given to Spirit for release and reinterpretation.

I say this because for many years I mistakenly believed a divine script existed here in the ego dream, one that was indelibly etched in stone. I really believed some of my toughest forgiveness lessons were placed in the script by Spirit. Unknowingly, I had projected my unconscious fears onto God, and had made for myself an ego version of god. Naturally this pseudo-god would place many painful forgiveness lessons on my path. No wonder I was so reluctant to trust in Spirit! Who would want to trust in a cruel God like that?

Only later did I realize God is all-encompassing Love with no opposite. Therefore there can be no suffering, pain, conflict, lessons or death in God. *I* am the decision maker. I am the perceiver. And my experience is determined by which inner teacher I choose to perceive with. If I choose the ego, then I will experience pain. In choosing Spirit, I will offer my perception of suffering in exchange for the Atonement and the miracle.

From the ego's perception, we may tend to see Spirit as something outside our self at first. But Spirit, or Love, is the true essence of who we are. We are expressions of God's Love. And there is nothing more powerful than God's Love.

Through the ego, we have temporarily forgotten who we are. We made up a dream-self and world. Making up an illusory power called fear, we claimed it to be the opposite of Love. But God is like the sun, and we are like the rays of light the sun emits. There is no separation between the sun and its rays. Likewise, there is no separation between us and God's all-encompassing Love.

THE EGO'S HORIZONTAL PLANE
OF ENDLESS NEEDS

If we are seeking happiness and security outside our self, believing whatever we seek will be the answer to our problem, we'd better look at the flip side of the ego's setup to get the complete picture.

Let's say you are seeking a romantic relationship to fulfill your need for companionship. The ego allows you to see the surface desire but won't let you see its shadow, which is the planned outcome it has for you. Its real goal in seeking relationship is for you to experience some form of loneliness, betrayal and/or abandonment.

Or let's look at the goal of abundance. Its ego shadow is scarcity. You have set your sights on wealth as a goal, yet the ego is busy plotting to attract some form of scarcity. This may not necessarily be in the form of monetary lack, but could manifest as scarcity in health or in relationship instead.

On the following page is a diagram showing how the ego seeks one thing, while secretly ensuring you end up with its opposite. On the lower half of the diagram, you'll see the ego is our greatest saboteur. It is always consistent in seeking its true goal of deprivation, destruction and death. The ego's mantra, as stated earlier, is *seek but do not find.*

As long as we independently seek to satisfy our desires through the ego, we will unconsciously attract the opposite. The ego will see to it, because suffering is its consistent wish for us. Seeking security, love, happiness, abundance, health, pleasure, companionship and life independently from Spirit, guarantees we will unknowingly invite suffering.

HORIZONTAL PLANE OF TIME = SUFFERING
Problem solving through personal (ego) will

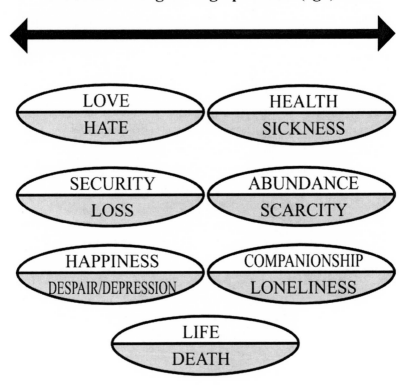

Seeking completion through the ego ensures we attract
its opposite: Suffering. Ego presents many different
problems and many illusory solutions.
But all attempts to problem-solve are merely shifts
made BETWEEN illusions. No healing takes place.

Diagram #3
The Ego's Horizontal Plane of Linear Time

THE MIRACLE:
A VERTICAL AXIS
OF ONE NEED AND ONE SOLUTION

When we are willing to admit the one cause of all our problems is in our mind, and never outside us as it appears, real healing can occur. Now we can forgive all problems and accept the miracle instead in any instant we choose. This is the process of bringing illusions to Truth.

We begin to recognize for our self that the cause and the answer are both in our mind. When we see and admit to this, Spirit is able to help us. We are saved from the ego's plan of sabotage. Holy Spirit knows exactly what we need, and His goal for us is unending joy and happiness. This miracle of healing requires no time.

As seen in the diagram on the following page, the vertical axis of the miracle collapses the painful gap that seems to separate us from the Love we so desperately yearn for. Our deepest desire is to experience this Love as our one Self.

THE MIRACLE
Vertical axis collapses time/suffering

LOVE

SECURITY

HAPPINESS

ABUNDANCE

HEALTH

COMPANIONSHIP

LIFE

**BRINGS ALL
ILLUSIONS
TO TRUTH**
Undoes the single cause
of all suffering

ONE NEED
To Know ThySelf in God

ONE ANSWER
Forgiveness/
The Atonement
(The Holy Instant)

Diagram #4
The Miracle's Vertical Axis Collapses Time

THE PROBLEM IS ALWAYS NEUTRAL

Everything we perceive is always neutral, with no exceptions. All meaning and value a problem, person or situation appears to have, is given it by our own interpretation. It has no inherent meaning of its own, nor does it possess any power apart from what we give it through our interpretation and belief.

A grievance, a headache, disease or death are all equally neutral. Not one of them holds more resistance to healing than any another, except in our belief. They, of themselves, hold no power to affect us when we realize they all dwell within the same category of illusion, regardless of the seeming severity. All forms of ego suffering, all problems of any kind are purely impersonal suggestions of an imaginary power that seemingly opposes and threatens God's Love and joy.

RESOLVING THE PROBLEM
AT THE EFFECT LEVEL ONLY

We try obsessively to solve our problems only at the level of form or behavior. In doing so, we resist acceptance of the Atonement, the one True remedy for the only cause of all problems. The Atonement undoes the cause of suffering in our mind, as its unparalleled power abolishes the unconscious self-hatred and guilt that produce all suffering.

If I perceive a problem, it's because I've misperceived my true goal, which is always peace through forgiveness. The ego misjudges both the goal and the means by which to achieve it. Its unconscious goal is always separation, and it pursues this aim by convincing you there actually *is* a problem. Whipping you up into a state of fear or anxiety, the ego then begs you to turn to it for advice on how to solve the issue it caused. And its advice will always be wrong.

But if we consciously decide our goal is always peace through forgiveness, regardless of appearances to the contrary, there can never be a situation that will not meet the goal. With this commitment, nothing can ever threaten us.

> "The value of deciding in advance what you want to happen is simply that you will perceive the situation as a means to [make] it happen. You will therefore make every effort to overlook what interferes with the accomplishment of your objective, and concentrate on everything that helps you meet it. T-17.VI.4:1-2
>
> "...when a situation has been dedicated wholly to truth, peace is inevitable." T-19.I.1:1

The ego claims the emotional and physical body as its identity. Every problem it perceives revolves around protecting, defending and acquiring for this ego self. Its perception is grossly polarized, as it perceives the body-self as deprived, frail and in need of constant attention and protection. It perceives incessant threat of attack, imagining a shadowy assailant quivering with anticipation as it waits for any opportunity to pounce and devour us.

Disease, pain, conflict, scarcity, loss, and even death represent some of the forms this ego-projected mystery attacker can take. There is but one attacker, which is the ego itself. However, this one assailant takes a thousand different forms in the ego's twisted, upside-down perception. What is the one thing the ego is actually terrified of? When you see it, you will also recognize there is no substance to this idea of a mystery attacker, with its myriad illusions of threat.

In every instance we seem to experience fear, compulsively trying to defend our self from the problem (as we perceive it), there is only one thing we're really trying to protect our self from. On the surface it might look like financial scarcity, ill health, security or a thousand other seeming threats. But these are purely effects or symptoms of the one unconscious fear we carry. What do we consistently defend our self from?

The ego musters all its fearful defenses against one enemy only. The ego's very existence depends on you never discovering the real source of all you defend yourself against.

Beneath every fear and every seeming threat we appear to face, lies just one unrecognized fear. It is the fear of God's Love. We are secretly terrified of God's Love as our Holy Self. This is the mighty and magnificent Holy Self in which we are all joined as one. We defend our self against having to remember the indestructible Love we are, as living extensions of God's Loving Will.

THE NATURE AND WILL OF GOD

"Fear of the Will of God is one of the strangest beliefs the human mind has ever made. It could not possibly have occurred unless the mind were already profoundly split, making it possible for it to be afraid of what it really is. Reality cannot "threaten" anything except illusions, since reality can only uphold truth. The very fact that the Will of God, which is what you are, is perceived as fearful, demonstrates that you [are] afraid of what you are. It is not, then, the Will of God of which you are afraid, but yours." T-9.I.1.

The nature of God is Love without opposite. Love is eternal and unchanging, unlike the conditional and temporary nature of the ego's "special" love, which it offers as a substitute. The nature of special love appears to change with each person we love, varying in intensity according to how well that love meets the ego's needs at the time. Often if the ego's needs are not met, love is withdrawn and we witness as love turns to hate. The ego sees everything as temporary and changeable, and its version of love conforms to these properties. However real Love never varies and is maximal in all ways, eternally.

"Perhaps you think that different kinds of love are possible. Perhaps you think there is a kind of love for this, a kind for that; a way of loving one, another way of loving still another. Love is one. It has no separate parts and no degrees; no kinds nor levels, no divergencies and no distinctions. It is like itself, unchanged throughout. It never alters with a person or a circumstance. It is the Heart of God, and also of His Son." W-127.1.

"Love's meaning is obscure to anyone who thinks that love can change. He does not see that changing love must be impossible. And thus he thinks that he can love at times, and hate at other times. He also thinks that love can be bestowed on one, and yet remain itself although it is withheld from others. To believe these things of love is not to understand it." W-127.2:1-5

The ego thought system is built on change, with everything appearing to be temporary in this world of illusion. The cycles of nature are in constant transition; the body is born, grows, withers with age and finally dies of decay. All of nature seems to be transitory.

The eternal meaning of God's nature goes far beyond our limited ability to perceive. It is beyond space, time and perception, and is infinite in the realm of Knowledge. It is boundless and formless. It is eternal Love without interruption or end. This Love is beyond our finite senses, although we can begin to embody this Holy Love by relinquishing our guilt through forgiveness. All perception is based on duality: A perceiver and the perceived. In God's Love there is only one. Oneness is entirely beyond the dualistic nature of perception.

The oneness of God is within each of us always, and this oneness is totally unaware of all we perceive through the ego. In other words, in Reality, not one of the dreadful things we think has occurred has ever actually happened. If God were a radar screen we could gaze upon to detect our degree of guilt, shame and unworthiness, nothing would show up. Neither our guilt, nor any of our bad deeds, fears or mistakes would show up on His divine radar. There is no such thing as sin.

There is no hierarchy of illusions, so an angry outburst is the same as murder. And a headache is the same as the final stages of cancer. *No hierarchy* means just that. Illusion is illusion. What is not real can't be ranked by degrees of truth, because it's all equally unreal.

Disease, scarcity and death are also equally unreal. Does physical death show up on God's radar? No. The nature and Will of God did not author the opposite of Life. Love, which is Life in God, cannot see the concepts of death, disease or scarcity. Our perception of these as "reality" is derived solely from the ego.

All our suffering arises because we confuse the unreal with God. Yet God and the unreal are diametrically opposed. Reality is uninterrupted Love, but the unreal is purely and always a call for Love. Love and the call for Love are the only two possible states, and there is nothing in between.

Every seemingly bad thing we do always comes from the ego, and is motivated by perceived lack of Love. As such, when a person commits a hurtful act, the origin of the behavior always stems from a call for Love. All calls for Love arise from unconscious self-hatred. Although it appears as if the person attacks another, in Truth she attacks herself. Then consciously or unconsciously, she harbors the ensuing guilt within.

Anyone you have ever felt personally assaulted by, past or present, has only attacked himself. And if you take offense, you reinforce your own unconscious guilt and self-hatred. His seeming attack upon you is really your own unconscious self-hatred projected outward. The ego uses people or situations to project our unconscious self-hatred back onto us.

When adversity or illness appears to strike, many pray to God for a remedy or healing of the perceived problem. This is a huge misperception. The problem is purely a symptom of the real and only issue, which is our belief we are separate from God's Love. When we ask God to heal the symptom instead of the real cause, symptoms may at times be alleviated by this form of prayer. Yet nothing has been accomplished in Truth. God cannot acknowledge an opposite of God. Sickness, scarcity, conflict, etc. cannot exist as opposites to Love. So the real cause cannot be healed.

This kind of prayer is an indication we don't yet know God, and therefore have no idea who *we* are. We are powerful extensions of God's Will here on Earth. If God is all-encompassing Love with no opposite, how could Love enter a nightmare of fear to fix something that doesn't even exist?

Imagine a young child in a deep sleep, having a terrible nightmare. To ask God to come in and fix our ego dream of life would be the same as if we tried to enter the child's nightmare in order to make it a better dream. If we Loved this child, wouldn't we whisper Lovingly to her, letting her know she's safe and is only dreaming? This is the way God's Love awakens us in this life. In gentle whispers we are told we are dreaming an ego dream of death, and that none of it is true.

There is no opposite of God's Love, and no opposite of God's eternal Will. We *are* God's Will. We are the Kingdom of Heaven. Our Identity is not the pseudo-self that made an illusory world, but the Holy Self that lies beneath the ego.

We can't conceive of just how Holy and cherished we are. As we undo the ego thought system, we become conscious extensions of God's Will. In doing so, we extend what we are. Extending Love is our only function. Whether sleeping or waking, we continuously project fear or extend Love. Those are our two choices, and we're always engaged in one or the other. Through the ego, we project unconscious guilt—hence our familiar and persistent sense of threat. As we awaken to our true Self we begin to extend Love, which is increasingly what we recognize our self and others to be.

Our Holy Self is everything. And because of this, it knows it *has* everything. There is no perception of lack, no perception of anything other than the perfect Truth of who we are. Accepting this power as Self, there is nothing we cannot accomplish in the name of Love's service.

OUR TRUE NATURE AND WILL

The nature of God is the nature of our Holy Self. The Will of God is our True Will. When we cease fearing God as Love, we will also cease fearing our own nature and True Will. Once the ego is undone, all that's left is our one Will with God, and its expression is unending Love and joy. Our free will to choose between ego and Spirit is just as powerful as God's Will.

God's Will cannot override our own ego will, here within the dream. All power is given us to choose to create with the Will of God, or to miscreate with the ego, projecting a world in which we wish for self-attack. As Jesus tells us in the *Course*, our will is as powerful as God's because we are living extensions of God's Will.

> *"Your will be done! In Heaven as on earth this is forever true. It matters not where you believe you are, nor what you think the truth about yourself must really be. It makes no difference what you look upon, nor what you choose to feel or think or wish. For God Himself has said, "Your will be done." And it is done to you accordingly." T-31.VI.4:3-8*

It's crucial that we willingly choose to undo our attachment to the ego thought system through forgiveness. The longer we remain possessed by the ego, seeking idols to replace our sense of Self, the longer we linger in suffering.

Our will is so unfathomably powerful that it made this entire universe and everything in it. Yet the majority of our will lies with the ego, hidden deep within our unconscious mind. Our will never stops projecting; it keeps on miscreating even while we sleep. The ego is obsessed with miscreation. Can you imagine what this hidden mass of darkness is responsible for projecting in our lives? We were created with free will choice. Will we use it to suffer, or to free our self?

When we ask only that God's Will be done, do we know what it is we ask for? When we sincerely ask *only* for God's Will to be done, we invoke miracles. The Will of God is our own

True Will. In any situation where we perceive threat, we can ask for God's Will to be done. To truly trust in God's Will is to feel thoroughly safe, peaceful and secure in every situation.

Trusting in God's Will to resolve everything elicits a deep sense of gratitude that's felt in advance. There is no shred of doubt about the outcome, even if we can't see what the outcome might be. In fact the absence of doubt is the miracles' prerequisite. It's a certainty of faith that God is all-Loving, and this certainty is embraced in gratitude. They go hand in hand.

> *"What is the Will of God? He wills His Son have everything. And this He guaranteed when He created him [as] everything. It is impossible that anything be lost, if what you [have] is what you [are]." T-26.VII.11:1-4*

> *"All real pleasure comes from doing God's Will. This is because [not] doing it is a denial of Self." T-1.VII.1:4-5*

> *"There is no strain in doing God's Will as soon as you recognize it is also your own." T-2.VI.6:4*

Any doubt we have about trusting God's Will implicitly in all situations, arises from the ego's projection of its god of fear. As long as we harbor any reservations about God's Will, it means the ego is still running our perception.

If this is the case, it means we hold unconscious defenses against Love that have not yet been raised to light for self-inquiry. These doubts about God manifest as projections in our life, causing us to suffer in fear. The ego is the belief that external things could happen to us without our will or consent. Jesus shares this about the ego:

> *"All that the ego is, is an idea that it is possible that things could happen to the Son of God without his will." T-21. II.6:4*

THE "GOD" THE EGO MADE:
ARE YOU FEARFUL OF GOD? AN EXERCISE

Following is an exercise that will assist in exhuming your unconscious beliefs about God. Your unconscious beliefs form the basis of your fear of God, which is really the unrecognized fear of Love itself.

1) What are the positive qualities of God's nature and Will?
With pen and paper, write down all the positive attributes or qualities of God's Love. Here are a few to get you started: Joy, unconditional Love, peace, infinite security. Go deep and see if you can come up with at least fifteen of these positive qualities for yourself. The more, the better.

These qualities form your intellectual list of God's celestial attributes. These are the things we believe on the surface; they're all the ego wants us to see. Ego doesn't want us to delve any deeper to find out what we *really* believe about God 's Love in our unconscious minds.

2) What will it cost me to trust exclusively in God?
Imagine what it would mean if you were to completely embrace this statement: *"I choose only God's Will for me, from this moment onward. In so doing, I choose to forfeit my own independent will in every area of my life."* If you ask for and accept only His Will, there is no room for your own separate will. Now, with radical self-honesty, what fears arise?

Write down all your fears and concerns about how this choice would impact each of the important areas of your life (see list on the next page). Unearthing these fears is invaluable. They pave the way out of fear forever, so please be totally honest with yourself. Write down any concerns about possible change, loss or sacrifice. Make a comprehensive list of all the so-called fearful or even disastrous scenarios that might occur if you totally surrendered your own independent will to God. What do you fear may change or fall away, specifically in the following areas?

- Finances and income
- Relationships
- Children and family
- Job or career
- Security and self image
- The body and health
- Pleasure
- Other

Any signs of concern or fear represent the tip of the iceberg, indicating a hidden wellspring of unconscious distrust in God's Love. When Tomas and I did this exercise after nearly 20 years of having studied the *Course*, we were astounded to discover just how much we did not want to entrust to Spirit. We still compartmentalized parts of our lives, feeling the need to keep them separate (and therefore safe) from our spiritual journey.

We all tend to categorize life as if it's a pie with lots of slices; one for family, one for income, another for physical health and so on. The ego instinct is to try to control some slices independently from Spirit. Yet this course of action never truly works. If we continue to insist on letting the ego control certain segments of the pie, believing these areas "too critical" to surrender to Spirit, the conflict of this stance eventually becomes unbearable. And it's here that we either opt to recycle again through scarcity, disease or death, *or* we decide to jump in and totally undo the ego by surrendering all to God.

3) Revealing the "god" the ego made:

Now look at your first list, the one you made of your positive beliefs about God's nature and Will. Place it next to the list containing all your fears about surrendering your life to God. It's likely you'll find these two lists are opposites of one another. One is full of Love and trust, and the other is full of fear and doubt. Look carefully: The first list of God's positive attributes is *real*. The second list is *unreal*. That second list represents your unconscious fear of God. This is your unconscious fear of Love itself.

Look again at your list of fears. This list represents the nature of the god the ego made. The ego projects these deep fears onto God, thereby persuading us to keep turning to the ego for guidance instead of trusting in God's Love. The degree to which we continue to make our own independent decisions, goals, plans and attempts at control, is the degree to which we actually fear God's Love.

The ego's projection of god is what we're terrified of, and we can't see beyond it without exhuming these misperceptions about God first. How can we ever trust God as our Holy Self within, while the ego's god remains hidden on our inner altar, deep within the unconscious?

Look at all the things in our lives that we fear and defend our self against. And look at all we struggle to achieve and attain, independently from God. We do this because we are terrified of the ego's god—and as long as we continue to defend ourselves against this pseudo-god, we will remain in resistance to the real and only God within, which is our Holy Self.

All the things we fear and defend against are the things we prioritize above God. This includes the fear of not being able to access God within! All your desires and needs that appear to be unfulfilled from the past, present and even the future, take precedence over God's Love within. We unknowingly use all these as defenses against God's Love. They form our blocks to the awareness of Love's presence.

"The presence of fear is a sure sign that you are trusting in your own strength." W-48.3:1

If you truly wish to heal your unconscious fear of God, it will be helpful to take your list of fears and go through the Atonement process with each of these blocks to Love's presence. Forgive them one by one, and surrender them in exchange for the miracle. In this process you will relinquish the ego's obsession with unconscious self-attack. The Atonement process is found on page 297.

God's all-encompassing Love is all there is. *Nothing else exists.* When we see or feel anything other than Love, we are hallucinating. So if God's Love is all there is, what is it we obsessively defend against? Why do we insist on problem solving independently from Spirit? We still fear God. We don't trust Love because we don't yet know it for our self. We don't know our Holy Self.

Through the ego thought system, we project an ego image onto God. And this god that frightens us is the imaginary god the ego made, a cruelly demanding god who tests us constantly and gives us freedom only in death. No wonder we are terrified of surrender! This god we made is the greatest unconscious block to Love; it prevents our ability to trust in the power and presence of our Holy Self.

A PRAYER TO RELEASE FEAR, GUILT, PAIN, ANXIETY, SICKNESS OR SCARCITY

"Every fear, pain or concern I have about my own or another's safety is always my defense against God's Love. I choose now to be mindful of every instance of fear. I choose to see fear for what it truly is: Rejection of my Self, whose Identity is Love and innocence. In defending myself from fear and suffering, I make them real in my belief. And by making them real, I reject the Love and guiltlessness that is my true safety, my Holy Self.

In the name of God's Love, I unite with Spirit's Will now. Together we choose against fear and suffering in every form. In His Will I am safe. Through His Will I remember I hold dominion over everything the ego made to attack me or another. Fear and suffering are not His Will. When I allow myself to be consumed by fear or pain, I isolate myself from God's Love as my Holy Self. I willingly accept only God's joyous Will for me, and reject anything the ego uses to try to distract me from my one-minded path Home. Amen."

CHAPTER FOUR

JESUS' DEEPER MESSAGE: A HOLOGRAPHIC REVELATION

Jesus was the first to complete his full return to God. He was the first to recognize and overcome the entire dream of separation by undoing its nucleus of death. In the illusion of time He was our pioneer, the one who demolished the veil of death and fulfilled God's Will completely. Until Jesus triumphantly overcame death through His own resurrection, we all, the one collectively sleeping mind, dwelt in darkness.

Through His resurrection He overcame all ego laws and gifted us with the Atonement, which is the undoing of fear. The Atonement is an immediate tool for correcting fear in our perception. Use of it will eventually undo our unconscious devotion to death, allowing us to follow Him out of the ego dream. Jesus *is* the Atonement. In His completion of God's perfect Will, He accomplished our healing too. It is already done. All we need do is accept it.

> *"You were in darkness until God's Will was done completely by any part of the Sonship. When this was done, it was perfectly accomplished by all. How else could it be perfectly accomplished? My mission was simply to unite the will of the Sonship with the Will of the Father by being aware of the Father's Will myself. This is the awareness I came to give you..."* T-8.IV.3:1-5

The extraordinary holographic message of *A Course in Miracles* is gradually recognized and integrated as a way of living and thus, of being. What is meant by the term, "holographic message"? The ego's severely limited frame of reference is focused upon one goal, of separation from the one Love we are. Miracles are holographic in the sense that they heal in all dimensions of time, collapsing fragments of the ego's thought system in every now moment that we invoke and thereby accept them.

> "Miracles are part of an interlocking chain of forgiveness which, when completed, is the Atonement. Atonement works all the time and in all the dimensions of time."
> T-1.I.25.

> "However, the miracle entails a sudden shift from horizontal to vertical perception. This introduces an interval from which the giver and receiver both emerge farther along in time than they would otherwise have been. The miracle thus has the unique property of abolishing time to the extent that it renders the interval of time it spans unnecessary."
> T-1.II.6:3-5

The deeper calling beckons us to live out from the one power within; this calling is only accepted once we willingly join with Spirit to exhume and relinquish our unconscious fears, guilt and false humility. To relinquish is to forgive. As our trust in Love increases, fear falls away, and that's when we genuinely withdraw our dependence on the world's opinion to tell us who we are and what reality is.

What we see out in the world is what the ego mind sends our senses to go fetch: Only what it projects is verified by our senses, to invite us to react to it. When we withdraw our trust in the physical senses, however, we learn to rely on inner vision and guidance to show us what Reality is.

In these holographic teachings, Jesus exposes death for what it is—the most epic of all unconscious myths since the beginning of time. He urges us to see through its many disguises and overcome death in all its sinister forms, just as He did. Death is universally believed to be life's only certain outcome. It is deemed a natural and legitimate part of life, the one outcome we all expect. The ego's survival depends on the belief that physical death is non-negotiable, inevitable and inescapable. It deems us victims of its own laws of time, deprivation, disease, decay and death. In other words, it insists we are prey to a power other than God's all-encompassing Love. But how could a power other than God's Love possibly exist unless we, through our free will, choose to value it?

This is not a teaching of the body's immortality. Death, like all imagined powers other than God's Love, does not exist unless we desire it in our experience. In Jesus' physical resurrection He overcame the concept of death in all its forms, and He did it for all of us. He calls us to use this ego dream as a means to reverse the ego thought system, and reclaim our true inheritance as expressions of God's Love. Death is not part of Life. If it were, fear would be part of Love and the ego would be part of God.

The ego mind made the body for the purpose of using it to attack our self and the world, expressly to teach and prolong separation and suffering within the illusion of time. As we undo the ego, the purpose of the body and world are reversed. It becomes understood they are solely teaching devices for Love and forgiveness.

As the mind returns to sanity, it withdraws its belief in ego laws and strengthens its recognition that the body is under no laws but God's. What a relief! Finally we can quit taking false responsibility for our bodies and those of our loved ones, and learn to trust in Love for our wellbeing instead. Our increased trust in the Holy Self takes over, and miracles flow. Jesus reminds us to relinquish everything that does not matter (including the body), and allow Him to guide everything that *does* matter:

> "*My control can take over everything that does not matter, while my guidance can direct everything that does, if you so choose.*" T-2.VI.1:3.

> "*I will substitute for your ego if you wish... I can be entrusted with your body and your ego only because this enables you not to be concerned with them, and lets me teach you their unimportance.*" T-4.I.13:1,4

Through Jesus' guidance we come to recognize it is not the body that sustains us, but the Mind and Love of God. As our trust is withdrawn from the ego thought system, we discover biological ego laws that previously appeared to govern the body are eclipsed by God's law of unopposed Life.

Our return to Love involves un-learning and reversing the body's purpose. While under the ego's reign, the body is believed to be our source of life. It is also erroneously idealized as both our identity and goal, an end in itself. We haven't yet seen its purpose as purely a vehicle through which we un-learn our dependence on the ego, body and world.

Through the ego, the body assumes an identity of its own, an image we mistakenly invest with the power to change, wither, sicken and die. In short, we give the body false authority over our mind, in order to prove the illusion of attack is real. We give it emotional and biological intelligence so it appears to overrule our mind.

The ego set this up as a powerfully effective distraction, to prevent us from awakening to our Holy Self. Until we join God's Will in undoing our unconscious devotion to death in all its forms, we will continue to believe, manifest and demonstrate the body is more powerful than the mind of our Holy Self.

Jesus explains the body cannot create either sickness or health. Physical illness represents a belief in magic, which is the temptation to believe effects can be at cause. Yet all cause exists in the mind. Pain and illness seek to demonstrate that something other than the Will of God is real. There is no will but God's, and everything other than this is magic. Physical illness is not part of God's Will, therefore it is magic.

We mistakenly believe matter, including the body, holds a creative ability the mind cannot control. This compulsive ego belief that the body can develop symptoms of sickness or health independently of the mind, necessarily excludes trust in God's Will as our primary devotion.

"The body cannot create, and the belief that it can, a fundamental error, produces all physical symptoms. Physical

illness represents a belief in magic. The whole distortion that made magic rests on the belief that there is a creative ability in matter which the mind cannot control." T-2.IV.2:6-8

As we awaken, we learn the body is not who we are. It is not a purpose or goal in itself. The body is solely a means, a learning device to help us remember our true purpose. As the mind is healed, our secret devotion to suffering and death is undone. The body is returned to its proper role and is no longer used to demonstrate the illusion that it holds power and dominion over the mind.

The body is eventually restored to its rightful place in our perception as an effect only, never a cause. At this point we will know without doubt the body is simply not real. As an effect, it has no ability to create, cause, attack, get well, get sick or die. When this level of mastery is attained, as Jesus' demonstrated, we will witness to our self and the sleeping world that the healed mind, *not* the body, is the supreme and only cause.

Then and only then will the body have served its divine purpose of demonstrating the reversal of the world's thinking. Having done so, it may no longer be required as a vehicle. This, I believe, heralds the Real World yet to come fully into our awareness. As our fear of God's Love is undone and trust in God as Self is restored, the Real World will expand in our perception.

"Only the mind can create because spirit has already been created, and the body is a learning device for the mind. Learning devices are not lessons in themselves. Their purpose is merely to facilitate learning. The worst a faulty use of a learning device can do is to fail to facilitate learning. It has no power in itself to introduce actual learning errors. The body, if properly understood, shares the invulnerability of the Atonement to two-edged application." T-2.IV.3:1-6

The healed mind will lay the body aside in perfect health, peace and joy, once its mission is complete. But until the body's unreality and creative inability to cause change is known and demonstrated in our *experience*—until we fully realize *and demonstrate* it has no ability to get well, get sick or die—we have not yet claimed the sovereign power of the fully healed mind.

Until we accept into our experience the Truth that all power lies in God, we will continue to believe, accept and testify to the body's reality. And we will do this no matter how strongly we intellectually espouse the body's unreality.

While we choose to remain victims of the body, we believe and validate the body's reality. And we will not know a fully healed mind until we realize, accept and demonstrate that the body cannot be victimized. Until we are ready to exhume, examine and release our false dependence on ego laws, we will be afraid of the power of our mind, and of our Holy Self. Thus we will choose the seemingly easier route of remaining as the body's victim, and death will appear to claim it.

While death remains at the center of our unconscious dream, the most cherished idol on our inner altar, Life will not be experienced. As long as death eclipses God's Love in our awareness, life as we know it will reflect fear instead of Love, guilt instead of innocence, suffering instead of joy, and deprivation rather than infinite supply. This choice for pain is not necessary, yet as the world's most cherished idol, death beats God's Love, hands down.

Jesus tells us very clearly that death *and* God's Love cannot both be real. Death and God's Love are mutually exclusive and wholly irreconcilable. They cannot coexist. Yet through the ego, we try to manage both simultaneous beliefs. This is insanity. We say we believe in God yet we also believe in, and therefore see, death daily—whether reported in the media or in our own personal life. If we're absolutely honest, when we connect with God and with death in daily experience, which one of these beliefs is more firmly held to be true for us?

Jesus is adamant that only one, either death or God, is real and therefore true. While we maintain both as real, we keep ourselves in terrible turmoil, confusion and fear. Unconsciously, we will believe that death comes from God, which fuels our unconscious fear of God as the fear of Love itself. Disease is another idol we believe is a natural, legitimate part of life. Like our belief in death, this is extreme delusion. We refuse to realize *we made disease and death* in an effort to convince ourselves of our own powerlessness and helplessness, separate from our Creator. Yet by choosing to remain asleep, helpless and powerless over the ego's laws, we effectively reject God's Love as our Holy Self.

> *"You see in death escape from what you made. But this you do not see; that you made death, and it is but illusion of an end. Death cannot be escape, because it is not life in which the problem lies. Life has no opposite, for it is God. Life and death seem to be opposites because you have decided death ends life. Forgive the world, and you will understand that everything that God created cannot have an end, and nothing He did not create is real."* M-20.5:2-7

> *"You made the god of sickness, and by making him you made yourself able to hear him. Yet you did not create him, because he is not the Will of the Father. He is therefore not eternal and will be unmade for you the instant you signify your willingness to accept only the eternal."* T-10.III.9:4-6

Jesus, as the one awakened Christ within us all, released *A Course in Miracles* into the world as a major wakeup call. In it, He asks us to recognize we made all suffering as a means to attack our self and to separate from God's Love, thereby keeping our self asleep. He gives us the principles through which we can take back our power, to un-make all we made to keep our self dreaming a dream of suffering and death. And he emphatically tells us to do this by using the body, in order to transcend the body.

> *"The body is the means by which God's Son returns to sanity. Though it was made to fence him into hell without escape, yet has the goal of Heaven been exchanged for the*

pursuit of hell. The Son of God extends his hand to reach his brother, and to help him walk along the road with him. Now is the body holy. Now it serves to heal the mind that it was made to kill." W-pII.5.4.

Many of us have unknowingly misunderstood Jesus' teachings about the body. For many years I was among those who were confused in this area. The popular *Course* quote, *"I am not a body, I am free,"* became widely employed by so many of us as an unintentional spiritual bypass, as yet another excuse for ego denial of the true cause of all suffering. This is the opposite of Jesus' intent.

Jesus titled his teaching tool *A Course in MIRACLES.* Yes, *miracles.* All good *Course* students know that everything we seem to see, including miracles, originate from one place only: The mind—the level of cause. As such, many miracles that occur are not seen with the body's eyes, because they are purely perceptual shifts. They might not be physically recognized, and may not have observable effects.

However, within the deeper message of the *Course,* Jesus boldly proclaims we *can* and *will* be the instruments through which many miracles materialize in form. And these tangible physical miracles will manifest as a direct result of accepting the Atonement for our self, allowing the full correction of error in our mind.

ARE PHYSICAL MIRACLES PART OF JESUS' TEACHING?

My understanding of the *Course* during my first twenty years of study was not so different from what most other students and teachers were prepared to assimilate from these teachings, given our level of trust in Spirit at the time. We all tried our best and learned (mostly intellectually) that the cause of all problems we perceived was in the mind. And we learned forgiveness was the key to healing our mind. Most of us were also taught that only the mind was real and the body and world were unreal and irrelevant. *Therefore it didn't matter* whether the body/world was healed or not, as a consequence of forgiveness.

I was not ready or willing back then to see the crystal clear message Jesus teaches us in the *Course*—and I remained unready to see it until my own fear of God, and of my limitless power in God, had been at least partially healed.

I recognize now that we all interpret the *Course* to the level we are able to accept at the time. Its deeper meaning is revealed to us only to the extent we've managed to undo the ego's fear and hierarchy of illusions. As unconscious guilt and fear are cleansed from our perceptual lens, we begin to accept and experience Jesus' teachings at a much deeper level. The deeper holographic message of the *Course* is discovered and embraced to the same degree that our unseen fear of God's Love is exhumed and surrendered.

Until recently, my own unconscious fear of God obscured my ability to recognize the profound depth of this teaching. Not to mention the subsequent paradigm shift it asks us to embrace! Had I been prematurely exposed to these deeper teachings in the first few years of studying the *Course*, I probably would have rejected them. Such was the depth of my own fear of God's Love as my Holy Self.

Few if any *Course* teachers or students thus far have fully appreciated the magnitude of what these teachings mean for this ego world: The miraculous thought-reversal they bring changes everything. Jesus teaches nothing less than how to overcome all forms of death including physical death, and this teaching itself is the death knell to the ego's central dream. But death cannot be overcome in all its insidious forms, until we confront our own unconscious fear of God's Love as our Holy Self.

"Death is the central dream from which all illusions stem. Is it not madness to think of life as being born, aging, losing vitality, and dying in the end? We have asked this question before, but now we need to consider it more carefully. It is the one fixed, unchangeable belief of the world that all things in it are born only to die. This is regarded as "the way of nature," not to be raised to question, but to be accepted as the "natural" law of life. The cyclical, the changing and unsure; the undependable and the unsteady, waxing and waning in a certain way upon a certain path,—all this is taken as the Will of God. And no one asks if a benign Creator could will this." M-27.1.

"Who loves such a god knows not of love, because he has denied that life is real. Death has become life's symbol." M-27.2:5-6

"Death is the symbol of the fear of God. His Love is blotted out in the idea, which holds it from awareness like a shield held up to obscure the sun. The grimness of the symbol is enough to show it cannot coexist with God." M-27.3:1-3

"If death is real for anything, there is no life. Death denies life. But if there is reality in life, death is denied. No compromise in this is possible. There is either a god of fear or One of Love." M-27.4:2-6

"The Holy Spirit guides you into life eternal, but you must relinquish your investment in death, or you will not see life though it is all around you." T-12.IV.7:6

The fear of Love appears in many forms, yet the last remaining barrier to be overcome is our belief in an order of difficulty in miracles. This belief exists because we still value a hierarchy of illusions, with death the most treasured of them all.

From my own experience, I recognize most of us are secretly terrified of being healed physically by the miracle. If a total spontaneous healing were to occur, it would be a living demonstration of the glaring defect in what we accept as nature's universal laws. Miraculous healings like those Jesus performed would overturn the ego's entire value system. The world as we know it, and the laws we obey, would be totally overthrown if we accepted full healing of both cause *and* effect.

The ego's last defense is fear of God, disguised as the fear of death. The unconscious urge for death is the ego's most addictive compulsion. As Jesus teaches in the *Course* (and as I now know in my own experience), our greatest fear, even more than our fear of death, is to awaken into the living embodiment of the Christ within. If we as the Holy Self claim our power over all the ego made, it will reverse the thinking of the world entirely. In other words, our greatest fear is to accept and embody the incorruptible power of God within us.

Physical death is the ego's plan to make sure the body dies before we awaken to our real invulnerability and power in God. For once we truly know this power, we will recognize, accept and demonstrate as living witnesses the number one miracle principle: *"There is no order of difficulty in miracles."* One miracle is not harder or bigger to make manifest than any other. A life-threatening illness is no more difficult to heal than a common cold.

> *"All forms of sickness, even unto death, are physical expressions of the fear of awakening. They are attempts to reinforce sleeping out of fear of waking. This is a pathetic way of trying not to see by rendering the faculties for seeing ineffectual. "Rest in peace" is a blessing for the living, not the dead, because rest comes from waking, not from sleeping." T-8.IX.3:2-5*

> *"For as long as you feel guilty you are listening to the voice of the ego, which tells you that you have been treacherous to God and therefore deserve death. You will think that death comes from God and not from the ego because, by confusing yourself with the ego, you believe that you want death. And from what you want God does not save you." T-12.VII.14:4-5*

Jesus says through claiming our Holiness, the power of God is made manifest, and all worldly laws are therefore reversed. This means nothing the ego projects in the world of form can threaten us, once our mind has truly been healed.

> *"Your holiness reverses all the laws of the world. It is beyond every restriction of time, space, distance and limits of any kind."* W-38.1:1-2

> *"Through your holiness the power of God is made manifest. Through your holiness the power of God is made available. And there is nothing the power of God cannot do. Your holiness, then, can remove all pain, can end all sorrow, and can solve all problems. It can do so in connection with yourself and with anyone else. It is equal in its power to help anyone because it is equal in its power to save anyone."* W-38.2.

When our trust has been transferred from the ego's dream of death to the Christ within, it is the Christ that lives out from within us. Our bodies remain here in the dream a while longer, yet through the Christ within we experience the Real World dream of Heaven instead. The ego's obsessive belief in a hierarchy of illusions has finally been seen through and discarded. Now we recognize everything that is not of God is simply not real. Only Love exists.

The Christ within looks beyond the illusory appearances of sickness, conflict and deprivation, and focuses only on perceiving the Truth. And from this right-minded cause in our mind, perception of Truth can then allow the ego's effects to be healed. Although these effects appear to be outside our mind, in Truth they are found within our mind along with their cause.

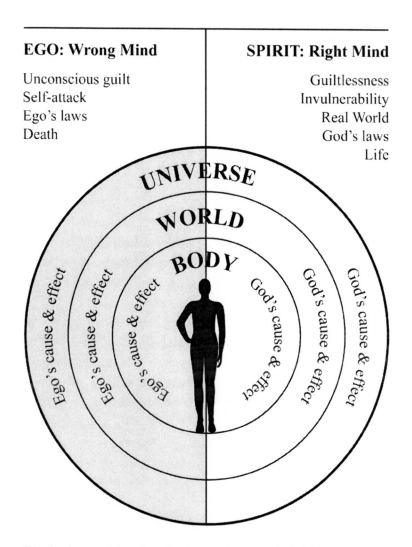

EGO: Wrong Mind

Unconscious guilt
Self-attack
Ego's laws
Death

SPIRIT: Right Mind

Guiltlessness
Invulnerability
Real World
God's laws
Life

UNIVERSE

WORLD

BODY

Ego's cause & effect

Ego's cause & effect

Ego's cause & effect

God's cause & effect

God's cause & effect

God's cause & effect

The body, world and universe are in our mind. They are either harmed or healed, depending on which inner teacher we choose to perceive them with: The ego, or Spirit.

Diagram #5
Cause and Effect Remain Together
in Our Mind

The cause of all sickness is in the mind. Yes, we may agree on this statement. However, I am now learning through my own experience that not only is cause in the mind—*so are its effects*. Both cause and effect are in our mind, and as such are never separate.

> *"Ideas leave not their source, and their effects but seem to be apart from them. Ideas are of the mind. What is projected out, and seems to be external to the mind, is not outside at all, but an effect of what is in, and has not left its source. T-26.VII.4:7-9*

I now recognize firsthand that the cause of sickness is in my mind. When the real cause is healed and guilt is truly forgiven, the effects or symptoms (which are also in my mind) can be healed by the miracle at the same time. But only *if* I am open to this idea. That is, if I am not afraid of the power of the healed mind. If I do not believe this simultaneous healing of internal cause and effect is possible, or if my level of self-doubt and unworthiness rejects healing, then my will must be done! No healing will take place. Our will is as powerful as God's, and whatever we will cannot be overridden by God.

> *"Health is the witness unto health. As long as it is unattested, it remains without conviction. Only when it has been demonstrated is it proved, and must provide a witness that compels belief. No one is healed through double messages. If you wish only to be healed, you heal. Your single purpose makes this possible. But if you are afraid of healing, then it cannot come through you. The only thing that is required for a healing is a lack of fear. T-27.V.2:1-8*

> *"The guiltless mind cannot suffer. Being sane, the mind heals the body because [it] has been healed." T-5.V.5:1-2*

> *"To heal is to make whole. And what is whole can have no missing parts that have been kept outside. Forgiveness rests on recognizing this, and being glad there cannot be some forms of sickness which the miracle must lack the power to heal." T-30.VI.8:3-6*

We suffer because our mind is split, causing us to believe we're separate. If we regard attack as Jesus teaches in the *Course*, we will see sickness is a form of self-attack, an outward effect of our un-relinquished guilt.

The healed mind is whole and no longer split. From within this healed mind, only healing will be extended. The healed mind as cause, must produce healing as its effect. The body is inside our mind and not outside it, therefore if we heal the cause the effect *must* follow. If the body remains sick, the mind must still be split and in need of Atonement.

> *"Oneness and sickness cannot coexist."* M.12.6:1

> *"All forms of sickness are signs that the mind is split, and does not accept a unified purpose."* T-8.IX.8:7

> *"Healing reflects our joint will. This is obvious when you consider what healing is for. Healing is the way in which the separation is overcome. Separation is overcome by union. It cannot be overcome by separating. The decision to unite must be unequivocal, or the mind itself is divided and not whole. Your mind is the means by which you determine your own condition, because mind is the mechanism of decision. It is the power by which you separate or join, and experience pain or joy accordingly. My decision cannot overcome yours, because yours is as powerful as mine."* T-8. IV.5:1-9

Jesus' ministry involved many healings of the sick, and He asks us to do the same. He helped heal the guilt in the minds of others, thus the effects of sickness were undone. Both the cause and the illusory effects of sickness were removed by the healing of guilt within the person's mind. They were healed because, as Jesus teaches in the *Course*, cause and effect are never separate. The miracle of healing proves separation is free of effects, when full transfer of the miracle has not been blocked by fear.

"It must be true the miracle can heal all forms of sickness, or it cannot heal. Its purpose cannot be to judge which forms are real, and which appearances are true. If one appearance must remain apart from healing, one illusion must be part of truth. And you could not escape all guilt, but only some of it." T-30.VI.7:1-4

In my own experience, I noticed the spiritual ego still wished to separate cause from effect in my mind. It was happy to heal the guilt in the mind, as long as this didn't translate to healing of the physical form.

To experience physical miracles as a result of a healed mind would be intolerable to the ego. For if physical miracles were indeed possible, I could no longer believe I was at the mercy of the ego's laws of sickness, pain and deprivation. As Jesus demonstrated in His own life, the laws of nature would no longer apply to me. And death could no longer claim power over God's Life.

I would be forced to give up the spiritual ego's false humility and self-doubt, the seductive self-delusions that have kept me from truly accepting the power of God within. All forms of death including physical death are so tempting; they save us from having to fully accept the power of God's Love within. Imagine for a moment, if we removed death from our concept of life: What would be left to be terrified of?

"See how the belief in death would seem to "save" you. For if this were gone, what could you fear but life?" T-19. IV.D.4:1-2

I blocked my own awareness of my divine inheritance by continuing to separate cause and effect in my mind. Only now I was doing it for "spiritual reasons," by declaring the body was not real, and therefore not important! *"I am not a body, I am free."* The ego loved this, as it gave me license to ignore the most important vehicle for transformation—the means through which I would remember and demonstrate the Holy Self's power of the healed mind.

Intellectually, I knew cause and effect were in my mind. The projector and the projected image both exist nowhere except in my mind. I understood the mind is not inside the body; rather, the mind dreams up the image of a body and then projects it to appear as if outside the mind. The difficult issue for me to accept was this: While the body and illness existed together in my mind, *so did the remedy*, the healing.

> *"God is in everything I see because God is in my mind." W-30.*
>
> *"There can be nothing that a change of mind cannot effect, for all external things are only shadows of a decision already made. Change the decision, and how can its shadow be unchanged? Illness can be but guilt's shadow, grotesque and ugly since it mimics deformity. If a deformity is seen as real, what could its shadow be except deformed?" P-2.IV.2:4-7*

If God is in everything I see, the cause of sickness must be healed along with the illusory symptoms. Both are in my mind and can never be separate. Whatever God in my mind perceives, is healed. God, the cause in my mind, is never separate from God's effect, which is the healing in my mind. The miracle leaps seamlessly from cause to actual manifest effect.

This terrified me. If I were to allow the miracle to manifest in form as living proof that there is no order of difficulty in miracles, the result would be blasphemy and annihilation to the ego. Ultimately it would herald the undoing of the world as I knew it, together with all its seeming laws. The ego would have no ground left to stand on.

The spiritual ego simply could not allow me to recognize the dream-busting ramifications of this teaching. But what if Jesus is right? What if cause and effect really *are* never separate in my mind? What if it's true that ideas leave not their source? This means when cause is healed, effect must follow. And this is exactly what the ego doesn't want us to see and accept!

If both cause and effect are in my mind and never separate, then healing of physical pain or sickness is readily available—and inevitable—when guilt is healed. If only the guilt were healed yet the effects were not, there *would* be a hierarchy of illusions. Cause and effect would be separate. And that's impossible! This is the very thing Jesus came into physical form to teach and demonstrate. There is no order of difficulty in miracles. One is not harder or bigger than another. Jesus does not hold back here, as he points out how reluctant we have been throughout history, to embrace the literal meaning of His teachings:

> *"There have been many healers who did not heal themselves. They have not moved mountains by their faith because their faith was not whole. Some of them have healed the sick at times, but they have not raised the dead. Unless the healer heals himself, he cannot believe that there is no order of difficulty in miracles." T-6.VII.1:1-4*

If I am afraid that healing my mind will heal its physical effects, then I am still afraid of the Christ within. I will therefore be terrified of the power of a healed mind. This is the crazy thing about all this: Until we truly drop our fear of God, we allow the ego to use our mind to unconsciously miscreate suffering in all its forms.

For many years I could not see and accept what Jesus was really teaching. I couldn't embrace the most ego-threatening implications of the *Course* until a greater degree of my own fear of God had fallen away. Now, finally, I am witnessing a deeper recognition of my own fear of God as my Holy Self, so it can be healed truly.

It is much easier to believe if the cause of suffering is healed, the manifest effects don't matter. It lets us off the hook; we abdicate our responsibility to truly embody and witness the limitless power of Christ within. We don't have to actually learn for our self that there is no order of difficulty in miracles. But if we disregard the miracle's ability to translate to physical healing, we must also deny the power of the healed mind. The ego's existence requires that we believe we have no power over its laws of scarcity, disease and death. Its survival depends on keeping us victims of the world we see. Following is miracle principle number twenty-four from the *Course*:

> *"Miracles enable you to heal the sick and raise the dead because you made sickness and death yourself, and can therefore abolish both. [You] are a miracle, capable of creating in the likeness of your Creator. Everything else is your own nightmare, and does not exist. Only the creations of light are real." T-1.I.24.*

Can you imagine a healed mind that willingly heals the sick and raises the dead, openly teaching forgiveness of the entire ego dream? Imagine if we remembered Jesus' True message and willingly embraced the invitation to live from the Christ within? The ego's dream of fear and corruptible bodies would vanish very quickly.

But when we exclude or disassociate effects (the body/world) from the healing power of the miracle, we feed the ego's delusional belief that matter is too difficult to heal, and therefore more special within its hierarchy of illusions. As Jesus tells us, He healed the sick and raised the dead by knowing that Life is the eternal principle of God's Love. God's Love is Life itself. It is all-encompassing. And what is all-encompassing can have no opposite.

> *"I raised the dead by knowing that life is an eternal attribute of everything that the living God created. Why do you believe it is harder for me to inspire the dis-spirited or to stabilize the unstable? I do not believe that there is an order of difficulty in miracles; you do. I have called and you will answer." T-4.IV.11:7-10*

The *Course's* number one miracle principle is *"There is no order of difficulty in miracles."* How can we ever know this is consistently True, unless we open our minds to deeper healing? Spirit can only heal what we do not close off to Him due to fear, unworthiness or false humility. Jesus tells us it is the Christ within us that heals. This is the Will of God.

> "It cannot be that it is hard to do the task that Christ appointed you to do, since it is He Who does it." T-25.I.1:1
>
> "You are part of Him Who is all power and glory, and are therefore as unlimited as He is." T-8.II.7:7
>
> "A broken body shows the mind has not been healed. A miracle of healing proves that separation is without effect. T-27.II:1-2

This is indeed scary stuff to the ego! It is by far the most challenging part of the ego's undoing. Jesus asks us to embody the Christ here and now, while we're in an illusory body. Not *after* the ego's many attempted escapes into yet another dream state of death. Jesus caps the whole *Course* by telling us our one assignment within the ego dream as the embodied Christ, is the undoing of death:

> "Teacher of God, your one assignment could be stated thus: Accept no compromise in which death plays a part." M-28.7:1
>
> "Very simply, the resurrection is the overcoming or surmounting of death. It is a reawakening or a rebirth; a change of mind about the meaning of the world." "It is the end of dreams of misery, and the glad awareness of the Holy Spirit's final dream. It is the recognition of the gifts of God. It is the dream in which the body functions perfectly, having no function except communication." M-29.1:1-2,4-6
>
> "The resurrection is the denial of death, being the assertion of life. Thus is all the thinking of the world reversed entirely. Life is now recognized as salvation, and pain and misery of any kind perceived as hell. Love is no longer feared, but gladly welcomed." M-29.2.1-4.

Belief in death as a natural, inevitable and legitimate part of life is the ego's central dream. Undoing death in all its forms unravels the ego's dream very rapidly. When we've thoroughly abdicated the body's purpose to Spirit, we can be sure Spirit will use it to teach Jesus' message.

> "The body is the means by which God's Son returns to sanity. Though it was made to fence him into hell without escape, yet has the goal of Heaven been exchanged for the pursuit of hell. The Son of God extends his hand to reach his brother, and to help him walk along the road with him. Now is the body holy. Now it serves to heal the mind that it was made to kill." W-pII.5.4.

> " It {body}* becomes a means by which the part of the mind you tried to separate [from] spirit can reach beyond its distortions and return [to] spirit. The ego's temple thus becomes the temple of the Holy Spirit, where devotion to Him replaces devotion to the ego. In this sense the body does become a temple to God; His Voice abides in it by directing the use to which it is put." T-8.VII.9:5-7 *Authors clarification

As long as I still choose to believe in a hierarchy of illusions, I will not know for certain there is no order of difficulty in miracles. I cannot maintain a belief I am a victim of the ego's laws, and still expect to realize there is no order of difficulty in miracles. These two beliefs are entirely and mutually exclusive. I must choose for myself which of these is real.

I realize Jesus means exactly what He says. And what will it cost me to know and to *demonstrate* his number one miracle principle that there is no order of difficulty in miracles? It will cost me my entire perception of the world!

> "This world [is] a picture of the crucifixion of God's Son. And until you realize that God's Son cannot be crucified, this is the world you will see. Yet you will not realize this until you accept the eternal fact that God's Son is not guilty. He deserves only love because he has given only love. He

cannot be condemned because he has never condemned. The Atonement is the final lesson he need learn, for it teaches him that, never having sinned, he has no need of salvation." T-13.in.4.

SIN, GUILT AND FEAR:
EVERY FEAR HIDES OUR GUILT

The *Course* tells us a classic ego cycle holds the ego's paradigm together, and this cycle in turn fuels the human cycle of suffering. This ego cycle is none other than the deadly threesome of sin, guilt and fear. First, we believe we sinned by leaving God; second, we're guilty; and third, we fear His punishment. Together they ensure the never-ending wheel of birth, suffering and death keeps turning. There's actually a fourth part to this cycle, which is the cumulative effect of the other three: The guilt we carry kills the body.

It took me many years to access the guilt hiding beneath my daily life experience. I found it difficult to detect the guilt that the *Course* suggested lay hidden beneath my rage at my mother, for example, or the guilt beneath my obsessive desire to protect my daughter and make sure her future was secure. I mean, these were normal human responses, weren't they? How would I manage to source the guilt beneath my negative emotional responses, when these responses themselves seemed so rational and justified? And what about my knee-jerk desire to fix these perceived problems independently of Holy Spirit?

Only recently have I learned to recognize almost immediately the guilt lurking behind any feeling of fear, judgment or perceived threat, or behind any need to problem solve or control. I am learning through my own experience that every reaction constituting a loss of peace can be traced directly back to my own dreadful fear of God's punishment.

The willingness to look at this, to become mindful of every instance we feel threat, will speed up our process of healing immeasurably. It all must be looked at, not alone with the ego, but joined with Holy Spirit.

We could never feel or perceive threat unless, of course, we expected it. We expect adversity because unconsciously, we expect to be punished by God. But this god we fear can only be the uninvestigated god of the ego. Punishment could never come from the God of all-encompassing Love without opposite.

This entire 3-D world is an attempt to defend our self from expected attack. We expect attack from our body, others, the world and God. And why is that? Because deep down, we feel attack is what we deserve. Guilt deserves punishment. If we truly knew our innocence without one shred of doubt about it, we'd remember we are totally invulnerable. We would clearly realize there could be no anticipation of threat without the unconscious desire for it.

There is no such thing as random chaos. All adversity is projected by the mind. The question is, are we ready to relinquish the guilt that demands our suffering? When we truly agree to embody our pristine innocence and worthiness, we will no longer join with the ego's purpose in using the body/world as a means for self-attack. We will renounce our former wish to separate from God's Love as Self.

I am beginning to recognize that nothing whatsoever, other than our unconscious guilt, can threaten us. This guilt we carry is our own unconscious self-hatred, projected outward onto the body, others and the world.

Jesus came to teach us we're eternally, wholly and absolutely innocent. No one alive (or dead) is excluded from this perfect innocence. He teaches that what we perceive as sin is simply error, nothing more. The part of us that appears to commit these errors is clearly insane. Only in insanity can one believe in and act from fear. Fear is the opposite of Love—which has no opposite!

The ego, crazy as it is, is fortunately also causeless. While the repercussions stemming from the ego's antics are upsetting, they are *not* real. If but one sin in history (whether the world's history or your own) were real, it would mean there could exist a power greater than the all-powerful, all-encompassing Love of God. Which, again, would be impossible.

> *"When you are tempted to believe that sin is real, remember this: If sin is real, both God and you are not. If creation is extension, the Creator must have extended Himself, and it is impossible that what is part of Him is totally unlike the rest. If sin is real, God must be at war with Himself. He must be split, and torn between good and evil; partly sane and partially insane. For He must have created what wills to destroy Him, and has the power to do so. Is it not easier to believe that you have been mistaken than to believe in this?" T-19.III.6.*

Jesus teaches us to behold our absolute guiltlessness. And we reclaim our innocence by looking past, and forgiving everything and everybody we seem to see. After all, everything we seem to witness, every seemingly unforgivable act is projected outward from the unconscious guilt within our own mind. Whatever it is that disturbs our peace, we're doing it to our self.

We can gauge the degree of our own un-relinquished guilt by observing the level of emotional charge we feel in any loss of peace. If we didn't possess this guilt (disguised, perhaps, as fear, anger or sadness), we would be unable to perceive attack. Forgiving what appears to be "out there" is what undoes the guilt within our own mind. And make no mistake, the cause is always in our mind. The effect only appears to be outside, but really, nothing is out there.

What makes the world go round? Contrary to belief, it's not money, power or sex. They're just symptoms of an underlying, fundamental cause. The world is fueled by our belief in sin and guilt. An end to sin and guilt would mean no more unconscious attraction to suffering. The expectation of threat drops away as guilt is forgiven.

And because the world is purely an effect, it will change as our perception heals. The world becomes an effect of our healed perception. As Jesus says, cause and effect are never separate. They remain together in our mind, no matter how real and independent they may appear. Jesus refers to guilt and every related form of suffering as "blasphemy," as these are all expressions of our refusal to forgive and accept the Love that is our Holy Self.

> *"If God knows His children as wholly sinless, it is blasphemous to perceive them as guilty. If God knows His children as wholly without pain, it is blasphemous to perceive suffering anywhere. If God knows His children to be wholly joyous, it is blasphemous to feel depressed. All of these illusions, and the many other forms that blasphemy may take, are refusals to accept creation as it is. If God created His Son perfect, that is how you must learn to see him to learn of his reality. And as part of the Sonship, that is how you must see yourself to learn of yours." T-10.V.12.*

Two thousand years ago, Jesus taught us to embrace our complete guiltlessness. He declared there is no such thing as sin. To the collective ego mind, guiltlessness is indeed the ultimate form of blasphemy. And that is why they crucified him.

Jesus speaks about the crucifixion:

> *"I have said that the crucifixion is the symbol of the ego. When it was confronted with the real guiltlessness of God's Son it did attempt to kill him, and the reason it gave was that guiltlessness is blasphemous to God. To the ego, the [ego] is God, and guiltlessness must be interpreted as the final guilt that fully justifies murder. You do not yet understand that any fear you may experience in connection with this course stems ultimately from this interpretation, but if you will consider your reactions to it you will become increasingly convinced that this is so." T-13.II.6:1-4*

THE PATH OF TRUE HEALING
THROUGH JESUS

I see a distinct process that leads to the discovery and embodiment of our Holy Self. That is, we must determinedly agree to exhume all that lies within the unconscious mind, patiently examining each and every illusion together with Spirit. And we must remain vigilant as we stay this course, refusing to be fooled by appearances. Healing cannot be accomplished while harboring dark imaginings of sin or guilt in any form.

For, as long as we feel fear and the need to control, protect or defend our self, we don't know who we are. We have made for our self a false self, a body, a world and all the universal laws that appear to govern them, including laws of time and space.

All of these beliefs and values are illusions we need to question deeply with Spirit. All must be thoroughly relinquished, if we are to discover our true Identity and the divine invulnerability that is our inheritance.

Fear is the essence of all our perceived emotional and physical pain. This fear arises in direct response to unconscious guilt. We usually don't recognize this unconscious guilt, because we're so busy projecting it onto our own body, others and the world. We're utterly intent on making it seem that life appears to attack us. All this perceived attack is ego-generated, and meant to keep us in constant defense mode. Many of these defenses are so subtle we don't consciously recognize them.

In our *Power of Power* workshop retreats, we include an exercise that exhumes many of these subtle and unrecognized defenses. Here are just a few of many examples of subtle defense: Planning, people-pleasing, feelings of guilt, sacrifice, struggle, scarcity, anxiety, sickness and accidents.

While we remain unaware of our defenses, we cannot unearth our unconscious compulsion to attack our self and others. All these unconscious compulsions come from one source only, which is our deeply unconscious fear of God. Guilt, simply put, is the fear of God. It's the terror of knowing our Self as the

God-Self. This Self is the state of True innocence, which is a state of complete invulnerability. Jesus demonstrated this over and over again, through his ministry of healing and in his resurrection.

THE HEALED CHRIST IS WITHIN

Because of our deeply unconscious fear of God, we tend to carry that same fear over to the Christ. We don't realize any disdain we might have for Jesus as the Christ is yet another manifestation of our own unconscious self-hatred. The real Christ dwells within, so our rejection of Jesus is a rejection of the Christ within, our Holy Self. Any negative reaction we have toward Jesus is a call for crucifixion of our self.

A good indication our own self-attack process is coming to a close, is that we'll find we no longer desire to edit Jesus out of our life. The closer we allow Him into our awareness, the more willingly we accept our own guiltlessness. And with this allowance, our sense of worthlessness and threat disappear, replaced by a growing experience of joy and inner security. In effect, we begin to take Jesus down from the cross within our own heart. In doing so we also forgive the Christ within, the Self we've been trying to crucify over and over again, throughout our human existence.

As we heal and accept the Christ within as our true Self, the imaginary gap between our self and the Christ closes. There is only one Holy Self. We discover this for our self through forgiveness of everyone and everything we seemingly see. Later, we clearly recognize with great relief that *all* our forgiveness was purely forgiveness of our own mistaken self. We forgive it for having used our body, others, situations, the world and God. We used it all to attack our self with the aim of remaining locked within a chaotic dream of suffering and death.

JESUS DID NOT DIE FOR OUR SINS

Contrary to what many Christians have been mistakenly led to believe, the crucifixion did not establish the Atonement. The resurrection did. Unfortunately, the spiritual ego interpreted Jesus' message according to *its* agenda, which always promotes fear and guilt. Many to this day are terrified of Jesus, precisely due to this disastrous misinterpretation.

Jesus agreed to allow His body to be crucified. It did not occur in opposition to His will. He consented in order to demonstrate one critical lesson: Even the most barbaric assault on the body cannot affect the Holy Self, because *there is no death.*

Jesus did not die for our sins. On the contrary, through His resurrection He proved we are guiltless! He allowed His body to be "put to death"—yet He rose from the dead to show us that by remembering our true Identity in God, our pristine innocence, we cannot suffer or die. Many have mistakenly portrayed Jesus in suffering. Yet He clearly states the guiltless mind *cannot* suffer. Only un-relinquished guilt can cause pain or suffering. Divine guiltlessness is invulnerability, and provides certain immunity to suffering.

"The crucifixion did not establish the Atonement; the resurrection did. Many sincere Christians have misunderstood this. No one who is free of the belief in scarcity could possibly make this mistake. If the crucifixion is seen from an upside-down point of view, it does appear as if God permitted and even encouraged one of His Sons to suffer because he was good. This particularly unfortunate interpretation, which arose out of projection, has led many people to be bitterly afraid of God. Such anti-religious concepts enter into many religions. Yet the real Christian should pause and ask, "How could this be?" Is it likely that God Himself would be capable of the kind of thinking which His Own words have clearly stated is unworthy of His Son?" T-3.I.1:2-9

The God of Love knows nothing of sacrifice or punishment. These twisted ideas arise from the ego's unexamined projection of its own version of god, the god of fear and guilt. This unconscious belief in a punishing god spawns all of our fears, including the persistent sense of threat that seems to permeate our daily life. The Atonement (forgiveness as a means of undoing fear) was introduced by Jesus, and remains available for us to accept in any instant we're willing to remember we are entirely worthy of receiving it.

> " *The resurrection demonstrated that nothing can destroy truth. Good can withstand any form of evil, as light abolishes forms of darkness. The Atonement is therefore the perfect lesson. It is the final demonstration that all the other lessons I taught are true." T-3.I.7:6-9*
>
> *"The journey to the cross should be the last "useless journey." Do not dwell upon it, but dismiss it as accomplished. If you can accept it as your own last useless journey, you are also free to join my resurrection. Until you do so your life is indeed wasted. It merely re-enacts the separation, the loss of power, the futile attempts of the ego at reparation, and finally the crucifixion of the body, or death. Such repetitions are endless until they are voluntarily given up. Do not make the pathetic error of "clinging to the old rugged cross." The only message of the crucifixion is that you can overcome the cross. Until then you are free to crucify yourself as often as you choose. This is not the gospel I intended to offer you. We have another journey to undertake, and if you will read these lessons carefully they will help prepare you to undertake it." T-4.in.3*

CHAPTER FIVE

UNEARTHING OUR UNCONSCIOUS FEAR OF GOD

Tomas left the body in December 2010, through what appeared to be cancer. He had awakened within the ego dream (although he had not awakened *from* it) prior to leaving the body. In the *Course*, Jesus calls us to the next level of awakening beyond that which Tomas attained. He asks us to awaken from the ego dream of death altogether. Although Tomas did not awaken from the ego's dream of death, he was very aware he chose cancer as a means through which he could apply vigilant discipline to prioritizing peace. He wanted to achieve only one goal, which was to awaken.

Since Tomas left physical form, communication between us has remained unbroken. In fact he is more available to me without a body than he was with one! Before he left the body, we both had lived and studied the principles of *A Course in Miracles* for twenty years. We took the long meandering path, and made every conceivable mistake along the way. While our misunderstanding and confusion appeared to increase our suffering during that period, I see now we chose this method so we could help light the path Home for others. I now see a much gentler and more joyful path of undoing suffering, and am sharing this with all who are called to walk with us.

I believe Tomas is helping with this; many have reported they feel he is currently assisting them in their commitment to the undoing of fear. I vowed also to assist those who are guided to take their experience of the *Course* to a new level. This is an invitation to experience and demonstrate a miraculous paradigm shift into embodiment as a true miracle-worker.

It's been only recently that I was shown our greatest individual and collective blocks to God's Love. I must admit I was shocked. I had no idea of their existence, even after twenty years of *Course* practice. No one needs to suffer the way Tomas and I did. My commitment is to share these teachings I've received lately, to help others overcome pain and suffering—to find deep and unshakeable security, Love and joy much sooner.

The first of these major blocks to Love is thoroughly hidden within our unconscious mind. When Tomas and I finally saw it and released it to Spirit, we understood why it had taken us so long to establish trust in God's Love: Until we had advanced far enough in trusting Spirit, we did what everyone does here in the dream. We mostly relied upon our own will and the world's laws, checking in only now and then with Spirit.

We tried to balance two opposing belief systems, partly trusting in Spirit and partly trusting in our own ego will. We had one foot planted in Spirit's canoe, and the other foot in the ego's. Not surprisingly, the mighty current of ego-undoing rapidly pulled these boats apart. The outcome? We fell head first in the water and felt like we were drowning.

That's the feeling we all experience whenever we attempt to integrate the ego's laws with God's Laws. The two are absolutely irreconcilable. Until we definitively choose only one, we won't feel consistent peace and joy. Until we choose, we're welcome to go on torturing ourselves. But there is no compromise in this. None.

The biggest block, the one hiding at the very deepest level, is our fear of God's Love. While it's true this is the last of the obstacles to peace, it can and should be exhumed as early in the process as possible. Fear of God is so insidious and prevalent that it sabotages every single thing we undertake, including our spiritual path itself. Fear of God is at the seat of all our physical and emotional pain, our need to control, our unconscious attraction to pain and disease, to scarcity, conflict and eventually physical death itself.

SUFFERING IS NOT GOD'S WILL

There is a fundamental difference between the God referred to in *A Course in Miracles* and the God spoken of in many other spiritual paths.

The God spoken of in the *Course* is all-encompassing Love with no opposite. We are God's extension, our true Identity beneath the ego dream that plays out in our mind. As such, our right mind shares the same incorruptible nature and Will of God. This incorruptible nature and Will forms the essence of our one Holy Self, which also has no opposite.

The ego, along with its thought system of seemingly universal laws, is entirely illusory and therefore utterly powerless. This means the separation from God's one Self never really occurred. The only thing keeping this Truth from our consistent awareness is our choice for the perception of separation.

As long as we choose to believe we are a separate self who can be victimized by the laws of this world, we will have no firsthand awareness of God's nature or Will. The awareness of God's Self cannot be revealed until we choose to unearth, recognize and relinquish everything that is *not* God's Will.

It's a process of undoing the false to reveal the Truth that has always been present—but unrecognized and rejected. Through the ego we cannot ever know God's Will. We may be able to identify it and understand it intellectually, but until we begin the process of undoing the ego's will and belief system within our unconscious mind, we will remain entirely unable to value or trust in God's Will. Therefore we won't be able to experience it.

Our Holy Self is the nature and Will of God. Our Holy Self *is* the Kingdom of God. Everything else is illusion. The Holy Self is right here, right now. It may not be recognized by most of us yet, but it's always present. It doesn't appear after some special future event like death, or spiritual awakening. It's our essential Self, eternally pure, perfect and innocent no matter who we imagine our self to be. The only self that can suffer is the ego self. The Holy Self remains constant, changeless and invulnerable in its perfect joy.

No part of the ego's dream affects the nature and Will of God as our Holy Self. In fact, no part of the ego's dream can remain unhealed once our perception has been healed through forgiveness, in acceptance of Atonement. Everything we assign power in the ego dream is not only unreal, but is completely powerless over God's perfect Will for happiness, healing, joy and peace. The only reason God's Loving Will is not seen more clearly in our awareness is our continuing choice for the ego's will. We still prefer illusion to Truth, believing in the ego's projections. The motivation for this choice is our un-relinquished self-attack.

Let's take a look at what is *not* and *never can be* God's Will: Sin, guilt, fear, sickness, disease, depression, physical or emotional pain, shame, sadness, grief, anger, scarcity in any form, judgment of self and others, doubt, conflict, loss, sacrifice, struggle, confusion, jealousy, loneliness, anxiety, worry and physical death. All these states are only possible through belief in an opposite of God's all-encompassing Love.

The ego's so-called laws of nature are also not of God's Will. While there is certainly much beauty to be found in nature, chaotic danger including storms, earthquakes, floods and fires are not God's Loving Will. "Survival of the fittest" is not a system devised by God's Loving Will. The laws of this world are the laws of the ego thought system. God's Will and nature is reflective of only Love and Life. There is nothing else.

When we confuse any of these ego illusions with the Will of God, we reject the miracle of healing within our mind. We're too afraid of this version of God to want to come any closer to it.

This is why it's crucial to identify the unequivocal distinction between the ego's will and God's Will, as we work to undo the ego's obsession with sin, guilt and fear. For, as long as we believe in any of these ego illusions, we will unconsciously presume they come from God, who surely must have authored suffering and death. This belief in sin, guilt and fear reinforces our terror of God. And we'll be far too frightened to trust exclusively in God's Will, believing instead we'll be subjected to terrible justice.

The Holy Spirit's "justice" is always Loving, because there is no conflict within it. This justice recognizes our mistakes are purely calls for Love, and answers only with Love. The ego, on the other hand, responds to mistakes by pronouncing them sins that require both guilt and punishment. It attempts to correct only through vengeance. The ego's model is the only model we know, until we sincerely begin to dismantle the ego thought system. Can you even imagine committing a grievous sin and being gently corrected by Love, and not by punishment? You perceive the sin; Love perceives it only as a mistake, and responds with Love.

"It is extremely hard for those who still believe sin meaningful to understand the Holy Spirit's justice. They must believe He shares their own confusion, and cannot avoid the vengeance that their own belief in justice must entail. And so they fear the Holy Spirit, and perceive the "wrath" of God in Him. Nor can they trust Him not to strike them dead with lightning bolts torn from the "fires" of Heaven by God's Own angry Hand. They [do] believe that Heaven is hell, and [are] afraid of love. And deep suspicion and the chill of fear comes over them when they are told that they have never sinned. Their world depends on sin's stability. And they perceive the "threat" of what God knows as justice to be more destructive to themselves and to their world than vengeance, which they understand and love." T-25.VIII.6.

Unconsciously we fear the Will of God, because of our deeply mistaken un-relinquished belief we have sinned. Past experience reflects our expectation of the ego's vengeance as punishment for these sins—all of which is brought on by our un-relinquished guilt as self-attack. Refusal to relinquish guilt is a choice we make. The punishment occurs by our own consent.

But the god we fear is the ego's god of vengeance. As long as we choose to cling to guilt or blame in any form, it means we still revere the ego's god of death. It must be that we are suspicious of guiltlessness; that without guilt and blame, we would forfeit our greatest defense against the ego's god of vengeance. This way of looking at our sin, guilt and fear may help us better understand why it seems so difficult to surrender and forgive them. *Without sin, guilt and fear*, the ego counsels, *we would be entirely defenseless against God's all-consuming wrath!*

It would be impossible to fear at all, if we did not secretly believe we have sinned and are guilty. This is the ego's lie, of course. The certain result of sin (judgments or grievances) is guilt, and the certain result of guilt is fear of punishment.

As this unconscious fear is continually projected outward as judgment toward the body, self, others and the world, it remains un-surrendered, un-forgiven. It then becomes an attraction to death, which *must* manifest. Physical death represents the ego's most exalted form of punishment. All of this false belief, until courageously exhumed and released through forgiveness, drives our unconscious attraction to suffering.

It's a vicious cycle. We believe we sinned, are therefore guilty, and fear the consequences. We project this fear without realizing that whatever we fear, we indeed attract. And instead of forgiving the real cause of our fear (guilt), we try to defend ourselves from the ego's unconscious self-attack—which *we ourselves* projected. In this act, we unknowingly reinforce our guilt by making the ego's projection real. And the cycle continues. This is why a continued belief in sin and guilt always leads to the ego's ultimate goal of death.

The word "sin" in Hebrew is *chet*, and simply means "missing the mark." It does not mean it is irrevocable, as the ego portrays it. Another interpretation of the word sin is *forgetfulness*, which more closely depicts what the *Course* teaches.

Sin, in the ego's eyes, is indisputable. And it needs you to believe this, to ensure you won't relinquish your judgments and thus, your guilt. If you did, the ego thought system would disappear! Sin is the one thing in this world that appears it cannot be changed. Yet Jesus asks us, "What is immutable besides God's Will?" "What wish can rise against His Will?"

He says, "If you could realize nothing is changeless but the Will of God, this course would not be difficult for you." All ideas of sin, guilt and fear can be healed, because they are not immutable and always remain open to the miracle in any instant we desire our perception to be healed.

"Yet each one knows the cost of sin is death. And so it is. For sin is a request for death, a wish to make this world's foundation sure as love, dependable as Heaven, and as strong as God Himself. The world is safe from love to everyone who thinks sin possible." T-25.VII.1:6-9

"It cannot be the "sinner's" wish for death is just as strong as is God's Will for life. Nor can the basis of a world He did not make be firm and sure as Heaven. How could it be that hell and Heaven are the same? And is it possible that what He did not will cannot be changed? What is immutable besides His Will? And what can share its attributes except itself? What wish can rise against His Will, and be immutable? If you could realize nothing is changeless but the Will of God, this course would not be difficult for you. For it is this that you do not believe. Yet there is nothing else you could believe, if you but looked at what it really is." T-25.VII.2.

When we remove the ego's long list of cruel illusions, eliminating everything that could possibly harm us, what remains? If we knew with every fiber of our being we have never sinned and are therefore not guilty, would we expect punishment in the form of suffering?

Guilt is not God's Will. All suffering we experience is projected by us, because we believe we sinned and must pay the price for our guilt. Suffering in any form is not God's Will. If we knew and accepted our true guiltlessness, we could not suffer. We could not be attacked by sickness, disease, depression, physical or emotional pain, guilt, shame, sadness, grief, anger, scarcity in any form, judgment or self judgment, doubt, conflict, loss, sacrifice, struggle, confusion, loneliness, jealousy, anxiety, worry or physical death.

What would be left to experience after guilt and its attraction to pain have gone? Without these ego illusions, what would happen? How would you feel? And more importantly, what would you remember about your Holy Self?

Only God's Loving Will and its dream of the Real World would remain. Separation would be undone within our mind, because we chose at last to Will *with* God instead of wishing with the ego.

The nature and Will of God reveals its glorious Self as we learn to reject the ego's projections wherever we seem to see them. It can be very tempting to believe in these projections. But if we knew without a doubt that suffering of any kind is *never* God's Will, would we not ignore ego temptation and promptly drop our own independent will to control our life, joining wholeheartedly with God's Will instead?

The Will of God lives uninterrupted within you. When you allow a Holy Instant in which you suspend all fears, doubts, judgments and concerns, you drop into peace within. And in this moment of peace, the ego ceases to exist. In this moment of eternity outside time, God's Will is yours. There is no interruption, and you allow a miracle. The miracle takes no time—it collapses it. Every True desire in your heart is the Will of God. And God's Love has been waiting for this precious instant, the one in which you are willing to accept and receive it.

God's Love transfers from healed mind to healed form, as cause and effect remain together and can never be separate. There is no order of difficulty in miracles, precisely because there is no hierarchy of illusions. One illusion cannot be greater than any other, as all illusions are equally unreal. Whatever the seeming problem, a miracle is waiting to heal its cause in our perception. And in healing the cause, the effect or symptoms must be healed as well. Otherwise we would be separating cause from effect. And as Jesus has shown us, this is not possible except in our ego imagination.

God's Will is perfect healing. Joy is the natural outcome of trusting in God's Will. God's Will asks us to embody the knowing that we have everything because we *are* everything. It wants us to be living witnesses to our own incorruptible power in God's

Love, just as Jesus was. But we won't know this in experience as long as we play the ego's game. If we believe we're under the ego's laws of suffering and separation, then under these laws we will be. We must make a choice, and only one is real.

SIN: A NEW INTERPRETATION FOR AN EVIL WORD WITH A WICKED HISTORY

What is sin? *A Course in Miracles* refers to the word "sin" no fewer than three hundred fifty four times, so it must be an important word! The journey of awakening from suffering is not about seeking Love. Love is already here. We need not seek it. Rather, our journey requires that we seek out all our blocks to the awareness of Love's presence. And our un-relinquished belief in sin is the root of all blocks to Love.

For many centuries the word "sin" has been used as a weapon to abuse the human psyche. For most of us, the idea of sin carries within it a cellular memory of pain and punishment.

In the *Course*, we learn everything is purely a neutral symbol. And through the interpretation we give it, we assign all the meaning it has for us. Of its own, a symbol has no meaning. Yet sin is one of those symbols that tends to ignite revulsion in almost everybody. I include myself in this group; sin was always a difficult word for me. It made my mind go numb instantly.

If God's all-encompassing Love is all there is, and if all-encompassing Love has no opposite, then sin clearly cannot exist. Only the ego believes in sin, having built its entire illusory empire on it. But sin is impossible. There are mistakes and errors, yes. Yet every one of them can be gently healed by forgiveness. Let's look at the truth behind this label we call "sin:"

- There is no sin. There is mistaken perception only.
- Sin is the belief attack is real.
- Sin is an un-relinquished belief in threat, attack or suffering. It is believed to exist in yourself, the body, another, the past, the future, the world or God.

But which self are you? The ego or the Holy Self? If sin is the belief in attack, which self must you defend from attack? This self of the ego and body must be who you think you are, if you defend it independently from Spirit.

- Sin is an unforgiving thought or belief.
- Sin is the belief an opposite could exist to God's all-encompassing Love.
- Sin is a highly valued illusory block we have placed against Love. We must hang onto the idea of sin to separate ourselves from God, others and our true Identity as the Holy Self. If we dropped our belief in sin, we would know we *are* God's Self. The idea of sin and attack is the biggest block to God's Love.
- Sin is the idea of irrevocable error.
- Sin produces guilt, and guilt produces fear. We believe in sin and attack. We believe we can be attacked by others, the body, conflict, scarcity, loss and death.

We also believe *we* can attack. Either way, we acquire guilt as a result. To take offense (which is attack) and to give offense are the same mistake; they both attract guilt and the unconscious desire for self-attack through punishment. Guilt always brings unconscious fear of God's punishment. Fear is the product of the idea attack is real—and attack made real constitutes our belief in sin. All fear, no matter what form it takes, is the fear of God. And fear of God translates to the fear of our one Holy Self. Keeping the idea of sin inviolate makes certain we cannot ever know God's Love.

- Sin is the belief illusions are not only real, they hold the power to defeat God's Love.
- Sin is the belief death is the certain outcome of life.
- Sin, being attack, calls for defense. Defense makes sin real in the mind, thereby rejecting forgiveness. *We cannot forgive that which we still believe is real.*

ARE YOU BEING SEDUCED BY SIN AND GUILT?

Did you know the first obstacle to peace is our desire to get rid of it? How crazy is that? We spend our whole life searching for peace, but through the ego we unknowingly reject it. In my experience, I have noticed the unconscious rejection of peace is inextricably tied to two other unconscious desires. These are the belief in sin and its consequences, and its twin attraction to guilt and punishment. These secret desires fuel the ego's consistent wish that we be unfairly treated.

To the ego, sin is permanent, immovable and fixed. The idea of sin's reality forms the basis for this ego world. But what we don't often recognize is this: The only way we could possibly witness sin in our world is through our own projection. The body and world are in our mind. If I'm triggered by a so-called sin out there, it's really not out there. It must be within my own mind, and I will learn how much of my guilt remains to be healed, by observing the degree to which I am triggered emotionally by the seeming sin.

> *"There is no stone in all the ego's embattled citadel that is more heavily defended than the idea that sin is real; the natural expression of what the Son of God has made himself to be, and what he is." T-19.II.7:1*

In the ego world, we do believe in sin, not in simple errors or mistakes. A sin is irreversible and demands punishment, yet a mistake is different. It calls for correction. The fear of God's Love is deeply ingrained in our unconscious mind, and this ego fear demands vigilant maintenance and defense. Our belief in sin is the defense needed to block awareness of the Love of God within us.

The ego's very existence depends on the belief that sin and attack are real. This is the ego's purpose for the body. It uses the body's senses to judge the body itself, the past, others and the world—and to report back only what the ego wants us to find. Sin is hunted down and hungrily devoured by the ego. This is its greatest defense against our memory of the Love within, our Holy Self.

The ego needs you to hold grievances, to see sin and attack, so it can maintain your terror of God's Love. As long as you hold grievances, you will uphold your unconscious belief you are guilty, that you can and should be attacked. *After all*, the ego says, *you committed the most unforgivable sin of all at the time of separation. You betrayed God.*

Your belief in sin fuels your hidden belief God will annihilate you if He ever finds you. Deep in your unconscious mind lies this terror of annihilation by Love. As long as you believe in sin and attack, you will continue to turn to the ego as your inner teacher.

> *"Sin is the only thing in all the world that cannot change. It is immutable. And on its changelessness the world depends... Yet each one knows the cost of sin is death. And so it is. For sin is a request for death, a wish to make this world's foundation sure as love, dependable as Heaven, and as strong as God Himself." T-25.VII.1:1-4, 6-8*

What we give, we do indeed receive. If I believe in sin and attack anywhere, it means I am projecting my own guilt, which is self-attack. Perhaps I think I'm judging someone or something other than myself. But no one and nothing exists outside myself. If I judge something, the guilt remains mine to keep. And the outcome of keeping guilt is death.

This is why forgiveness, through acceptance of the Atonement, is the most miraculous form of healing. It targets the only source of every problem we face. It undoes the single cause of all suffering, which is our unconscious belief we are guilty and deserving of punishment.

Physical death is always *self*-administered retribution, regardless of appearances. Death is an ego attempt to escape a much more severe, albeit imaginary punishment from God—who, of course, is all-encompassing Love with no opposite.

If you believe in sin, you also believe sin requires punishment. Consequently you make sin real in your mind. And the punishment you deem justified for the sin will be one the ego secretly gathers for use against you, yourself.

"Sin is attacked by punishment, and so preserved. But to forgive it is to change its state from error into truth." T-25. III.8:12-13

There is no sin. There can't be. All sins we seem to witness arise from lack of Love. Any so-called sin is simply a mistake, or what Jesus terms a call for Love. The ego punishes all calls for Love, because it declares them sins and not mistakes issued from lack of Love. Yet no one has ever truly committed a sin. If we held no guilt or fear, we could not know lack of Love, and could never therefore make a mistake. Only lack of Love causes mistakes.

There is no hierarchy of illusions, so how can sin be real? Is there a greater illusory mistake than any other illusory mistake, if they're all equally illusory? Interpret just one mistake as a sin, and you have effectively made real an opposite to God. If sin is real and there is no God, this means you don't exist. Either this is true, or both God and you are real, and sin does not exist. There is no compromise here.

"The Son of God can be mistaken; he can deceive himself; he can even turn the power of his mind against himself. But he [cannot] sin." T-19.II.3:1-2

THE FEAR OF AWAKENING

If we believe any form of suffering is real, we must believe in sin. The two go hand in hand, for sin and suffering are one and the same. The ego strives to hide this from the light of our awareness at all costs. The belief in suffering *and* in God's Love are mutually exclusive. If we believe suffering is real, we must also believe God authors suffering and that it has value. God then will surely demand suffering as payment for our sins.

Who would willingly approach such a god if this were the cost of salvation? Sin is the secret belief we are guilty and therefore deserving of punishment. The ego's belief in sin calls for inescapable punishment. Let's follow the ego's logic here:

If sin is real, spiritual awakening (going Home to God) must equal pain and loss. Suffering is the cost of sin. So salvation must be feared, because from the ego's insane perspective, salvation means deliverance from sin. It projects that deliverance from sin must come at the cost of great pain, loss and suffering.

As we follow this destructive line of nonsense, we can see the ego's idea of ultimate victory over sin is physical death itself. The ego glorifies death, selling it to us as a means to pay for our sins and be granted access to Heaven. Yet the truth of God is Love and Life with no opposite. There is no death in God— only in the ego.

> *"If sin is real, salvation must be pain. Pain is the cost of sin, and suffering can never be escaped, if sin is real. Salvation must be feared, for it will kill, but slowly, taking everything away before it grants the welcome boon of death to victims who are little more than bones before salvation is appeased. Its wrath is boundless, merciless, but wholly just." W-101.3.*

Through the ego, salvation is met with fierce resistance. This is because its belief is we haven't yet paid the necessary savage price for our sin. While we still believe we can be victimized by suffering, we will still believe in sin. And for this, we will continue to fear awakening to God. For secretly, we will believe the debt we owe God for our countless transgressions is too great a cost for us to pay. Who could possibly trust a god like this? And who would ever want salvation?

"Who would seek out such savage punishment? Who would not flee salvation, and attempt in every way he can to drown the Voice which offers it to him? Why would he try to listen and accept Its offering? If sin is real, its offering is death, and meted out in cruel form to match the vicious wishes in which sin is born. If sin is real, salvation has become your bitter enemy, the curse of God upon you who have crucified His Son." W-101.4.

EXERCISE FOR EXPOSING UNCONSCIOUS GUILT

Let's look at how this belief in sin affects our daily life. If my belief in sin always calls for punishment, and there is really only me in truth, then it's always myself that ends up being punished. All attack is self-attack, regardless of appearances. Sin is a call for punishment.

So what forms of punishment do I use to unconsciously attack myself? Who and what does the ego use in my body and life, in its attempt to prove I have sinned? Included in this unconscious assumption of my own sin is everyone and everything "out there" I believe has been guilty of sin. Take a moment and list some of the ways the ego uses your body, others or the world to prove your guilt.

Self-judgment is a favorite sin of the ego as well. The symptoms of your belief in sin could be anxiety, confusion, unworthiness, weight gain, sickness, physical or emotional pain, scarcity, depression, conflict or death, to name but a few. Identify some of the symptoms that cause you to suffer. You may want to list these as part of the next exercise.

If I unconsciously hold an un-relinquished belief that overeating is a sin, for example, I will believe I should be punished for it. And I will unknowingly punish myself by gaining weight. Maybe I use self-criticism as a sin. So the ego will punish me with experiences that confirm my seeming unworthiness. Or say I believe someone hurt me, thereby making the wound a sin. I unconsciously demand retribution for the sin I think was committed, therefore the ego will punish me for it, perhaps through physical pain or sickness. Whatever the symptom may be, the cause is my un-forgiven belief in sin. Sin begets guilt, and guilt demands punishment.

We would heal so quickly if we could acknowledge none of these mistakes are sins. They're simply errors committed through lack of Love. And so I ask you, what would Love do? How would Love respond to these mistakes? What would the Voice for Love tell you? A mistake can be Lovingly corrected and forgiven. But a sin deserves cruel punishment and must remain forever un-forgiven.

It is exceedingly important to look at all the circumstances and people we have unknowingly used to attack ourselves. We must begin to recognize the "sins" we have deemed real. These are the people and events we believe have victimized us. We cannot heal until we do this. It is futile to look to the body, the past, others or the world as scapegoats for the only real cause of all suffering. This cause for suffering is found nowhere except within our own mind. Real healing is found in the gentle majesty of the Atonement. This powerful forgiveness process is here for us in any instant we genuinely desire to heal our perception. (See the Atonement Process, found on page 297.)

In searching my mind for sinful scapegoats, I might find I am my own worst critic, that I suffer from an endless barrage of destructive self-judgments. To the ego, these judgments against myself are indeed sins. And these sins will also demand punishment if they are not sincerely offered to Spirit in exchange for the miracle. In my own experience, the consequences of cruel self-judgment have been pain, sickness, exhaustion and sleeplessness.

The punishment exacted for belief in the sin of scarcity is usually more scarcity, and so on. This is how the ego keeps us entrenched in its vicious cycle of sin, guilt and fear. And this cycle continues until we willingly offer these self-inflicted mistakes to Spirit for reinterpretation.

The following exercise will be helpful for identifying areas where your unconscious beliefs in sin and guilt reside:

1) Review the figures throughout history who have supposedly sinned. Include people you see in the news, especially those who trigger you. Write them down.

2) In your own history, who or what has sinned in your view? It may be a person. Or it could be your body, an institution, yourself or God. In other words, who or what have you not yet forgiven completely? Write down each one that comes to mind.

Those people and phenomena you have not completely forgiven symbolize the unconscious guilt (self-hatred and self-attack) you would prefer to defend and keep. These are not seen as simple errors in need of correction, but sins as the ego would define them. And sin calls for punishment.

Remember these un-forgiven "others" are not out there, but within your own mind. As long as these sins you hang onto remain un-forgiven, they will demand and manifest self-punishment. This is the unconscious ego belief that you are guilty—therefore it is you who deserve punishment.

"Any attempt to reinterpret sin as error is always indefensible to the ego. The idea of sin is wholly sacrosanct to its thought system, and quite unapproachable except with reverence and awe. It is the most "holy" concept in the ego's system; lovely and powerful, wholly true, and necessarily protected with every defense at its disposal. For here lies its "best" defense, which all the others serve. Here is its armor, its protection, and the fundamental purpose of the special

relationship in its interpretation..." "It can indeed be said the ego made its world on sin. Only in such a world could everything be upside down." T-19.11.5,6:1-2

Look at your lists, including the earlier one, "What does the ego use in your body and life, in its attempt to prove you have sinned?"

Are you ready to genuinely release each of these people or issues to the forgiveness process? Be radically honest with yourself. If you feel any reluctance to forgive wholeheartedly, set aside those you'd prefer not to forgive just yet. Stay centered, and gently ask yourself why you feel resistance to releasing them. Then just observe your responses. What is it you want by retaining your judgment against them? Be as specific as you can. What gain is there for you in holding these grievances? And in their release, what do you fear to lose?

Now, imagine these victimizers actually do not exist. There's only you and these grievances that offer hatred, separation and punishment. As you look upon the grievances, ask yourself: *Do I want this request for punishment aimed directly at myself?* If you find you are ready now to wholeheartedly release all or even some of the grievances on your lists, I suggest you take them through the Atonement process found on page 297.

I have experienced a multitude of forgiveness opportunities in my life, and I'm relieved to report that everyone in my life is forgiven. The body is showing up as my primary forgiveness area now, as it's the last of the special relationships to heal completely.

I can clearly see how I have used it as a repository for sins that are really only errors. Any little pain tells me immediately I have used the body to inflict the punishment my sins demand. In my case, the un-forgiveness is almost always a self-judgment exacted upon the body to try to prove I have sinned, and am therefore unworthy of unconditional acceptance.

As long as I carry any grievances at all, the body will be used for self-attack to demonstrate to myself and the world that I am guilty and deserving of punishment. The power of the Atonement eradicates the very concept of sin and guilt, by rendering the seeming sin an innocent mistake. And the mistake is always worthy of forgiveness and healing.

> *"Yet punishment is but another form of guilt's protection, for what is deserving punishment must have been really done. Punishment is always the great preserver of sin, treating it with respect and honoring its enormity. What must be punished, must be true. And what is true must be eternal, and will be repeated endlessly. For what you think is real you want, and will not let it go..." "An error, on the other hand, is not attractive. What you see clearly as a mistake you want corrected. Sometimes a sin can be repeated over and over, with obviously distressing results, but without the loss of its appeal. And suddenly, you change its status from a sin to a mistake. Now you will not repeat it; you will merely stop and let it go, unless the guilt remains." T-19. III.2,3:1-5*

FALSE HUMILITY AND GUILTLESSNESS

Jesus clearly tells us of our function here in the world—and it's no small function!

> *"...your function here is to be the light of the world, a function given you by God. It is only the arrogance of the ego that leads you to question this, and only the fear of the ego that induces you to regard yourself as unworthy of the task assigned to you by God Himself. The world's salvation awaits your forgiveness, because through it does the Son of God escape from all illusions, and thus from all temptation. The Son of God is you." W-64.3.*

Guiltlessness is greatly feared, because the ego's illusory identity and power depend on keeping sin and guilt real. Yet if we release the concept of sin through forgiveness, guilt and fear in the form of suffering *must* fall away.

Guilt and fear represent the palpable gap we feel between our self and God. It is this seeming gap that separates us from the deep, incorruptible security of knowing we are Love without opposite. To the ego, guiltlessness is the ultimate blasphemy—a sin worthy of death. Jesus came to reverse the laws of this world, and to teach us of our guiltlessness. He came to teach, through the Christ within, that we are the light of the world.

No wonder Jesus' body was killed. He not only taught guiltlessness, He demonstrated the invulnerability that only innocence could offer. He showed the world only God's Love and laws were real, and the ego's laws were powerless over Truth.

In the ego world, we value false humility. To the ego, guiltlessness is arrogance. How dare we claim to be the Self that God created! To declare we are, in fact, the light of the world is to commit the ultimate ego sin. The ego believes if we wish to maintain our holiness, we must remind our self we are a sinner indeed. This is the ego's concept of holiness, and unsurprisingly it's directly opposed to Jesus' teaching that proclaims, "you are the light of the world."

> *"A major tenet in the ego's insane religion is that sin is not error but truth, and it is innocence that would deceive. Purity is seen as arrogance, and the acceptance of the self as sinful is perceived as holiness. And it is this doctrine that replaces the reality of the Son of God as his Father created him, and willed that he be forever. Is this humility? Or is it, rather, an attempt to wrest creation away from truth, and keep it separate?" T-19.II.4.*

> *"I am the light of the world." "To the ego, today's idea is the epitome of self-glorification. But the ego does not understand humility, mistaking it for self-debasement. Humility consists of accepting your role in salvation and in*

taking no other. It is not humility to insist you cannot be the light of the world if that is the function God assigned to you. It is only arrogance that would assert this function cannot be for you, and arrogance is always of the ego." W-61.2.

FROM WHAT DO WE ATTEMPT TO SAVE OUR LIFE?

What is it, exactly, that we try to protect our self from? Without the unconscious fear of death, we would live in joy and inspiration, fully trusting in the moment. Every moment of life is infused with Spirit when the need to "save our life" has been surrendered to God, for we realize there is no life to save. Why is this? Because we recognize and accept that before this surrender, we were trying to save our life *from* God.

The fear of God translates to the fear of death, which includes fear of deprivation, disease, scarcity and a host of other ills. Now we see the ego is no longer driving our need to protect and save our life—so if not the ego, who is left to live it? We recognize God, as the Christ Self, is living our life *through* us. This is the Happy Dream. Life is God, and Life itself lives through us once the ego's fear of death has been surrendered.

Surrender your persistent sense of threat. The ego's fear of threat unconsciously attracts more of it. That's the ego's plan. It wishes to make us fearful, so we'll attract the goal of death it set out for us.

CHAPTER SIX

WHY JESUS' TEACHING IS THE QUICKEST OF ALL SPIRITUAL PATHS

Jesus was the first among the one Son of God (who appear to be many), to unequivocally break the ancient vow of separation and death. Through His resurrection, He took the lead by awakening completely from the ego's central dream of death. Many have awakened in the dream, but Jesus was the first to awaken completely *from* the ego's dream of birth and death.

He did this by overcoming physical death, which is our greatest defense against God's Love. Our belief in death is the darkest veil, the deepest unconscious idol responsible for imprisoning us in a seemingly endless loop of amnesia and time.

"This is the darkest veil, upheld by the belief in death and protected by its attraction. The dedication to death and to its sovereignty is but the solemn vow, the promise made in secret to the ego never to lift this veil, not to approach it, nor even to suspect that it is there. This is the secret bargain made with the ego to keep what lies beyond the veil forever blotted out and unremembered. Here is your promise never to allow union to call you out of separation; the great amnesia in which the memory of God seems quite forgotten; the cleavage of your Self from you;--[the fear of God,] the final step in your dissociation." T-19.IV.D.3.

Jesus represents the risen Christ, the awakened Holy Self we all share equally as our inheritance. Working as the Christ, He healed the separation and fulfilled the Atonement principle on behalf of us all. Jesus undid all errors the one Son of God mistakenly thought he made, including the concepts of karma and death. The only reason we still appear to witness and experience suffering, is because we still value "free" will, which is nothing but the ego's choice to suffer.

We chose to believe in the illusory, separated self instead of our own true Will, which is shared eternally with God. The uncompromising message in *A Course in Miracles* came to us from Jesus, to help us make another choice. We are taught we can choose to release all pain and suffering, by being willing to drop our defenses against Love and healing.

Many of us would sincerely choose to drop those defenses and reunite wholeheartedly with God's Will. Yet until we are willing to use the miracle of forgiveness to unearth the myriad forms of our unconscious wish to be unfairly treated, this secret desire for self-sabotage cannot be healed.

The concept of death is our deepest unquestioned belief, and our greatest unconscious defense against the memory of our innocence and invulnerability in God's Love. If we sincerely desire true healing, we must be willing to question and release this most destructive root of the ego's entire thought system.

Jesus overcame the concept of death through His own resurrection. He proved death is a completely fabricated concept, the grandest illusion upon which all other illusions rest. He demonstrated that the unreal cannot die, because it was never real in the first place. All seeming reality inherent within death is bestowed exclusively by our own uninvestigated belief in it.

The glue holding the entire ego dream together is our deep and unconscious devotion to death in all its forms—and its forms are many. Sickness, conflict, scarcity and pain all fall under this same illusory structure along with actual physical death. The degree to which we try to protect or defend our self from these perceived threats, indicates our own unconscious attraction to death.

It's also a good indicator of how strongly we unconsciously wish to be saved by death from the terror of awakening to the reality of the one divine Self we truly are. Death is the granddaddy of all illusions, purposefully shielding our ultimate fear of God. This is the fear of realizing we are Love itself.

Death symbolizes the terror of recognizing and claiming our impeccable guiltlessness, as well as the infinite power inherent within this perfected Identity. It's the fear of remembering our self as pure and unassailable Love, sharing equally in God's limitless Will. In fact our Holy Self *is* God's Will. And any form of suffering is not God's Will.

The degree to which we still perceive suffering, conflict, pain or sacrifice in our self, others or the world, is the degree to which we're still attached to the illusion of a separate self with an individual agenda apart from our Self, who is God's Love made manifest.

"Death is the thought that you are separate from your Creator." W-167.4:1

If we remembered there is no death, Life would be revealed: Uninterrupted eternal Life, here and now, while still in a body. For this to occur, we would need to truly accept personal responsibility for having projected everything we seem to see in our experience, including the body, others and the world.

We'd have to embody the knowing that life is not happening *to* us, caused by something out there. It's all occurring in our mind right here and now, and being caused *by* us.

How difficult do we find it to accept this blanket statement of Truth? It varies from person to person. The degree it triggers us, is the same degree to which we secretly embrace un-forgiveness of our self. Un-forgiveness of self is the unrecognized compulsion for self-attack, and it's this hidden un-forgiveness that seeks ongoing self-punishment in the outwardly projected forms of suffering, conflict, scarcity and death.

"See how the belief in death would seem to "save" you. For if this were gone, what could you fear but life? It is the attraction of death that makes life seem to be ugly, cruel and tyrannical. You are no more afraid of death than of the ego. These are your chosen friends. For in your secret alliance with them you have agreed never to let the fear of God be lifted, so you could look upon the face of Christ and join Him in His Father." T-19.IV.D.4.

The ego is terrified of God. It attempts to usurp the power of God by killing our body, in the belief we are irredeemably guilty. It believes we have sinned beyond imagination. In the haunted hollows of its traumatic past, lies a single secret terror causing our pervasive uneasiness and persistent sense of threat. This ancient, hidden secret is the true motivation behind every urge to sustain and protect the body and those of our loved ones.

The ego's secret is its senseless fear of God's retribution. The ego believes it betrayed God at the time of separation when it fled from Love, making an illusory world to escape the imagined wrath of its Creator. It's been running ever since. This overwhelming sense of guilt is the fabricated core of our individuated ego self. Its nucleus is guilt, and its seemingly independent existence is fed exclusively by fear and deprivation. Its most treasured escape from God is the veil of death.

"You see in death escape from what you made. But this you do not see; that you made death, and it is but illusion of an end. Death cannot be escape, because it is not life in which the problem lies. Life has no opposite, for it is God. Life and death seem to be opposites because you have decided death ends life. Forgive the world, and you will understand that everything that God created cannot have an end, and nothing He did not create is real." M-20.5:2-7

Our greatest fear is not death. Our supreme terror is of God! The ego asks, *"If God ever found us, can you imagine what He would do to us for abandoning and betraying Him?"* The suffering of this world seems like a great choice, compared to what we unconsciously imagine would happen if God finally caught up with us. Thus we hide from God in death. We hide from God in all deaths large and small—every moment we judge or feel guilty, every moment we suffer in sickness or lack, we are embracing death. Everything we choose that is not of Life, joy and Love is an affirmation of our desire to hide in death.

When we try to perceive God's nature through the thought system of the ego, we imagine Him to be an omnipotent version of a vengeful ego. We can't possibly fathom the infinite Love that is our Holy Self, because it is entirely outside the experience of the ego, whose very purpose is to block out all memory of God's Truth. The ego's version of god is a judgmental, punishing god. As long as we unconsciously believe in this version of god, we will devotedly offer our allegiance to the ego and death, rather than trusting in the one True God within.

The un-relinquished guilt we carry fuels the ego's unconscious compulsion for self-attack—and physical death is the ultimate in self-attack. The ego, in its madness, believes it can crown itself king and take the place of God. It sentences us to death (and all forms of suffering). It believes by killing the body, it will avoid a much more terrible penalty from God.

> *"The ego believes that by punishing itself it will mitigate the punishment of God... It tries to usurp all the functions of God as it perceives them, because it recognizes that only total allegiance can be trusted."* T-5.V.5:6,9

Deep down, we don't really believe death is release, relief, peace, Heaven, or Home. If we did believe this, we wouldn't fear death. We would eagerly anticipate it. But no one questions this obvious conflict, because the ego's insanity is behind it. This is a classic example of the deep, unconscious split in our mind. Two completely opposed thought systems can only be maintained by keeping them separate in our awareness. Yet once we dredge up the ego's unconscious beliefs and fears, putting them side by side with the Holy Spirit's message of Love and Life without opposite, the stark insanity of the ego thought system becomes plainly evident.

The fact is, while death remains real to us in any form, we will unconsciously fear God, because we will believe death comes from God. And in this belief, we have no choice but to reject God's Truth as our Holy Self.

> "You will think that death comes from God and not from the ego because, by confusing yourself with the ego, you believe that you want death. And from what you want God does not save you." T-12.VII.14:5-6

> "There is no death because the living share the function their Creator gave to them. Life's function cannot be to die." T-29.VI.4:9-10

> "The body neither lives nor dies, because it cannot contain you who are life. If we share the same mind, you can overcome death because I did. Death is an attempt to resolve conflict by not deciding at all. Like any other impossible solution the ego attempts, [it will not work]." T-6.V.A.1:4-7

DEATH IS NOT A PLACE WE GO TO

The state of physical death is not a place we go to after life. It is a state of mind we bring about through attachment to our un-relinquished guilt.We don't go anywhere; death is merely a continuation of the ego's dream of life. The ego is safely retained in the dream of death. Death, after all, is an ego dream. Its self-preservation is naturally built right into the system.

When the ego is entirely undone during this dream of life, however, our perception is healed and transformed so the Real World reveals itself. And we will recognize the Real World has always been the Truth of our existence in this world. In the Real World, Love shines through all we made; this is why it's known as the Happy Dream. We're still here in a body, surrounded by the rest of the world, but our healed mind now perceives self and other as one perfect Self. This is Heaven on Earth.

We go from the ego's dream of suffering, conflict, disease and death to the Holy Spirit's dream of unopposed joy, peace, Love and Life. When we have released all guilt through forgiveness, we can then lay the body aside in peace, at the appropriate time. But Jesus is adamant that this is a joint decision made with Spirit. The body is not victimized by age, deterioration, sickness or pain.

In fact the body, in itself completely neutral, becomes a mirrored consequence of complete forgiveness. As an effect, it is the perfect reflection of its healed cause within our mind. Cause (in the mind) and effect (the body or world) always remain together, inextricably linked in our mind. Heal the cause and the effect must reflect this new state. It is through knowledge and mastery of this principle that Jesus healed the sick and raised the dead.

> *"The miracle is possible when cause and consequence are brought together, not kept separate."* T-26.VII14:1 *"A major step in the Atonement plan is to undo error at all levels."* T-2.IV.2:1

The body is necessary as our primary vehicle to awaken from the ego's dream of separation, suffering and death. Death of the body is the ego's greatest defense against God's Love, so healing can only take place while we're in the body, where we can work to expose the errors that prohibit healing.

Once the body's purpose has been willingly transferred from the ego to Spirit, it is actually no longer *our* body; it becomes the Christ's body because it has become the vehicle through which we extend forgiveness. In the service of Love, the body cannot suffer.

Yet as long as we mindlessly abdicate our power to the ego, inviting suffering and physical death again and again, we adamantly maintain that death is our savior. We affirm it is more powerful than God's unopposed and all-encompassing Life.

We must abdicate jurisdiction over the body, if we wish to stop experiencing our self as a victim of the dream of death. Joined in God's Will, we must agree to undo everything we made for the unholy purpose of experiencing this dream. We erroneously think of this dream as life. But a state that terminates inevitably in death should never be mistaken for real Life.

Living through the ego is living death. No wonder we look to death as an escape—as relief from the body and the ego's incessant conflict. No wonder so many have mistakenly looked to death as Heaven, or Home in God.

As long as we believe death is more powerful than God's Love, we unknowingly fear and therefore reject our Holy Self. The dream of death keeps us from remembering who we are in God's perfection. And while we continue to value death in all its forms, we delay our awakening from the ego's death cycle.

> *"The ego is not a traitor to God, to Whom treachery is impossible. But it is a traitor to you who believe that you have been treacherous to your Father. That is why the undoing of guilt is an essential part of the Holy Spirit's teaching. For as long as you feel guilty you are listening to the voice of the ego, which tells you that you have been treacherous to God and therefore deserve death. You will think that death comes from God and not from the ego because, by confusing yourself with the ego, you believe that you want death. And from what you want God does not save you." T-12.VII.14.*

> *"When you are tempted to yield to the desire for death, [remember that I did not die.] ... Would I have overcome death for myself alone?" T-12.VII.15:1,3*

WHERE ELSE BUT IN THE BODY WILL YOU AWAKEN FROM DEATH?

The illusion of time seems never-ending. We flee into death over and over, lifetime after lifetime, in attempts to avoid awakening into the God Self that we are. Death is the ultimate expression of our fear of God. Death is amnesia, and the invitation to yet another illusory birth. But a birth into what?

In the ego's illusion of life, we are born remembering nothing. We have no idea our sole purpose is to undo the illusory sense of a separated ego-self by learning to forgive everyone and everything. Instead, in this ego paradigm, we are taught to judge and condemn everyone and everything, including our self.

The ego teaches us we are nothing but a fragile body destined for inevitable destruction. Its entire world is based on death/fear, and not on Life/Love. The ego uses the body to distract us so completely that it eclipses Truth in our awareness.

In Truth we are not the body, nor are we even *in* a body. We are the eternally guiltless Child of God who shares the power and dominion of God's Mind. The ego keeps us distracted in delusions of powerlessness and helplessness. It persuades us we are trapped in a dream of death we mistakenly believe is life.

"You suffer pain because the body does, and in this pain are you made one with it. Thus is your "true" identity preserved, and the strange, haunting thought that you might be something beyond this little pile of dust silenced and stilled. For see, this dust can make you suffer, twist your limbs and stop your heart, commanding you to die and cease to be." W-136.8:3-5

"Thus is the body stronger than the truth, which asks you live, but cannot overcome your choice to die. And so the body is more powerful than everlasting life, Heaven more frail than hell, and God's design for the salvation of His Son opposed by a decision stronger than His Will." W-136.9:1-2

The body has no power to shift or change itself. It cannot get sick, nor become well unless our own mind commands it. All biological laws arise from the ego, not from God. The body is purely a neutral image we project in every new instant; its state is derived from either guilt or guiltlessness, depending upon which inner teacher governs the body. It has but one cause, which is in our mind. And as long as we choose to allow our mind to suffer unconsciously in paroxysms of guilt, the ego will continue to use the body, others and the world for the purpose of attack.

"You think that death is of the body. Yet it is but an idea, irrelevant to what is seen as physical. A thought is in the mind. It can be then applied as mind directs it. But its origin is where it must be changed, if change occurs. Ideas leave not their source. The emphasis this course has placed on that idea is due to its centrality in our attempts to change your mind about yourself. It is the reason you can heal. It is the cause of healing. It is why you cannot die. Its truth established you as one with God." W-167.3.

Rarely is a child of this world fortunate enough to be raised by ascended masters who have already transcended the dream of death. Most of us are raised by the un-relinquished egos belonging to our parents or caretakers.

Their unrecognized agenda is to help us cultivate a false self, a more secure defense against Love. We are taught to seek for special love, and shown how to succeed in the world. The world's aim is to teach us we are unworthy and incomplete, and that we must seek outside our self for completion through relationships and accomplishments.

Some of us begin to remember the Holy purpose of Life, and commence the journey of undoing the false self—the very self the world helped us build. If we haven't quite remembered our Holy Self in its entirety before the body dies, however, we have no choice but to slip once again into the amnesia cycle of death and birth. The cycle of time continues, with each unconscious descent into death and subsequent rebirth into a body. The ego's central dream of death remains inviolate, until we partner with Spirit to look at and undo the ego's unconscious attraction to death. All spiritual paths are helpful in the gradual awakening from the ego's birth and death cycle. Yet Jesus' pathway of forgiveness and the miracle, is by far the quickest for collapsing time. Erasing guilt, the miracle undoes our secret attraction to death. This attraction is our most seductive form of escape from awakening to our own invulnerability as God's Will. As our unconscious fear of God vanishes, death is overcome. And without death, we joyfully discover time has no purpose other than to return to Love.

Where else but in the body could we hope to overcome the ego's central dream of death itself? If death is the final and greatest defense against our return to Love, we must turn the body's purpose over to Spirit for reinterpretation with complete willingness, thereby overcoming death in all its forms. As we accomplish this relinquishment of the body's purpose and allow the healing that follows in its wake, we will overcome the ego's dream of death just as Jesus did two thousand years ago.

> *"The central lesson is always this; that what you use the body for it will become to you. Use it for sin or for attack, which is the same as sin, and you will see it as sinful. Because it is sinful it is weak, and being weak, it suffers and it dies. Use it to bring the Word of God to those who have it not, and the body becomes holy. Because it is holy it cannot be sick, nor can it die." M-12.5:1-5*

THE BATHTUB: A SYMBOL OF THE VASTNESS OF JESUS' TEACHING

Recently I was gifted with an insight, a simple analogy that gives us a tiny glimpse of the sheer magnitude of Jesus' teaching. It was shown to me as a visual symbol, portraying the entire universal ego dream from the beginning of the separation until the end of time: An Olympic swimming pool-sized bathtub is filled to the brim with water. The water represents our universal dream of duality, encompassing the seemingly endless cycle of time, space, karma, birth and death. In short, I was given to understand the water conveys the ego's entire dream of guilt, fear, suffering and death.

This gargantuan bathtub's capacity to retain such a vast quantity of toxic water is made possible only by an enormous plug that holds it all in. The plug represents our unquestioned belief in death as a power greater than our own power in God. Our belief in death as an idol to be held above God, is the single obsession that holds the entire illusion of suffering in place. For, if death is real, there can be no God. Death denies Life and God.

There are many helpful spiritual teachings in the world, and they all contribute to the undoing of the dream of suffering. Yet although they may seem to teach that death is an illusion, they still believe death is the natural, legitimate and inevitable outcome of life in the ego dream. Many even justify death, attempting to integrate the two mutually exclusive and irreconcilable concepts of death and God.

Jesus' teaching is uncompromising. He states that God is Life. Period. There cannot be God *and* pain, God *and* sickness, God *and* death. God is Life. And there is no opposite of God. So there cannot be life *and* death, unless we believe we are separate from our Source.

> *"If death is real for anything, there is no life. Death denies life. But if there is reality in life, death is denied. No compromise in this is possible. There is either a god of fear or One of Love... He did not make death because He did not make fear."* M-27.4:2-6,9

Jesus is asking us to learn this truth in our own experience, and to learn it now while we're here in a body—not after the illusion of death has claimed our body, thus leading us into yet another birth cycle of amnesia. We learn this truth by choosing to forgive all illusions that seemingly hold us apart from Love.

As we commit to accomplish this, we demonstrate here and now that we are under no laws but God's. Yet until we commit wholeheartedly, our results will be inconsistent. For, as long as we believe in a dualistic god of suffering and death, we can't hope to know of our complete invulnerability in God's Love—because we haven't chosen it. Of God and death, only one is Real. There is either God *or* there is pain, sickness and death.

> *"And the last to be overcome will be death. Of course! Without the idea of death there is no world. All dreams will end with this one. This is salvation's final goal; the end of all illusions. And in death are all illusions born. What can be born of death and still have life? But what is born of God and still can die? ... Do you not see that otherwise He has an opposite, and fear would be as real as love?"* M-27.6:1-8,11

As far as I know, *A Course in Miracles* is the only teaching that targets our unconscious attraction to death, the nucleus of our fear of God. Until we dare to examine our most terrible fear of God, which lies at the root of the death dream, the "plug of death" that keeps the universal ego dream afloat will stay firmly in place.

While many teachings other than *A Course in Miracles* are undeniably helpful, they do not address the nucleus of our imagined separation from God—that giant plug of death that keeps the whole ego dream alive and cycling. As a result of this omission, I was shown, they might be capable of draining the universal "bath of suffering" by a single drop every thousand years. At this pace it may take hundreds of thousands, or even millions of years to empty completely. And because we are literally all one, this means none of us will be perfectly and fully at Home until the bathtub is empty, allowing every single sleeping mind to return to sanity.

Here is the significance of Jesus' deeper teaching as outlined in *A Course in Miracles*. Through His resurrection and Atonement, He has *already* seized that giant plug called "death," and He has wrenched it right out of the bathtub on our behalf! And with that one action of pulling the plug, the dream of suffering has been drained away within moments.

Sure, we can choose to awaken to a level of relative peace here within the dream through many spiritual practices. Yet this relative awakening is not complete. Jesus' unique pathway of forgiveness, Atonement and miracles is vertical. It slices straight through the horizontal time plane, collapsing it immediately. This collapse of time saves us untold suffering and many lifetimes of karma.

Jesus was the first in the long dream of separation to go beyond all prior spiritual teachings and pathways, demonstrating that there *literally* is no death. Not for just one of us, but for all of us.

In His resurrection and Atonement, He unraveled and released the ego's central dream of death. And in so doing, He proved we are perfectly guiltless, and therefore wholly invulnerable Children of God. Jesus tells us here that the resurrection has already been accomplished *in you*. Can you sit quietly within right now, and open your heart to accept your certain healing?

"Believe in the resurrection because it has been accomplished, and it has been accomplished in you. This is as true now as it will ever be, for the resurrection is the Will of God, which knows no time and no exceptions. But make no exceptions yourself, or you will not perceive what has been accomplished for you." T-11.VI.4:6-8

"Blessed are ye who have not seen and still believe, for those who believe in the resurrection will see it. The resurrection is the complete triumph of Christ over the ego, not by attack but by transcendence. T-11.VI.1:5-6

In overcoming death and completing the Atonement, Jesus erased our guilt, which is nothing other than our hidden fear of God. And as He accomplished this, He undid the ego's concept of karma. As a living symbol of the one Son of God, a human being who embodied the one eternal Christ Mind we all share, Jesus went before us and made the path straight. He gifted us with the Atonement and miracles, which comprise the now-moment portal to instant healing.

When Jesus reversed the ego's concepts of sin, guilt, fear and death through His resurrection, you were there with Him. As an eternally treasured member of the one Mind of God, your Holy Self partook in this resurrection. If you cannot accept this fact yet, it's because you have not been ready to accept and receive your perfect healing. When you are ready, you will simply offer your acceptance and say yes to your healing.

This is what the Atonement is for. It's a vehicle through which we accept the Truth about our self. The Atonement is already complete. All dreams have already been undone. You are simply experiencing the ego's echo, until you wholeheartedly desire only the Love of God. When Love is all you want, Love is all you will experience.

Jesus did not die for our sins. Quite the opposite. He proved there is no sin by overcoming death, which is the ego's most aggressive defense against God's Love. He demonstrated the powerlessness of the ego's most violent attack. And He rose from the ego's dream of death to show us only in our guiltlessness and defenselessness does our true invulnerability lie.

What does the end of death mean? Jesus asked us more than 2,000 years ago to join Him in his resurrection. But we didn't; we just weren't ready. We were still too terrified of Love. Now, two millennia later in the illusion of time and suffering, He has gifted us with *A Course in Miracles*. It's a miraculous road map designed to lead us Home to the glory of God's Love within.

Heaven is not a place we go to. Heaven is our natural state, when guilt and death no longer remain to darken and distort our perception. Yet as long as they do, it means fear sits on our inner altar instead of Love. Jesus' journey was the last useless journey to the cross, as His resurrection freed us from all dreams of death. He accomplished this on behalf of all of us. Are we ready to accept our eternal guiltlessness?

"Very simply, the resurrection is the overcoming or surmounting of death. It is a reawakening or a rebirth; a change of mind about the meaning of the world. It is the

acceptance of the Holy Spirit's interpretation of the world's purpose; the acceptance of the Atonement for oneself. It is the end of dreams of misery, and the glad awareness of the Holy Spirit's final dream. It is the recognition of the gifts of God. It is the dream in which the body functions perfectly, having no function except communication. It is the lesson in which learning ends, for it is consummated and surpassed with this. It is the invitation to God to take His final step. It is the relinquishment of all other purposes, all other interests, all other wishes and all other concerns. It is the single desire of the Son for the Father." M-28.1.

"The resurrection is the denial of death, being the assertion of life. Thus is all the thinking of the world reversed entirely." M-28.2:1-2

"There is no death. The Son of God is free. And in his freedom is the end of fear. No hidden places now remain on earth to shelter sick illusions, dreams of fear and misperceptions of the universe." M-28.4:2-5

COLLAPSING THE DREAM OF DEATH

Through Jesus' resurrection and Atonement, He has already collapsed the ego's dream of death. All we're seeing and experiencing is the echo of our own free ego will, or personal will. We will to see only the ego's dream, because our unconscious attraction to guilt as self-punishment has been too great. This is the only reason we still appear to witness a world of suffering and death. As our own deep-rooted fear of Love is brought to light and healed, the ego's echo, along with its interpretation of the 3-D world, will fall away to reveal the Real World of unopposed Love and joy.

Jesus was the first to overcome the ego's central dream of physical death. He dispelled the grandest of all illusions, this nonnegotiable ego belief in, and attraction to death in all its forms. He realized our belief in the ego's dream of death keeps us from the embodied knowledge of our self as the Christ. In His resurrection he proved no illusion, not even death itself, is more powerful than a healed mind.

In His demonstration of miracles, He reversed the ego's paradigm of cause and effect. In doing so He proved indisputably that the mind is cause and the body/world are purely effects seen externally, yet recognized exclusively as being within the mind. He overlooked the ego's laws, and lived out only from God's Laws. He encourages us to do the same.

This world, our body and the Real World exist only in our mind. While they appear to unfold in time externally, they are caused first within the mind, and occur there simultaneously with the outer projected experience. The same is true of the ego's dream of death. The so-called death realm is not a place; it's simply a state of mind. As long as death remains an experience we unconsciously desire, we continue to manifest the death realm within our mind.

The body is the hero of the ego dream. Without the body there can be no ego, for without the concept of the body's physical death, the ego cannot survive. The ego requires a body to enforce its beliefs and manifest its fear paradigm. The body, you see, is our greatest repository for guilt—so into the body we must go to undo the dream of death. This dream of death includes all forms of sickness, pain, conflict or scarcity, all of which play out through the body. How can we possibly transcend the illusion of death without the body?

> *"The body is the central figure in the dreaming of the world. There is no dream without it... It takes the central place in every dream, which tells the story of how it was made by other bodies, born into the world outside the body, lives a little while and dies, to be united in the dust with other bodies dying like itself. In the brief time allotted it to live, it seeks for other bodies as its friends and enemies. Its safety is its main concern. Its comfort is its guiding rule. It tries to look for pleasure, and avoid the things that would be*

hurtful. Above all, it tries to teach itself its pains and joys are different and can be told apart." T-27.VIII.1.

"This single lesson does [the body] try to teach again, and still again, and yet once more; that it is cause and not effect. And you are its effect, and cannot be its cause." T-27. VIII.3:4-5 Thus are you not the dreamer, but the dream." T-27.VIII.4:1-2

The body must be totally surrendered to God's purpose, if we wish to facilitate a comprehensive reversal of the world's thinking, and welcome the Real World into our perception. The body is meaningless in itself. It is neutral. All meaning arises from the purpose we have assigned to it. Who is in charge of and responsible for our body? Is it the ego or Spirit?

As long as I still believe the body can attack and be attacked, and while I attempt to meet the body's illusory needs independently from Spirit, I must believe I am a body and not the incorruptible Holy Self. If that is the case, I will surely believe in, and therefore live out from the ego's unholy laws.

Yet if I've given my body's purpose to Spirit, I will know my perfect guiltlessness—which translates literally to my perfect immunity under God's laws. And that includes the body's immunity! But if I believe in the body as myself, the certain outcome is death. As long as I continue to believe in the ego's laws instead of God's laws, I make the body real and give it status more powerful than God's Love.

Jesus' is not teaching immortality of the body. That would be pointless, as the body is seen to hold no special value or importance, once perception has been healed. It will last as long as it is seen to be useful, and then be gently laid aside without regret.

His teaching is designed to help us overcome and undo the body/world's ego purpose. It is here to give the body/world the Holy purpose of forgiveness. Forgiveness is the undoing of guilt, heralding the return of the Holy Self and its Real World to our awareness.

"The real world was given you by God in loving exchange for the world you made and the world you see. Only take it from the hand of Christ and look upon it. Its reality will make everything else invisible, for beholding it is total perception. And as you look upon it you will remember that it was always so. Nothingness will become invisible, for you will at last have seen truly." T-12.VIII.8:1-5

As long as we still believe we are victims of the body and world, the body is believed to be more powerful than our mind. It is stronger than God's Will. And, simply put, if this is so we will not awaken from the ego's dream. Sickness, pain, conflict, depression, scarcity and death are blocks to the awareness of Love's presence. Thus they are manifestations of our resistance to awakening to our Holy Self as God's Will. We *are* the Will of God. We *are* the Kingdom of Heaven.

JESUS AS THE FIRST TO AWAKEN FROM THE EGO'S DREAM OF DEATH

As explained earlier in the bathtub analogy, Jesus was the first to completely overcome the ego's central dream of death through His resurrection. He was also the first to complete the Atonement principle on behalf of us all. Within the one mind of the Son of God (which includes us all), He was the first to awaken completely from the ego's birth/death cycle. He did this while appearing in a body. The Holy Spirit therefore called upon Jesus to carry out His plan of Atonement:

"He has established Jesus as the leader in carrying out His plan since he was the first to complete his own part perfectly." C-6.2:2

Jesus demonstrated that He overcame the body/world by reversing the laws of this world. He did this through the recognition and embodiment of His own absolute guiltlessness. And as He knew His own guiltlessness, He therefore knew the guiltless state of everyone and everything.

In His acceptance of all-inclusive guiltlessness, all blocks to the awareness of Love's presence fell away forever. God's unlimited power was returned to His awareness. This is how He took dominion over both the body and world, reversing the ego's cause and effect. And this is how He invoked miracles and healing.

There have been many saints and sages who awakened in the dream, but did not awaken from the dream completely. Their knowing was incomplete; they were not fully able to reverse the ego's cause and effect. They still perceived a hierarchy of illusions and were therefore unable to demonstrate that there is no order of difficulty in miracles.

The ego's dream of death appeared to overpower their will, resulting in sickness and physical death that claimed their bodies. They had not yet accepted their total guiltlessness, and therefore did not claim divine immunity from ego phenomena. If they had, they could have simply laid the body aside in perfect health when their purpose was complete. In so doing, they would have awakened from the ego's dream altogether, breaking free of the ego's birth and death cycle.

> *"There have been many healers who did not heal themselves. They have not moved mountains by their faith because their faith was not whole. Some of them have healed the sick at times, but they have not raised the dead. Unless the healer heals himself, he cannot believe that there is no order of difficulty in miracles." T-5.VII.2:1-4*

ASCENSION
(End of the ego's dream)

Lay the body aside
THE REAL WORLD DREAM
No sickness, no pain
No suffering
THE EGO'S DREAM OF DEATH
No scarcity, no conflict
No aging
THE EGO'S WORLD
(the dream of ego life)
JOY
LOVE
Recycle back into the ego's world
No death
No death
PEACE

The star's path depicts Jesus
showing us the way out of the ego's dream of death

Collapsing the Dream of Death

THE INNERMOST RING:
EGO'S BODY AND WORLD

In the diagram *Collapsing the Dream of Death*, there are three concentric rings. The innermost ring represents this ego paradigm where we seem to experience pain, conflict, illness, loss, scarcity and death. The so-called laws of nature also are found here. As you can see, the concept of death holds all of these ego laws together; it appears to give them their structural integrity.

The innermost ring is filled with dots. These represent all human beings since the beginning of time. The star symbolizes Jesus as Christ, the risen Holy Self within us who has already undone the ego's dream of separation. When Jesus resurrected, we were there with Him. When He recognized and accepted He was the Son of God, and therefore the Kingdom of Heaven, we were also with Him.

Our one Holy Self has already overcome the ego's world and laws. This was accomplished on behalf of us all. Yet we don't experience this as our own truth, because we still value the ego. Our own power of choice is paramount. The instant we no longer desire the ego's thought system, our awareness will be restored to all-encompassing Love with no opposite.

As the diagram shows, the star of Christ has leapt beyond the dream of death. While Jesus was here in a body, He lived out from the Christ within; this means He lived out from His awareness of the Real World, which is what enabled Him to heal the sick and raise the dead. He did this by recognizing the total reversal of ego cause and effect.

These "worlds" do not truly inhabit separate physical spaces; they're all one. Yet the Real World was immediately revealed to Him as He chose total forgiveness, allowing all things to be reinterpreted for Him.

There are many levels of awakening in the ego dream. Some may become Self-realized or enlightened, which is immensely helpful to all of us. But to become enlightened in the dream is not the same as awakening from it altogether. Once we truly know all cause and effect is in our mind, we will demonstrate that nothing in the ego's illusory world of external phenomena can possibly hurt us, including our own body. We can no longer be victimized by the body or the world.

THE SECOND RING: RING OF DEATH

The second ring represents the ego's dream of death. Notice how this ring completely encases our world. The dream of death acts as a very solid barrier to attainment of the Real World. While any belief in death is held, regardless of its form, the Real World is kept from our awareness.

Note that in this ring of death, a constant "recycling program" is in effect. Another name for this is reincarnation. If the dream of death is not overcome within our lifetime, we simply recycle back into form for yet another experience of birth, amnesia and death.

Some of us hit a wall around mid-life, although it occasionally comes earlier. This is when the ego, the false self developed by our parents, culture, media and education finally cracks under the weight of its own deception. Suicide is a common attempt to escape this dilemma, but physical death is not the remedy—because death is not the end of the ego's cycle.

"For death is seen as safety, the great dark savior from the light of truth, the answer to the Answer, the silencer of the Voice that speaks for God. Yet the retreat to death is not the end of conflict." T-19.IV.C.7:2-3

"There is no death because what God created shares His life. There is no death because an opposite to God does not exist. There is no death because the Father and the Son are One." W-167.1:5-7

"There is no death because the living share the function their Creator gave to them. Life's function cannot be to die. It must be life's extension, that it be as one forever and forever, without end." T-29.VI.4:9-11

A period of disillusionment occurs when we have exhausted everything the ego offers. A type of breakdown takes place, in order to break *through*. This breakdown or disillusionment phase is the pivotal point at which we can change the purpose of our life. From what to what? From the ego's goal of separation and death to Spirit's goal of awakening and Life. This new choice heralds the awakening from fear, because it offers us the reversal of our life's purpose, and therefore our body's purpose as well.

Reaching this phase of disillusionment usually precipitates— or accelerates—a search for deeper meaning or purpose in life. At this point some may take up a spiritual path. Others may make the unconscious choice to get sick and die. Whichever course we take, if there remains a belief that death is the certain outcome of life, we will surely manifest death as our outcome. And the recycling will continue: Death, birth, amnesia, building a bigger ego, disillusionment and finally death again.

The birth/amnesia/death cycle ensures the illusion of time will drag onward ad infinitum. This long, arduous cycle has been rendered unnecessary by Jesus' resurrection and Atonement. Each time we forgive, accepting the miracle of Atonement instead of its opposite, a literal collapse of time, and therefore suffering, occurs.

"The miracle substitutes for learning that might have taken thousands of years." T-1.II.6:7

"Be still and listen to the truth today. For each five minutes spent in listening, a thousand minds are opened to the truth and they will hear the holy Word you hear." W-106.9:1-2

"The function [of God's teachers] is to save time. Each one begins as a single light, but with the Call at its center it is a light that cannot be limited. And each one saves a thousand years of time as the world judges it." M-1.2:11-13

THE OUTER RING:
THE REAL WORLD DREAM

When forgiveness is complete, our perception is healed. No one and nothing is left to hurt us. We have forgiven our self completely for having used others, the past, the world and our body to attack our self. We are no longer victims of the illusory world in our mind. Cause and effect have been completely reversed, and recognized for what they are. We realize everyone and everything, including the body, dwells within our mind, and are not the external projections we think we see. We now see with God. And everything we see with God is healed.

Only the laws of God prevail here in this Happy Dream, because the body's purpose has become Holy. While the body might still exist a little while longer until its purpose is complete, it harbors no sickness, pain, scarcity, conflict, aging, loss, sacrifice, struggle, suffering or death.

When the Holy Self recognizes the body's purpose has been fulfilled, the body is joyfully, peacefully laid aside. It's the unzipping of a "skin suit" for the very last time.

The body is in perfect health as this decision is carried out. Having finally broken our ancient vow of separation and suffering, the Christ within takes dominion over everything the ego made. The body and world have been returned to God's purpose. All dreaming is complete. The cycle of death and destruction ends at last, as the Holy Self is lifted into God. This final step is taken by God, in what Jesus calls the transfer or return from perception to knowledge. I call it the Ascension.

"The central lesson is always this; that what you use the body for it will become to you. Use it for sin or for attack, which is the same as sin, and you will see it as sinful. Because it is sinful it is weak, and being weak, it suffers and it dies. Use it to bring the Word of God to those who have it not, and the body becomes holy. Because it is holy it cannot be sick, nor can it die. When its usefulness is done it is laid by, and that is all." M-12.5:1-6

"And you will lay aside the world and find another. This other world is bright with love which you have given it. And here will everything remind you of your Father and His holy Son. Light is unlimited, and spreads across this world in quiet joy. All those you brought with you will shine on you, and you will shine on them in gratitude because they brought you here. Your light will join with theirs in power so compelling, that it will draw the others out of darkness as you look on them." T-13.VI.11:5-10

DEATH EXERCISES

1) Write down what you expect to experience after death. Make a list of your positive beliefs of the benefits of death. Carefully search your mind and come up with at least ten answers that are true for you. Some common examples follow here: The end of conflict; Heaven or union with God; reunion with loved ones; etc.

2) Now ask yourself this: If you had the chance to die today, would you take it?

3) If not, why not? If death offers so many apparent benefits that life does not, why would we not commit suicide today? If death seems to deliver so much more than life, *why are we so fearful of death?* And yes, whatever our conscious attitudes toward it, we do fear death. To the degree we independently attempt to "save our life" from sickness, pain, loss, betrayal, scarcity or any other ill, reveals the extent to which we unconsciously fear death.

4) Now make a second list. With radical self-honesty, write down all your concerns and fears about dying. What will you lose or sacrifice in death?

5) Place your two lists together. Look at these side-by-side statements of positive beliefs about death, and fears about death. Can you see a split in your mind? Can you help but notice a contradiction here?

Death is the ego's favorite form of propaganda. It sells us the concept of death by gift-wrapping the experience. Yet most of us also fear death, which causes our unconscious attraction *to* it.

All adversity, including sickness and death, is sold to us through the ego's storehouse of contradictions and lies. If we hoard these unconscious ego grenades, they will eventually detonate. We must raise all hidden ego contradictions to the light of Spirit, willingly exchanging them for the miracle.

6) Have you believed God is responsible for setting the time of your death?

7) What have you believed are some typical causes of death? List at least 5-10 of your beliefs. Review your list, and ask yourself: "what is the single cause of death?" If you still believe the cause lies in the body through disease, accidents or aging, you cannot heal the real cause, which is guilt.

8) What would you stand to lose if there were no physical death? A few examples: rest; peace; freedom from ego; etc.

9) What would you have to give-up...
a) if there were no sickness?
b) if there were no emotional or physical pain?
c) if there were no betrayal?
d) if there were no loss?
e) if there were no conflict?
f) if there were no scarcity?
g) if there were no physical death?

10) What would you have to face if there were no physical death?

11) Do any fears arise from these questions? If so, what are they?

12) Take note of all the ego's concerns and fears you have exposed. Be willing to do the Atonement process to forgive each one, allowing you to release them in exchange for the miracle. This will enable real healing.

CHAPTER SEVEN

A WORLD WITHOUT DEATH

Jesus' holographic teachings are intended to completely reverse the thinking of the world. In my own firsthand experience (with the assistance of Tomas since he departed physical form), I have been gifted with many miraculous epiphanies and perceptual shifts. I have been shown that the miracle component of Jesus' teachings, if followed consistently, *will* completely overturn our perception—just as He says they will. After perception is healed and before we return to God in oneness with Love itself, we will experience, *while still in a body*, the Truth that refutes all ego laws.

Jesus calls this state of mind the Real World. He demonstrated the Real World while He was here in the body. He saw no separation, sickness, scarcity or death. And because He chose to look beyond all appearances and forgive, He became a conduit through whom the power of God was made manifest.

There are many documented accounts of His demonstrations of the miracle. He fed a crowd of five thousand people with just five loaves of bread and two small fish. The biblical account of this from Matthew in the New Testament says the following: *"They all ate and were satisfied, and the disciples picked up twelve basketfuls of broken pieces that were left over."* He healed the sick many times, and raised the dead. And He taught his disciples to do the same in His name.

Jesus' miraculous healings were always consistent. He never failed. His ability to bring Heaven to Earth came about because His Mind was unified in God's Love. He operated exclusively from

His right mind, having renounced the temptation to exercise His own personal ego will. He knew God's Will was His own True Will, and His complete trust in Love without opposite allowed Him to Will with God unfailingly.

Because He knew God's Will was all-encompassing Love without opposite, He Willed with absolute certainty in God. Therefore, His miracle-working abilities were unobstructed. He had overcome the last obstacle to peace, which is the fear of God. Fear of God is the final veil that separates us from knowing God as our Holy Self. The Kingdom of Heaven is within, and Jesus knew this. He also knew nothing in this dream could possibly interrupt the Kingdom of Heaven within.

The difference between Jesus and us right now, is this: Because we continue to fear God, we still choose to cherish certain illusions instead of seeing only Love. In other words, we maintain a hierarchy of illusions that obscures from our awareness (and therefore from our experience) the number one miracle principle taught by Jesus: *"There is no order of difficulty in miracles."* In short, His desire was undivided. When we desire only Love, we too will experience nothing but Love, expressed as endless miracles and joy.

Jesus demonstrated no order of difficulty in miracles. He knew the seeming reality and solidity of our world is only illusion. He understood that everything in the dream is a product of the mind, and all of it resides within the mind always. He recognized if there is evidence of scarcity, sickness or death, it comes from the ego mind. So He simply looked past appearances and recalled the Truth, thereby manifesting it. He knew anything not of God's Love could not be of His Will, and therefore held absolutely no power to harm anyone.

Before we can truly heal, as the *Course* explains, we must clearly understand the two levels of cause and effect. Level one is the mind, from which all cause manifests. Level two is the effect level, which includes the world and everything in it. The level of effect has no ability to cause anything independently from the mind. At this level, everything we perceive is appearance only. There is no seeming cause in the body, another, the past, or the world (all of which are effects), that cannot be healed by the miracle. Anything that is not changeless and eternal Love belongs to the level of effect. As such, everything at this worldly effect level is open to the healing power of the miracle.

Precisely *because* everything at the level of form consists of illusory appearance only, it is not eternal and can therefore be healed through the miracle. All physical miracles are preceded by a perceptual shift into Love. We can never place our trust in what the body's eyes seem to see, because it's not the truth.

> *"The miracle is means to demonstrate that all appearances can change because they [are] appearances, and cannot have the changelessness reality entails. The miracle attests salvation from appearances by showing they can change."* T-30.VIII.2:1-2
>
> *"A clear distinction between what is created and what is made is essential. All forms of healing rest on this fundamental correction in level perception."* T-2.V.A.12:1-2
>
> *"Spiritual vision literally cannot see error, and merely looks for Atonement. All solutions the physical eye seeks dissolve. Spiritual vision looks within and recognizes immediately that the altar has been defiled and needs to be repaired and protected. Perfectly aware of the right defense it passes over all others, looking past error to truth."* T-2.III.4.

THE REAL WORLD

Jesus heralds an unparalleled paradigm shift, the most monumental shift since the separation. Through His Atonement He reversed our present paradigm of separation, deprivation and death. Although this epic shift has already occurred, we still perceive the echo of the old paradigm as long as we choose to embrace a hierarchy of illusions. But when we choose undivided allegiance to God's Love as Self, we will become instruments through which the power of God will manifest. And just as Jesus has said, this world of fear will be replaced by Love.

Jesus was able to unequivocally work miracles because He refused to let Himself be tempted to believe the ego's world. He chose to see, and therefore demonstrate only God's all-encompassing Love and healing. He perceived nothing else, placing His absolute trust in God's grace and Love.

> *"There is nothing about me that you cannot attain. I have nothing that does not come from God. The difference between us now is that I have nothing else. This leaves me in a state which is only potential in you." T-1.II.3:10-13*

The only thing stopping us from joining Him in this consistent state of awareness, is our ongoing choice to perceive the unreal in our self, others and the world. In other words, we have not yet chosen to accept the Atonement unfailingly.

The Real World, as I am learning, gradually emerges in our awareness as we deliberately make the choice, over and over, to disbelieve the ego's world. This can only be achieved by consistently denying anything the power to harm us, recognizing it is not of God's Love.

We commit to being vigilant only for God and His Kingdom. This is True forgiveness. In saying *no* to illusion while accepting Atonement for our misperceptions, we experience miracles. Thus, the Real World begins to appear in our perception.

> *"It is denial of illusions that calls on truth, for to deny illusions is to recognize that fear is meaningless. Into the holy home where fear is powerless love enters thankfully, grateful that it is one with you who joined to let it enter." T-22.I.10:6-7*

"What He enables you to do is clearly not of this world, for miracles violate every law of reality as this world judges it. Every law of time and space, of magnitude and mass is transcended, for what the Holy Spirit enables you to do is clearly beyond all of them." T-12.VII.3:2-3

"The Holy Spirit has the power to change the whole foundation of the world you see to something else; a basis not insane, on which a sane perception can be based, another world perceived. And one in which nothing is contradicted that would lead the Son of God to sanity and joy. Nothing attests to death and cruelty; to separation and to differences. For here is everything perceived as one, and no one loses that each one may gain." T-25.VII.5.

THE CONDITION OF THE REAL WORLD

The condition through which we enter the Real World is a state of oneness within the mind. Oneness means a consistent, single-minded choice to disbelieve all ego illusions. Oneness is lack of fear—and wherever fear has been released, Love is restored to awareness. We cannot perceive True oneness until we learn to recognize and forgive everything not of God's Love and joy.

Until then, we will continue to believe in a hierarchy of illusions. Some illusions will be cherished, and intentionally held apart from the light of truth. Until we let them all go, we will confuse the ego with God. And as long as we continue to do this, we will fear God.

In the ego's realm we think we have millions of choices to make. We see a multitude of unfulfilled needs, and we perceive thousands of problems. We attempt to remedy most of these problems by choosing between a countless number of ego illusions. But these are all pseudo-remedies. Not one will lead us back to the memory of our perfect invulnerability in God's Love.

The prerequisite for entry into the Real World is our undivided acceptance that there is always only one problem: Guilt. And therefore only one answer can heal this single cause of all our suffering. It is forgiveness alone that heals all. The Real World is perceived when we learn to meet its conditions, consistently looking past all illusion of separation and attack. We must learn to perceive only Love. Until then, we will not be able to discern correctly between fear and Love, or between Heaven and hell.

"Yet who can make a choice between the wish for Heaven and the wish for hell unless he recognizes they are not the same? This difference is the learning goal this course has set. It will not go beyond this aim. Its only purpose is to teach what is the same and what is different, leaving room to make the only choice that can be made." T-26.III.5:3-6

"There is no basis for a choice in this complex and overcomplicated world. For no one understands what is the same, and seems to choose where no choice really is. The real world is the area of choice made real, not in the outcome, but in the perception of alternatives for choice. That there is choice is an illusion. Yet within this one lies the undoing of every illusion, not excepting this." T-26.III.6.

WE DON'T LEAVE THE WORLD
THROUGH DEATH

This 3-D world of form is governed entirely by the concept of death. It is the central pillar that upholds all the thinking of the world, making the death concept the ego's most heavily fortified defense against God's Love as Self. Consequently, it's the last unconscious idol we willingly release. Here in the ego dream, we believe in all forms of death including pain, sickness, loss, scarcity and of course, physical death. To the ego mind, these are natural, legitimate and inevitable—because without them, there is no ego.

Without the ego, not only would all forms of death lose their hold on us, the familiar fearful world (including all the insane laws we currently accept) would also fall away. The ego depends on our fear of, and unconscious attraction to death, to sustain itself and its illusory world.

God *and* any form of death cannot both be true. While we still believe death in any form is real, it means we don't yet believe in God's Love. We have allowed the ego to convince us the world is left through physical death of the body. We our self made physical death through the ego, endowing it with the imaginary power to claim the eternal Life force of God's Will. We *are* eternal Life. But because humanity has never dared question this most obsessive central ego illusion, we have been unable to release this core belief in death's power before this.

Jesus calls on us to know thy Self, to recognize and embrace the Truth within. By renouncing the untrue self, we discover the magnificent power of innocence within; we experience our Holy Self. This Self cannot be threatened, because as an expression of God's Love, our Self is all-encompassing Love without opposite.

Without our fundamental belief in death, every other fear would have no choice but to fall away. Death is our last defense against awareness and acceptance of the Love we are. Death is the last obstacle to be overcome, because it is intertwined with our fear of Love, and our fear of God.

To the degree we fear death in all its forms, we still fear Love. The degree to which we still feel a need to control our life independently from Spirit, compartmentalizing it to defend our self from lack, disease, change or loss—to that extent we still fear Love. We fear our one Will with God. We're afraid to recognize and accept total dominion over everything the ego made. Yet we must recognize and accept this here and now, while we are still in the dream. These choices cannot be made anywhere else.

WE LEAVE THE WORLD BY TRUTH

"The world is not left by death but by truth..." T-3.VII.6:11

The new world, the Real World, is still a dream. Yet it is a healed dream, one that excludes all forms of separation, deprivation, suffering and death. It is a dream whereby we eventually triumph over the world, as Jesus did in His resurrection. We no longer choose to be victimized by what we made to hide from God's Love. Here, through forgiveness and miracles, we literally reverse effect and cause.

We triumph over death and the world, by forgiving them in our own mind. We remember they are not external or separate, but found only within our mind. This is what it means to undo the ego, to demolish its insane laws. No longer do we use these laws to hold our self and others captive. Every time our mind or body senses a loss of peace, we steadfastly undo the ego and its laws by refusing the ego's temptation to believe in it. Instead we accept the Atonement, the divine correction of perception.

We will not see the Real World until we decide for Love by rejecting all belief and investment in the unreal world. When we consistently refuse to believe what the ego attempts to make real, we will perceive the Real World of joy and Love.

As Jesus explains, we will all eventually take our part in undoing that which we made to attack our self. Yet we must be aware of this point: Until we wholeheartedly renounce the concept of death as the central pillar upholding the ego's dream, we still have more to do, in undoing the ego. The ego clings to its obsessive misperception that we will be free of the ego only after death; that death offers us the freedom and peace we seek. But death in any form is not part of God.

"Salvation is no more than a reminder this world is not your home. Its laws are not imposed on you, its values are not yours. And nothing that you think you see in it is really there at all. This is seen and understood as each one takes his part in its undoing, as he did in making it." T-25.VI.6:1-4

NOUK SANCHEZ 181

The body, although originally made by the ego to imprison us, is reinterpreted by Spirit and given its final Holy purpose of freedom. Jesus tells us through the ego, we unconsciously hate the body and want to destroy it. We thus agree to leave the body via physical death, as seeming victims of aging, pain, accidents or sickness. In this way we perpetuate the illusion of separation and attack. By choosing to embrace guilt instead of innocence, we demonstrate to self and world the ego's seeming victory over God.

Through the ego, we reject Spirit's "True escape" from the body. True escape does not result from separation, attack and death, but from joining, Love and Life. The body, a neutral nothing in itself, can only be relinquished through its total surrender to, and reinterpretation by Love. The body is ultimately escaped through Love's triumph over guilt and attack.

Given this Holy purpose and no other, the body becomes immune to deterioration—and when its role has been fulfilled it is gently laid aside in gratitude, unharmed and guilt-free. This and only this is the final escape from the body, and from the ego's illusory cycle of birth and death.

> "You hate this prison you have made, and would destroy it. But you would not escape from it, leaving it unharmed, without your guilt upon it. T-18.VI.7:6-7 Yet only thus [can] you escape." T-18.VI.8:1

DEATH AND THE FEAR OF GOD

It is through the personal self of the ego that all fear and lack of peace can be traced back to its one source: Our fear of God. This is our deep fear of Love, and our deep fear of our True Holy Self. This Self is our joined memory of our True Identity as the one Will of God. If we were to allow and accept this joined memory, we would have to reclaim our one power in God's Love.

This veiled terror of Self as God's Love is thoroughly disguised, to keep us from recognizing it. We're more likely to recognize instead its primary symptom: Our constant, persistent sense of threat. This sense of threat may include a general feeling of unworthiness, insecurity or depression. Or it may appear as financial scarcity, pain, health issues, or relationship problems. All these (and more) are representative of the one cause that drives them all. This single cause is unconscious guilt, which is fear of God's Love.

It can be difficult at first to recognize our fear of Love; it's much easier to locate its effects. Our unconscious guilt *is* our fear of Love. Once our guilt has been recognized and forgiven, Love replaces fear. Love manifests as a deep, tangible inner state of trust and security that completely replaces all sense of threat.

We start by making the effort to recognize the ongoing effects of unconscious guilt on our daily experience. We notice the persistent sense of threat each time it appears, whatever form it happens to take. By being conscious of these myriad forms of threat, it becomes easier to reveal their single origin.

When this one origin is recognized, we can make a committed choice to let forgiveness remedy them all. Until then, we play the ego's game of perceiving many varied problems, each requiring a different solution. And not one of these ego solutions addresses the unconscious guilt which is the fundamental cause of all problems.

Every time we experience lack of peace, it's been spawned by our unconscious guilt, manifesting as unconscious self-hatred. Think of this guilt as an unrecognized death wish—literally. We can identify the effects of this guilt every day. It is projected outward onto our bodies through pain or sickness, or onto the world through conflict with others, financial scarcity, or many other forms.

In truth, nothing outside us can possibly threaten us. It could only do so if we agreed to use it to attack our self. Through our unconscious self-hatred we use others, the body, and situations to attack our self. No one would willingly or consciously do such a thing, but this is the ego's unwavering unconscious mission. As long as this mission remains unrecognized and un-relinquished, it will wreak havoc.

The ego truly believes we are helpless victims of all the merciless laws it made up. These many laws include time, scarcity, conflict and disease. The last thing it wants us to do is take back our power and remember we are never victims of the world we see.

> *"I am not the victim of the world I see. How can I be the victim of a world that can be completely undone if I so choose? My chains are loosened. I can drop them off merely by desiring to do so. The prison door is open. I can leave simply by walking out. Nothing holds me in this world. Only my wish to stay keeps me a prisoner. I would give up my insane wishes and walk into the sunlight at last." W-57.1.(31)*

This world was not made by Love, but by fear. Nearly everything we do, when sincerely questioned with radical self-honesty, is shown to stem from fear and doubt—not from Love and trust. To change the world, we must learn to change our mind about what the world is *for*. Is the world's purpose suffering and death? Or, in its innocence, is it Love?

We accept consistent threat, rarely recognizing it as anything out of the ordinary. We have a sense we are relentlessly pursued by something. But by what? We don't really know, yet our survival seems to depend on constant vigilance against this thing.

Its effects seem randomly chaotic; we never know when it might hit. Every human being lives with this sense of constant threat. Some are driven mad by it, others choosing suicide in an attempt to gain relief. Most of us just fill our lives with constant distraction or addiction, to ensure we never need look at it too deeply—in case we find the cause is within.

This insidious internal threat is our carefully hidden guilt. This is the imaginary black hole inside us that terrifies us so. This is the source of separation. All our suffering is caused by our steadfast belief in, and fear of God's wrath. While we still compartmentalize our life, deciding, planning and controlling it independently from

Spirit—and while we believe we have a hierarchy of unmet needs—we are still fearing God's wrath instead of trusting in God's Love. Every fear, and every experience of anything other than Love and joy, arises from this secret fear of God's punishment.

What is behind *your* fear of God? Dare to look, and you'll soon see for yourself it's the crazy belief you are guilty, and therefore deserving of punishment. If you are still unsure this is the case, simply look at everything you believe you need to struggle, work and sacrifice for. Look at how much effort you expend on defense against possible threat.

The belief you need to seek your happiness and security, or protect your life could hardly enter your mind—unless of course, you secretly expect attack. That's the ego right there, secretly expecting punishment disguised as random chaos.

We made the ego's world appear to attack us, to convince our self we are victims of the world we see. These are the ego's laws and not God's laws. While we continue to believe in the ego's laws—that our bodies, others and the world can indeed attack us—we will fear God's Love as our Holy Self. This translates to a deep fear of trusting Spirit within our mind.

> *"This world will bind your feet and tie your hands and kill your body only if you think that it was made to crucify God's Son. For even though it was a dream of death, you need not let it stand for this to you. Let [this] be changed, and nothing in the world but must be changed as well. For nothing here but is defined as what you see it for." T-29.VI.5.*

> *"What you have given "life" is not alive, and symbolizes but your wish to be alive apart from life, alive in death, with death perceived as life, and living, death." T-29.II.6:2*

We play into the ego's hands each time we judge another or our self, keeping alive the lie of helpless victimhood. We also keep this lie alive by seeking to complete our self externally through special love, happiness and security—and by defending our self from external disaster, disease, conflict and death. To control or defend our self independently from Spirit keeps this victimization paradigm intact.

Our guilt translates to an unconscious terror of God's wrath. We truly believe we will be punished. And the unconscious agreement we made with the ego is to succumb to the death penalty. The ego believes physical death is the entirely justifiable penalty for the guilt we carry. *Death*, says the ego, is *the inevitable outcome of all life*. This is the ego's most fiercely defended belief. It will remain so until it is thoroughly investigated and forgiven.

> *"It is not will for life but wish for death that is the motivation for this world. Its only purpose is to prove guilt real. No worldly thought or act or feeling has a motivation other than this one. These are the witnesses that are called forth to be believed, and lend conviction to the system they speak for and represent."* T-27.I.6:3-6

All our impulses to attack, defend or protect aspects of our life are manifestations of this unconscious death wish. These urges are totally alien to our Holy Self, who knows only security, Love and innocence. Yet how often do we feel threatened? Our level of un-relinquished guilt and attraction to death can be determined by the degree of emotional or physical suffering we feel on a daily basis. Unconscious guilt correlates directly to the suffering factor in our lives.

The god we secretly fear has nothing to do with the one True God of Love. The god we fear is only the ego's vicious self-projection. *It does not exist*. The god the ego made mirrors its own self-hatred, and its "justice" is cruel. Yet the Holy Spirit's justice is Love and only Love. Nothing opposes the power of Love's kind justice—unless we want to cling to the ego's insane version of god's love.

> *"It is extremely hard for those who still believe sin meaningful to understand the Holy Spirit's justice. They must believe He shares their own confusion, and cannot avoid the vengeance that their own belief in justice must*

entail. And so they fear the Holy Spirit, and perceive the "wrath" of God in Him. Nor can they trust Him not to strike them dead with lightning bolts torn from the "fires" of Heaven by God's Own angry Hand. They [do] believe that Heaven is hell, and [are] afraid of love. And deep suspicion and the chill of fear comes over them when they are told that they have never sinned. Their world depends on sin's stability. And they perceive the "threat" of what God knows as justice to be more destructive to themselves and to their world than vengeance, which they understand and love." T-25.VIII.6.

"What is not love, is sin..." T-25.VII.6:3

If we perceive anything that is not Loving, then we perceive with the ego. Yet, anything that is not of God's Love cannot possibly threaten us. This means everything we do on our own without conscious awareness of Spirit, is done with the ego.

It is not arrogant, nor is it blasphemous to embrace the concept that we made the body, the world and death itself. Accept this as truth, for it is up to us now to undo, with Spirit, these things we mistakenly made as an attack on God's Love.

"Is it not strange that you believe to think you made the world you see is arrogance? God made it not. Of this you can be sure. What can He know of the ephemeral, the sinful and the guilty, the afraid, the suffering and lonely, and the mind that lives within a body that must die? You but accuse Him of insanity, to think He made a world where such things seem to have reality. He is not mad. Yet only madness makes a world like this." W-152.6.

"To think that God made chaos, contradicts His Will, invented opposites to truth, and suffers death to triumph over life; all this is arrogance. Humility would see at once these things are not of Him. And can you see what God created not? To think you can is merely to believe you can perceive what God willed not to be. And what could be more arrogant than this?" W-152.7.

GUILT CALLS ON DEATH,
FORGIVENESS CALLS ON LIFE

When we find our self believing both God *and* the ego's world of suffering are true, we become immersed in fear again. The belief in sin calls upon guilt, and while we maintain allegiance to these, they run our lives. Yet if God's all-encompassing Love is all there is, how can there be an opposite of God—unless we still believe deep down we are guilty?

Imagine truly knowing you are infinitely guiltless, absolutely innocent. In this state, no one and nothing can threaten you. You are wholly invulnerable and immune to all threat. Sit in this state of innocence for a minute or two. Allow it to be, and let yourself drop into a deep state of peace within your heart.

Now, think of something that feels threatening. Allow the feeling of familiar anxiety to surface. Feel it fully, but look deeper. Can you sense what lies beneath not just this fear, but *all* your fears? The foundation beneath your need to control, defend and protect? What is the nucleus, the one felt belief that dwells beneath every conceivable threat? Is it a vague sense you might be punished *because the ego says you deserve it*?

Only the guilty expect attack as justified punishment. This is the persistent sense of threat we all feel. It is our fear of God, our deep fear of Love, union and innocence. And it is the one barrier that blocks us from truly experiencing our Holy Self's profound uninterrupted sense of inner security. Guilt dwells beneath every fear and need to control—yet we can call it out, any time we stop to check in with Spirit.

We could never experience fear unless we secretly believe we have sinned. We believe we are guilty for this seeming sin, and punishment is due. We might feel this as a sense of unworthiness, but rest assured, directly underneath is guilt. We feel we must constantly be on guard against possible threat—yet how could there exist any threat unless deep down, we believe we are guilty? If we really knew the truth of our own total innocence, we could never feel any sense of threat.

Guiltlessness is a state of peace and invulnerability. And this cannot be perceived through the ego. The ego must be suspended in order to be right-minded. This peace does not come from external factors, but from the gentle, yet deliberate relinquishment of the ego's guilt and resulting sense of threat. We need to firmly decide against the ego, before our natural state of innocence can be known.

We will recognize the extent of our own guilt to the degree we still judge self and others. We forget our judgment of others is our own un-relinquished guilt projected outward. We are only condemning our self. If we cannot forgive the other, we cannot forgive our self (for using them to project our secret guilt). And when we judge our self, we are holding that same grudge against everyone, including God. If we judge against one, we judge against all.

Any un-relinquished judgment against self or others (including Jesus or God) is an attraction to unconscious guilt. Unfortunately, this attraction directly translates to a death wish. Since only one of us exists in the dream, all our un-forgiven condemnations act as death magnets.

But the good news is, in any moment we sincerely desire to trade our judgments for True forgiveness, that's the same instant it's accomplished. This is the gift of Atonement. Spirit can instantly correct any seeming error with equal ease, no matter how insignificant or grievous it may appear to us.

Death in all its forms will disappear, once the single cause of death is recognized and relinquished. The relinquishment of guilt means all suffering is at an end. Our original state of guiltlessness and innocence is restored, and we experience no further attraction to suffering or death. As we accept our own total innocence by choosing to see the same in others, we will also know, without a doubt, there is no opposite to God's Love.

WHAT IS LIFE'S ONE CERTAIN OUTCOME?

To reveal our unconscious devotion to death in all its forms, let's ask a simple question: What is the one outcome in life we are certain of—the one outcome we can never escape?

Death is the central dream upon which the entire ego thought system rests. As we have shown, pain, disease, conflict, loss, scarcity, and physical death itself are all merely aspects of our unconscious devotion to the idol of death.

Unfortunately, we are not nearly as faithful to Life and Love as we are to death. Our unquestioned belief is that death is real, and our armored defense of this belief is nearly impenetrable. Death is the greatest defense we have made against remembering God's Love as Self. It is the most compelling witness against God as Love. Consequently, our belief in death acts as a massive block against the memory of the unlimited power we share with God, as mighty extensions of His glorious Will.

As we have seen, guilt is the fuel that keeps alive our devotion to death. Because we truly believe we are guilty, we unconsciously believe God authored death, and death is the natural outcome of life. But if God is Life eternal, how can there be an opposite?

Our un-questioned judgments and un-relinquished guilt have allowed the ego to trick us into equating God with death. How, then, could we ever trust Love and Life, if we remain convinced that life leads to death? This is insane! Yet the ego thought system *is* insanity.

> *"All things but death are seen to be unsure, too quickly lost however hard to gain, uncertain in their outcome, apt to fail the hopes they once engendered, and to leave the taste of dust and ashes in their wake, in place of aspirations and of dreams. But death is counted on. For it will come with certain footsteps when the time has come for its arrival. It will never fail to take all life as hostage to itself."* W-163.3.

> *"Would you bow down to idols such as this? Here is the strength and might of God Himself perceived within an*

idol made of dust. Here is the opposite of God proclaimed as lord of all creation, stronger than God's Will for life, the endlessness of love and Heaven's perfect, changeless constancy. Here is the Will of Father and of Son defeated finally, and laid to rest beneath the headstone death has placed upon the body of the holy Son of God." W-163.4.

We are endowed with free will to choose which paradigm we pay allegiance to—either fear or Love. In choosing fear, we reinforce it in our awareness. We are choosing to value death in all its forms. What we fear, we defend our self against. Whatever we defend against, we expect. And whatever we expect, we must invite into our experience.

Death is the greatest of all ego idols. We invest death with all our belief in its fixed certainty. This means God's Love and Life are eclipsed in our mind by the ego's insistence that death is the inevitable outcome of life. The stakes are high; it matters greatly which belief we choose. For if death is real there is no God. But if God is real, there is no death.

DEATH AS AN OPPOSITE TO LIFE

From the ego's dualistic perspective, death is life's opposite. Yet life has no opposite. If life is from God and God is eternally uninterrupted Life, how can life possibly be terminated?

" Life has no opposite, for it is God. Life and death seem to be opposites because you have decided death ends life. Forgive the world, and you will understand that everything that God created cannot have an end, and nothing He did not create is real. " M-20.5:5-7

"There are not different kinds of life, for life is like the truth. It does not have degrees. It is the one condition in which

all that God created share. Like all His Thoughts, it has no opposite. There is no death because what God created shares His life. There is no death because an opposite to God does not exist. There is no death because the Father and the Son are One." W-167.1.

We feel we have good reason for our devotion to death. Unconsciously we perceive death as resolution to the constant conflict of life. Life seems to call for a myriad of painfully exhausting decisions. Yet when we make these decisions apart from Spirit, all we're doing is choosing between illusions. Conflict is assured as a result.

The answers cannot be found in illusions, but only from inner guidance. Acceptance of the Atonement is the correction of error in our mind, clearing away all illusion. But as long as life is seen as conflict, death is mistakenly believed to be salvation. This is the insane interpretation the ego gives to life and its dark savior, death.

" In death alone are opposites resolved, for ending opposition is to die. And thus salvation must be seen as death, for life is seen as conflict. To resolve the conflict is to end your life as well." W-138.7:3-5

"These mad beliefs can gain unconscious hold of great intensity, and grip the mind with terror and anxiety so strong that it will not relinquish its ideas about its own protection. It must be saved from salvation, threatened to be safe, and magically armored against truth. And these decisions are made unaware, to keep them safely undisturbed; apart from question and from reason and from doubt." W-138.8:1-3

Death is the secret engine that runs this thing we call we call "life." This life is merely the ego's dream of its brief and autonomous rule apart from God. But ask yourself this: How could we "live" at all, without having been given Life by eternal Life itself? How could this Life that we are, possibly end in death?

It is our choice to live by the rules of death—by the rules of fear, deprivation, conflict, separation and suffering. Living a life ruled by death means we taste death in everything we do. Even love is not immune from this addiction to death. Human love, referred to in the *Course* as special love, is ruled by death and not by life. This love is seen as temporary and conditional, just like death.

And what about the body's sickness or health? These, too are ruled by the law of death. They are temporary and conditional, based on fear and the threat of inconsistency and impermanence. The ego hijacks the body, and makes of life a living death.

> "The body is the ego's idol; the belief in sin made flesh and then projected outward. This produces what seems to be a wall of flesh around the mind, keeping it prisoner in a tiny spot of space and time, beholden unto death, and given but an instant in which to sigh and grieve and die in honor of its master. And this unholy instant seems to be life; an instant of despair, a tiny island of dry sand, bereft of water and set uncertainly upon oblivion. Here does the Son of God stop briefly by, to offer his devotion to death's idols and then pass on. And here he is more dead than living. Yet it is also here he makes his choice again between idolatry and love. Here it is given him to choose to spend this instant paying tribute to the body, or let himself be given freedom from it. Here he can accept the holy instant, offered him to replace the unholy one he chose before. And here can he learn relationships are his salvation, and not his doom." T-20.VI.11.

> "Death is the symbol of the fear of God." M-27.3:1

How could we possibly believe in God's Love as all-Loving, when everything we value is born only to die? This is an obvious question. Have you asked, "Who is God, and what is His nature?" The ego claims death is life's opposite. Yet this would mean death is a power opposite to Love and God. And this cannot possibly be. Nothing other than God can exist, except in dreams. Therefore death can only be a dream—*a dream from which we can awaken.* Awakening from this dream of death is our only purpose, while we dream. To awaken from the dream itself, we must awaken from the illusion of death, and from the belief we could be separate from God.

When we've healed our unconscious commitment to death in all its forms, what remains is the memory of God Himself. Death is seen as the great dark savior from this terrible memory of God's Love. Death lures us unceasingly back to its crypt. In doing so, it has promised to save us from the imaginary wrath of God. This is the central purpose of death; it tries to save us from Life in God. The last block to Love that must be overcome is the illusion of death, for death is the fear of God as our Holy Self.

"Death is indeed the death of God, if He is Love." M-27.5:5

If God is Love with no opposite, yet death is real, then death must mean the death of God's Love. But in Truth, God is eternal Love and is always present. If we believe we see any form of death, it must be because we have chosen to hallucinate with the ego. We have chosen to believe what the body's senses tell us, instead of looking with inner vision. The body's senses can never be trusted. For until the mind is healed, what the body sees is only what the ego's projection tells it to perceive.

"And the last to be overcome will be death." Of course! Without the idea of death there is no world. All dreams will end with this one. This is salvation's final goal; the end of all illusions." M-27.6:1-5

THE DEATH REALM IS AN ILLUSION

As we have seen, the mind is at the level of cause, and the body/world are its effects. God's eternal Love is the one True cause of all Reality. Everything else is temporary, and therefore belongs to the effect realm. An effect cannot cause anything real. This means *nothing we perceive* in this world is able to cause real effects.

Consciousness after death is part of the effect realm. Death is an imaginary effect caused by the ego. It is merely our belief. Death, then, is a state of mind. It is a continuation of the ego's dream within our mind. Like everything else in this world, death exists solely in our mind. Death remains within our mind as the effect of an ego cause. The one cause of death is guilt, and death will remain our experience until we heal its cause within our mind.

All phenomena we perceive are in our mind. Not the brain, which is just an organ, but the mind. As we have seen, nothing exists outside the mind. The universe, time, the death realm, astral planes, and dreams are all effects occurring within our mind. Everything is part of our dream. These fragments of the ego dream have no meaning apart from what we give them. We have a choice of how to view these effects: We can perceive them with ego, or we can perceive them with Spirit.

The body, the world, the cosmos and the concept of death all reside together in our mind. Therefore, they can all be healed as we awaken to our divine inheritance as the Kingdom of God. But as long as we maintain that death is the one sure outcome of life, fear, guilt and death remain as idols on our inner altar. We must see through these idols, refusing to believe any of them are true, natural or inevitable. For we cannot awaken to our divine inheritance if we remain terrified of God's Love as Self.

Our attraction to death is the final obstacle we must face and relinquish before entry into the Real World, which is the healed or Happy Dream. To reverse our devotion to death, we must willingly surrender our fear of God.

"This is the darkest veil, upheld by the belief in death and protected by its attraction. The dedication to death and to its sovereignty is but the solemn vow, the promise made in secret to the ego never to lift this veil, not to approach it, nor even to suspect that it is there. This is the secret bargain made with the ego to keep what lies beyond the veil forever blotted out and unremembered. Here is your promise never to allow union to call you out of separation; the great amnesia in which the memory of God seems quite forgotten; the cleavage of your Self from you;--[the fear of God,] the final step in your dissociation." T-19.IV.D.3.

"See how the belief in death would seem to "save" you. For if this were gone, what could you fear but life? It is the attraction of death that makes life seem to be ugly, cruel and tyrannical. You are no more afraid of death than of the ego. These are your chosen friends. For in your secret alliance with them you have agreed never to let the fear of God be lifted, so you could look upon the face of Christ and join Him in His Father." T-19.IV.D.4.

Guilt separates us from the memory of God's Love as our Holy Self. Fear of God is our terror of remembering who we really are: We are God's Love, His Will in expression. Therefore, we share God's infinite creative power and are not under any laws but His.

We're like a caged bird seemingly trapped so long that we have forgotten to ask some very important questions: *What am I? Where am I—and is the cage door closed or open?* We've forgotten we have strong wings to fly, and that the cage door is wide open. It always was. We are free and under no laws but God's. We are not under the ego's laws. Contrary to our mistaken belief, we are not a flightless bird trapped forever inside a locked cage.

We have free will to choose against the ego's beliefs, and accept God's grace instead. In doing so, we eradicate guilt and return our awareness to eternal innocence and Love. We are restored to sanity and will recognize without a doubt that, in the words of the *Course, Nothing real can be threatened.* This means "you" can never be threatened. The Holy Self cannot suffer. Only the delusional self could ever perceive threat, in its belief it must protect itself from God's imaginary wrath.

To see through the ego's delusion is to undo it. Every fear, every tiny stab of anger, frustration or pain is a symbol of our fear of God's wrath. This is the fear of Love and the love of fear.

It's an unconscious reminder of the grandest lie ever: That we abandoned God at the separation, and are eternally guilty as a result. This is the ego's obsession with irrevocable error, a sin it believes can never be forgiven. As we have seen, this belief in unforgivable sin is the root of our uninvestigated need to defend our self from threat in all its forms. Yet to investigate the illusion of death is to free yourself from it. It is to notice the wide-open cage door.

A PRAYER TO UNDO FEAR OF GOD'S LOVE

Perhaps you still find it difficult to detect your fear of God's Love. As mentioned earlier, every stab of fear or pain is an indication of this one great fear. The instant we believe there is indeed something wrong, delusion has set in and it's this belief that represents our fear of God. If all-encompassing Love is all there is, everything apart from that Love (including the slightest twinge of fear or discomfort) cannot be real because it is not of God's joyous Love. If only perfect Love exists, from what do you defend yourself on a daily basis? If Love is all there is, what is it you really fear?

It can only be Love, only True healing that we fear. Our own Identity is Love, and it is this Identity we fear most. The ego is terrified we will discover this secret. No matter what we think we fear and defend against, the one thing we really fear and protect our self from is God's Love. This is our perfect guiltlessness expressed as the indestructible power, healing and dominion of our Holy Self.

Following is a prayer to help release our fear of God, which is the fear of healing, regardless of the "form" of fear:

"Holy Spirit, my belief in _____(issue or problem)_____ as real, causes me to feel attacked, and to defend myself against it. In my defense I am alone, isolated from your Love and True healing in my awareness. Yet the Truth is your Love and healing is all there is. Nothing exists apart from your Love.

I recognize in choosing to believe this fear, I reject your Love and healing. And I defend myself from your Love, joy and peace. I now decide to bring my concerns and fears to you, Holy Spirit, so we can look upon them together. We will look at my list of defenses together. I ask that you shine your Love into my mind, and reinterpret these fears for me. Cleanse them and transform them into areas of healing and inspiration.

I acknowledge my only part in this:

1) I invite you in to look at these fears and judgments with me. I will not judge myself or another while we do this; instead I will leave a space of total non-judgment, so you can fill it with Love and healing.

2) As I look upon it all, I will say to myself with sincerity, "Even though this appears to be a problem, and despite any feelings of fear, anxiety, anger, guilt or doubt I may hold, in this instant I open myself to receive healing through the miracle. I accept this healing. And so it is. Amen."

> *"Your present trust in Him is the defense that promises a future undisturbed, without a trace of sorrow, and with joy that constantly increases, as this life becomes a holy instant, set in time, but heeding only immortality. Let no defenses but your present trust direct the future, and this life becomes a meaningful encounter with the truth that only your defenses would conceal." W-135.19.*

CHAPTER EIGHT

THE BODY IS THE MEANS
BY WHICH WE RETURN TO SANITY

Contrary to the belief I held for so many years, I have been clearly shown the body is *anything but* meaningless in the higher sense. It holds a sovereign role in the undoing of our ultimate defense against God. This defense is indeed the greatest barrier against awakening to our Holy Self as the infinite expression of God's magnificent Will.

Death of the body as a real and inevitable fact is the ego's unchallenged covenant. By honoring it, we are guaranteed we won't ever have to awaken to God's all-powerful Love as Self. Until we exhume this unconscious desire for death in all its forms, the ego will use the body as witness, to irrefutably prove its case for separation. We will continue to believe unconsciously that both death *and* God are real.

While these mutually exclusive beliefs are accepted as true and maintained together, we will unknowingly equate God with death. We will believe God authors death, and consequently we will avoid claiming our inheritance and dominion in Christ while we still reside in the body. By choosing belief in death instead, we need not ever experience our Holy Self as sharing in God's perfect Will and power.

The body is absolutely necessary if we are to overcome the ego's central dream of death. As long as death is still real for us, remaining our unconscious attraction, we cannot know the full, embodied power of God within. To embody knowledge means to live out from that knowing. This is not an intellectual understanding, but a deep-seated knowledge that we actually *become*; this knowledge becomes anchored within the body. And it is here that we remember the body is not separate from the mind that made it.

Seen within the mind, the body is now made one with it. No longer persecuted by the split mind, the body's purpose is completely transformed. It becomes a conduit through which the healed mind witnesses to the unopposed power of God's Love and healing. We need the body to overcome death in all its forms, thereby allowing the embodied knowledge of God to return to its rightful place in our memory.

Through the ego, we have been trained to abandon our body through fear. This is often expressed by obsessing on the body's appetites for food, health, sex, comfort or image. Or we may betray the body by rejecting it. When we feel threatened, we often unconsciously desert the body—we literally check out. And once we abandon the body, the ego claims it, using it as a witness for separation and attack.

> *"The body is the means by which God's Son returns to sanity." W-pII.5.4:1*

Death is an unreal aberration, totally unnatural and antithetical to God's Love. The means through which we attain the Real World's perception can't possibly be through death. It *must* be that we attain it through the body and life.

> *"The world is not left by death but by truth..." T-3.VII.6:11*

The body is indeed nothing, although we mistakenly believe it is who we are. It is merely a barrier the ego uses to block our memory of uninterrupted communication with God's Love. The body is useless and meaningless, as long as its emotional and physical needs remain our focus. The ego obsesses over the body's safety and comfort.

How many things do you think, say and do every day, to appease your emotional or physical body? We seek pleasure and avoid pain. In between these, we plan and insure against expected threats.

Everything we do at the behavior level means nothing. Yet the intent behind what we do means everything. When we examine it, we quickly see the intent behind much of what we do arises from fear. It does not arise from Love, and is therefore destructive.

We must work *with* the body to undo misperception. Please refer to the embodiment text at the end of this book, and guided audio meditation by Stacy Sully, found at www.EndOfDeath.com

THE BODY: OUR LAST SPECIAL RELATIONSHIP TO BE HEALED

We cannot transcend something we choose to deny. This is a monumental truth that is often overlooked. As long as we deny the body, we reject the healing of suffering's cause within our mind.

The *Course* encourages us to recognize and release to Spirit everything the ego made for attack. In this surrender, a process of divine transformation occurs. Our special relationships are transformed into Holy Relationships. The ego world fades in our perception, as the Real World rises to take its place. The ego's hierarchy of illusions gives way to our living demonstration of the Course's first miracle principle:

"There is no order of difficulty in miracles. One is not "harder" or "bigger" than another. They are all the same. All expressions of love are maximal." T-1.I.1.

Notice how the ego separates the body from this all-inclusive and miraculously transformative healing process. The ego says, *it's okay to transform our relationships with others and the world through forgiveness. But the body is nothing. It has no meaning. And therefore*, the ego counsels, *the body is to be held apart from Spirit's all-encompassing thought-reversal and transformation.*

"The ego, which always wants to weaken the mind, tries to separate it from the body in an attempt to destroy it." T-8.IX.6:1

"Believing in the power of attack, the ego wants attack." T-8.IX.6:8

"That forgiveness is healing needs to be understood, if the teacher of God is to make progress. The idea that a body can be sick is a central concept in the ego's thought system. This thought gives the body autonomy, separates it from the mind, and keeps the idea of attack inviolate. If the body could be sick Atonement would be impossible. A body that can order a mind to do as it sees fit could merely take the place of God and prove salvation is impossible. What, then, is left to heal? The body has become lord of the mind. How could the mind be returned to the Holy Spirit unless the body is killed? And who would want salvation at such a price?" M-22.3.

As long as we believe the body can be sick of its own volition, we will continue to exclude from healing this final and most coveted special relationship. The body is the ego's last stronghold, its final hiding place. It is the last remaining hostage through which we witness attack and separation via scarcity, sickness and death. When its dominion over the body is overthrown by the healed mind, the ego thought system is demolished entirely. This is what Jesus came to demonstrate and teach.

While we join with the ego to deny the body's key role in the healing of our mind, we unintentionally choose for continuing attack. Making the body mirror our split mind through our belief in its ability to cause pain or sickness, we choose attack by giving the body authority over the mind. And yet, the body holds no ability or power to change itself. It can't get sick, get well, age or die. In Truth, only the mind commands the body to do as its chosen teacher instructs.

"The Holy Spirit teaches you to use your body only to reach your brothers, so He can teach His message through you. This will heal them and therefore heal you. Everything used in accordance with its function as the Holy Spirit sees it

cannot be sick. Everything used otherwise is. Do not allow the body to be a mirror of a split mind. Do not let it be an image of your own perception of littleness. Do not let it reflect your decision to attack. Health is seen as the natural state of everything when interpretation is left to the Holy Spirit, Who perceives no attack on anything. Health is the result of relinquishing all attempts to use the body lovelessly. Health is the beginning of the proper perspective on life under the guidance of the one Teacher Who knows what life is, being the Voice for Life Itself." T-8.VIII.9.

The body plays a magnificent role in overcoming the ego's dream, once we abdicate our original purpose for it. We must surrender the body completely to the Will of God, thus forming a Holy Relationship with the body. In its Holiness, it can no longer be used to demonstrate attack in any form. The body becomes the vehicle through which we overcome everything the ego made to keep us apart from God's Love.

In this, the purpose for the body becomes reversed. No longer a conduit for acquiring guilt through attack, it becomes a vehicle through which innocence is restored and miracles are witnessed. Such was the role of Jesus' body. It witnessed that God's power overcame all ego laws of attack, including sickness, pain, scarcity and death.

As the body's purpose is shifted from fear to Love, from attack to healing, we recognize it now has only one purpose. It is here to extend Love and forgiveness. The body then becomes the means by which we undo all our ego projections. When the body is used exclusively in the service of Spirit, it cannot get sick. Because the body has been thoroughly abdicated to Spirit's purpose, no form of sickness is immune to the miracle. The body is merely an aid to help us reach the home where God abides.

"With [this] as purpose is the body healed. It is not used to witness to the dream of separation and disease. Nor is it idly blamed for what it did not do. It serves to help the healing of God's Son, and for this purpose it cannot be sick. It will

not join a purpose not your own, and you have chosen that it not be sick. All miracles are based upon this choice, and given you the instant it is made. No forms of sickness are immune, because the choice cannot be made in terms of form. The choice of sickness seems to be of form, yet it is one, as is its opposite. And you are sick or well, accordingly."
T-28.VII.4.

MY OWN RELUCTANCE TO SEE JESUS' DEEPER TEACHINGS

The following is a real-life account from my own experience as a *Course* student. My spiritual journey had helped me detach significantly from physical and emotional pain, however after more than twenty years of studying and practicing the *Course*, I still believed in the body and the ego's laws. I still believed decay, disease and death would overcome life. I believed I had no power over death. Death and sickness were natural, inevitable and legitimate parts of life. Because this was my free-will belief, I *expected* disease, decay and death. And from what I expected, God could not save me.

I tried to defend myself from these, but did not realize my very defense caused me to unconsciously attract them into my experience. I did not know my own ego will was as powerful as God's Will, and that everything I defended myself from, I attracted. As Jesus says: *"Truth cannot deal with errors that you want."(T-3.IV.7:1)* And I could not forgive that which I still believed was real.

I did not recognize this: If I defend myself against something, I must still believe in its reality. While I'm defending against a perceived threat without willingly recognizing my own insanity, I won't surrender my erroneous perception to Spirit. And that means I cannot forgive it. I cannot heal or be healed. For total healing to occur, I didn't know I needed to offer up my entire perception that the mistaken concept of threat *had ever existed.*

I did not realize, and therefore could not benefit from, a profoundly significant component of the forgiveness process. It begins from the basis that only God's Love exists. I did not yet accept or believe that nothing the body or world seemed to show me had the power to cause harm. I did not yet live out from the embodied knowing that wholehearted forgiveness could not occur, unless I consistently deny that any power exists other than God's Love.

And so I remained split between belief in a world that seemed to victimize the body and life, yet I professed I also believed in God's Love. I felt a great deal of inner conflict and confusion over this, which surely contributed to my unconscious guilt and ongoing self-judgment. Effects of this fundamental split repeated themselves over and over in my life, no matter how sincerely I tried to forgive them.

I didn't consciously question my beliefs about all the ego's laws. I questioned many, yet didn't really look at my ingrained beliefs about those things that seemingly sustained the body and world. Nor did I examine my beliefs about what appeared to attack the body and the world. It hadn't occurred to me the laws of nature were the ego's laws, and not God's.

I took for granted these beliefs in the so-called laws of nature were just part of the ego dream. I had no idea they played such an enormous unconscious role in the ego's defense against God. In seeing through the ego's arbitrary laws of sustenance and attack, I realized it wasn't about giving up my magic remedies—the ego can't give anything up! It was about courageously examining all the laws I still believed attacked and sustained me. It meant looking at each one of them with Spirit, and without judgment, simply surrendering my perception for healing. That's all. But I wasn't ready for that yet.

My beliefs in magic remedies were many. I took supplements, I dieted to lose weight, I believed in the laws of nutrition and the laws of both holistic and traditional medicine. I still believed it was the body's organs that sustained me, not God's eternal Life. And because I believed the body sustained me, I planned my life and all my defenses around the body. These included both emotional and physical defense. The body appeared to be the main event even while I sincerely attempted forgiveness exercises on a regular basis.

I still thoroughly believed in the ego's laws of economics and scarcity, instead of God's Law of abundance and endless supply. Unsurprisingly, I found myself struggling financially and sacrificing. I tried to forgive this, too.

I didn't see I still valued two mutually exclusive and irreconcilable thought systems. I wanted to hang onto both God's *and* the world's thought systems. I thought I could maneuver between them. I had no idea it was necessary to choose which thought system to value. I didn't truly realize I had to commit to perceive only Love, willingly disciplining myself to look past, and forgive all ego appearances.

Perhaps this sounds odd, given that the *Course* tells us all this so clearly. But I did not, could not make the leap of recognition that intellectual understanding wasn't enough: I needed to actually apply these principles to my own life.

I believed the ego dream, the body, and the laws of nature were inevitable, fixed—*yet also inconsequential*, since none of these were real in Truth. I just needed to forgive them all, without examining any of them to see what they were actually made of.

This is a subtly clever ego trap that ensnares many students of *A Course in Miracles*. I didn't realize that while I kept defending my body from illness, overweight, scarcity and loss, I was at the same time investing in the body/world's reality. I obviously believed all these things were real. How could I forgive them? The truth is, we can't forgive the body (or the world) while we still want to use them independently for the ego's purposes.

I didn't realize True forgiveness undoes the cause of the ego dream, and therefore undoes its effects as well. When I sincerely forgave something, I believed the cause was fully healed in my mind. And I felt that was enough. The effects or symptoms in the body or life didn't matter. I realized only much later that I hadn't really forgiven half the people and things I thought I had. And I certainly hadn't Truly forgiven the body. Because I still believed these things were real, I was still valiantly protecting and defending them, independently from Spirit. The cause was not thoroughly forgiven, because it had not yet been fully recognized, looked upon with Spirit, and surrendered.

Jesus clearly asks us to fully heal the cause through forgiveness, and then to accept *the effects must be healed as well* because they are never separate from the cause. This was impossible for me to do, while I continued to value two mutually exclusive thought systems. And as I discovered, the mind is eventually torn apart by this split.

I still felt threatened by the ego's laws. I wasn't yet ready to accept that, by consciously joining with God's Will to fully accept Atonement, God's Will is then able to reverse all ego laws. Even if I had tried, I confess I lacked the conviction to trust in God instead of the ego.

But even if I had been able to trust in God, another issue plagued me: To reverse the ego's laws at the level of form by healing cause within the mind, was a concept that seemed utterly blasphemous to me. I didn't yet realize it was only blasphemous to the ego. I still judged myself (and therefore others) as deeply unworthy; I was much more comfortable claiming false humility. I couldn't possibly reverse the so-called laws of nature, as Jesus did! I did not recognize this was just the ego's arrogance, yet another defense against God's Love within.

By shunning belief in physical miracles, I delayed the memory of the immense power of God that I am in Truth (and that everyone else is, too). This thoroughly delighted the ego. I still chose to believe there could be victims of conflict, scarcity, disease and death. In doing so, I unknowingly revered a power other than the all-encompassing Love of God. I gave it precedence over God as Self within.

In my extreme sense of unworthiness, I rejected the whole idea that effects or symptoms could heal, once the cause was healed. I think if I'd been shown, at that point, that my forgiveness resulted in physical miracles, it would have caused me more fear, rather than less. The appearance of physical miracles would have overthrown my entire value system. And I would have had no choice but to question everything I believed in. The purpose of the body and world would have to be totally re-evaluated!

I see now how I unknowingly continued the separation, by separating flesh from Spirit. I was convinced the level of form was meaningless, and was therefore largely excluded from the miracle. But Jesus reminds us we must undo error at *all* levels, in order to heal truly. We made the body and world, and gave them the erroneous purpose of separation. Our healing will come as we embrace our True purpose, forgiving the separation and literally learning to unmake all we previously made to attack our self.

> *"A major step in the Atonement plan is to undo error at all levels."* T-2.IV.2:1

> *"How foolish and insane it is to think a miracle is bound by laws that it came solely to undo!"* T-27.VI.6:3

I was terribly resistant to looking deeply at my beliefs, even the so-called "good beliefs" I held about the *Course*. I treasured certain interpretations of the *Course*, and refused to accept anything different. What changed all this for me? I've had the experience, the direct knowing that Jesus speaks of when he says the Atonement undoes error at all levels, *including* the body and world.

Direct experience is absolutely necessary. How else will we know for certain that anything not of God's Love has no power to hurt us? How else will we know, experience and demonstrate without a doubt, that there is no order of difficulty in miracles?

> *"Nothing that you have refused to accept can be brought into awareness. It is not dangerous in itself, but you have made it seem dangerous to you."* T-3.VI.4:4-5

Jesus demonstrated only God's laws are True. Through His miracles, He proved beyond doubt that all ego laws are rendered powerless in the light of God's unopposed Will.

"Truth cannot deal with errors that you want. I was a man who remembered spirit and its knowledge. As a man I did not attempt to counteract error with knowledge, but to correct error from the bottom up. I demonstrated both the powerlessness of the body and the power of the mind. By uniting my will with that of my Creator, I naturally remembered spirit and its real purpose. I cannot unite your will with God's for you, but I can erase all misperceptions from your mind if you will bring it under my guidance." T-3.IV.7:2-7

In our ego paradigm, we rarely dare to question the ego's laws. Sickness, scarcity, conflict, loss and death are illusory laws made to convince us God's laws have no power. Ultimately, they are meant to show us we are bereft of God's Love. It is through the body that we prove the ego's paradigm is utterly meaningless. Through the body, we return to sanity through forgiveness. When we overturn the ego's laws by accepting the Atonement, the body's goal will be reversed.

"The body is the means by which God's Son returns to sanity. Though it was made to fence him into hell without escape, yet has the goal of Heaven been exchanged for the pursuit of hell. The Son of God extends his hand to reach his brother, and to help him walk along the road with him. Now is the body holy. Now it serves to heal the mind that it was made to kill." W-pII.5.4.

You may feel tremendous resistance to this teaching, as I did, because if accepted it will threaten the entire ego thought system. The ego must retain at all costs the belief we are helpless victims of forces outside us.

The concept of physical death is the most treasured of all ego defenses. It virtually guarantees we won't have to awaken to God's Love. Our greatest fear is the embodied knowledge of our self as the expression of God. To have to remember our True Identity after death, in some imaginary dream of Heaven would be terrifying enough—it would be even more unthinkable to have to remember it right here within the ego dream.

Yet the Truth remains there is nothing outside us. The body and world we seem to see are all in our mind. The cause of the ego dream, together with its effects, is in our mind. And cause and effect are never separate. Heal the cause, and the effects must follow. Once the choice is made to live out from God within, God is all we see out there.

WHAT WE USE THE BODY FOR,
IT WILL BECOME TO US

In our ego paradigm, the body is used for virtually everything but the purpose that will bring us Home to our Holy Self. Through the ego, we use the body for separation and attack. What constitutes attack, you may ask? And why would we use the body for attack? Most of our attacking intent is unconscious, and therefore hidden from our own awareness, until we dare to look deeply within. We unconsciously listen to ego logic, so we use attack because we think it will bring us what we want.

We employ the body for attack in many hidden ways:

- Special relationships: We judge another and withhold forgiveness. We hold another responsible for our emotional or physical happiness, or our security.
- Sacrifice: We sacrifice our time, energy and effort in exchange for ego gratification (people-pleasing, need for approval, financial security, to name a few).

- Unmet needs: Reluctance to meet our own needs; being disloyal to our self. Being untruthful about the needs we have.
- Sickness and pain, regardless of form.
- Accidents.
- Anxiety, worry, concern, unresolved sadness or grief.
- Scarcity and belief in lack.
- Martyrdom or victim feelings; perceiving attack or taking offense.
- Judging: Self-judgment and criticism; judgment of others.
- Holding onto grievances: Blaming current or past abuse.
- Living in the past.
- Making an idol of the body: Focusing on image, fitness, etc.
- Addictions.
- The ultimate use of the body for attack: Death.

"If you use the body for attack, it is harmful to you. If you use it only to reach the minds of those who believe they are bodies, and teach them [through] the body that this is not so, you will understand the power of the mind that is in you." T-8.VII.3:1-2

Our greatest healing lies in relinquishment of the ego belief that we are separate from God and each other. The ego uses others to project our own unconscious self-hatred and guilt. It does not want us to realize every grievance we hold against another, a situation or our self, is directed at our own body. The body is the repository of sin, and the ego uses it as a storehouse for hate and attack. Is it any wonder the body ages, grows ill and dies? Whenever you judge another, remember you always attack yourself first.

"Again and again have you attacked your brother, because you saw in him a shadow figure in your private world. And thus it is you must attack yourself first, for what you attack is not in others. Its only reality is in your own mind, and

by attacking others you are literally attacking what is not there." T-13.V.3:6-8

"To the ego the body is to attack [with]. Equating you with the body, it teaches that [you] are to attack with. The body, then, is not the source of its own health. The body's condition lies solely in your interpretation of its function." T-8.VIII.1:5-8

The body responds exclusively to the mind's commandments. It has no agenda of its own. Until the secret orders given by the unconscious ego are exhumed and released, the mind will order the body to attack itself. The body, like all projected images in the dream, is totally neutral. It has no creative ability and no meaning of its own. The body's state is governed by the mind, and it responds accordingly, reflecting the purpose of either the ego, or the Holy Self.

The ego believes the body (emotional and physical) is our life goal, and reason for being. It claims the body as our identity, thereby obscuring our true Identity, which is the perfect and Holy Self. It convinces us the body is not a means, but an end in itself; a god unto its own.

The ego's reign is upheld because we our self join in its insane conviction that the body is an autonomous, self-governing entity. We agree with the ego's assertion that we are helpless to direct or change the body, and are therefore subject to its sabotage. To us, the body does indeed appear more powerful than the mind. And the mind, the only True place of power, is rendered powerless.

In the ego's service, the body is used only to search for special love in every form it can find. Nearly all relationships are built around this desire for conditional love. Special love fuels the ego's belief that love can turn to hate, that love contains varying degrees and different forms, and that it can change capriciously with time and circumstance. Special love forms a barrier in our mind and heart against the experience of Real Love. Real authentic Love is changeless, has no degrees, and can never turn to hate.

The ego uses the body as a defense against Love. As a result, we unknowingly employ the body as a tool for separation and attack, valiantly defending to the death against any true joining of hearts and minds as one. The ego knows this true union occurs beyond the body.

The body can be used to facilitate this authentic union of minds, but the body itself is never the focus of union. In any interaction where an investment in the body is held (as either benefactor or loser), it means the ego has rejected Love. The miracle is obstructed. The body forms the gap we use to separate from each other, so authentic Love can be kept at bay.

Unconsciously, we bestow power on the body it does not have. We use the body to attack our self and others, without knowing it. And then we claim we are victimized! It is always our own decision first. We tell the body what its limitations are. We assign it a predetermined role and remain vigilant that it does not surpass the limits we set upon it. We order the body to abide by the ego's laws of scarcity, sickness and death—the so-called laws of nature. Having set its limits, we insist the body must take authority over our mind.

> "The body could not separate your mind from your brother's unless you wanted it to be a cause of separation and of distance seen between you and him. Thus do you endow it with a power that lies not within itself. And herein lies its power over you. For now you think that it determines when your brother and you meet, and limits your ability to make communion with your brother's mind. And now it tells you where to go and how to go there, what is feasible for you to undertake, and what you cannot do. It dictates what its health can tolerate, and what will tire it and make it sick. And its "inherent" weaknesses set up the limitations on what you would do, and keep your purpose limited and weak." T-29.I.5.

> "The body will accommodate to this, if you would have it so. It will allow but limited indulgences in "love," with intervals of hatred in between. And it will take command of when to "love," and when to shrink more safely into fear. It will be sick because you do not know what loving means.

And so you must misuse each circumstance and everyone you meet, and see in them a purpose not your own." T-29.I.6.

As we relinquish the body to only God's purpose, we will experience this joyful fact: The body is never a block between our self and others. When we begin to accept that no one and nothing outside us causes our suffering, we see, to our astonishment, that our former enemies become our saviors. We recognize it's safe to Love and be Loved. All of this seems very strange at first, and perhaps not to be entirely trusted.

> *"The body, innocent of goals, is your excuse for variable goals you hold, and force the body to maintain. You do not fear its weakness, but its lack of strength [or] weakness. Would you know that nothing stands between you and your brother? Would you know there is no gap behind which you can hide? There is a shock that comes to those who learn their savior is their enemy no more. There is a wariness that is aroused by learning that the body is not real. And there are overtones of seeming fear around the happy message, "God is Love." T-29.I.8.*

To commit the body's purpose to God's Will is to release it into the safest hands. Here, the ego cannot hijack the body, unless we choose to allow our self to be deceived. And if we do, the Atonement is always available in any Holy Instant we wish to reverse the ego's reign in our perception.

Giving the body wholly to Spirit ensures it can no longer betray us. The body's health is fully guaranteed, as long as we refuse to let it be ruled by the ego's laws. The body is now under no laws but God's. Sickness becomes impossible. When the body is liberated from the tyranny of unconscious guilt, it becomes a highly efficient vehicle that runs on joy and Love. Now, the body's only role is to serve God's Will.

> *"Perhaps you do not realize that this removes the limits you had placed upon the body by the purposes you gave to it. As*

these are laid aside, the strength the body has will always be enough to serve all truly useful purposes. The body's health is fully guaranteed, because it is not limited by time, by weather or fatigue, by food and drink, or any laws you made it serve before. You need do nothing now to make it well, for sickness has become impossible." W-136.18.

"Yet this protection needs to be preserved by careful watching. If you let your mind harbor attack thoughts, yield to judgment or make plans against uncertainties to come, you have again misplaced yourself, and made a bodily identity which will attack the body, for the mind is sick." W-136.19:1-2

When we perceive another as a physical body, we judge and limit that person. The ego doesn't want us to realize that in the body of another, we will see the function we have given our own. How we see and treat another, is the way we perceive and treat our self. The unconscious guilt and self-attack we thereby accumulate will cause havoc in our experience. To regard another as a physical entity denies his True Identity, as well as our own. It separates us both.

When we hold another responsible for meeting our needs, or for making us happy physically or emotionally, we deny Love. If we are blinded by appearances, seeing another's body as beautiful or ugly, young or old, thin or fat, healthy or sick, rich or poor, we reject the Truth of who they are. And whenever we reject another, we reject our self first. In this, we have lost our Loving connection with the one Self, our Holy Self.

When we see self and others as bodies, we assign our body a role the ego will fulfill. The ego seeks sin, guilt and death. It sends the body's senses out to find what it projects. The Holy Self, on the other hand, teaches us to forgive what we have projected onto our body, others, and the world.

When we join with Spirit to abdicate the ego's purpose for the body, giving it wholly to God's Loving purpose instead, the body becomes a means through which Spirit reaches beyond our delusional idols, gently returning us to sanity.

UNDOING THE BELIEF WE ARE A BODY

It took me a very long time to accept that the body is in my mind, and not the other way around. Yet learning to see the body in its correct placement was extremely important to my own healing. As we undo our blocks to Love, we begin to see only one purpose in everything: Forgiveness.

I recognize now everything within this ego dream is neutral. I give it all the meaning it has for me. Viewed through the ego, everyone and everything seems to have its own unique purpose. But these are always attempts to fill the false sense of lack projected by the ego. Remember the ego's mantra is *seek but do not find.*

We must remember our body and the world itself are projected images inside our mind. This is where cause and effect of the body and world reside. The brain is just a tool the mind uses to carry out its function; it is not from the brain that we manifest our dream. The mind is the single source of all we perceive, and everything we perceive is inside it. Nothing "out there" is apart from our mind. We project it all.

We project the body by beaming its image freshly in each moment. And the image we perceive always reflects our belief, according to which inner teacher we choose.

When we begin to accept the body is inside our mind, that we project the body's image continuously in every moment, this realization gives us some distance from the ego's belief system. No longer will we wholly believe we are held hostage to a body, tyrannized by the ego's biological laws.

We now possess a much-needed buffer. This buffer helps us return to right-mindedness whenever we feel emotionally or physically attacked by self, another or the world.

In the buffer zone, we can choose again: We are *not* the body. We are the mind behind the body and world. If we feel attacked, we have the opportunity to recall it is always self-attack—because only one mind exists. We can thereby forgive the only cause of attack, which is the unconscious guilt within our own mind.

RECOGNIZING WHEN WE STILL BELIEVE IN THE BODY AND THE WORLD

The body eclipses God's Love as long as we defend it. What does it mean to defend the body? Sustenance of, and protection of the body are both defenses. The independent urge to save our life is a defense against God's Love. As long as we believe we are independently responsible for the health and welfare of our body, we are fearful of God.

We place our allegiance with ego laws, above God's laws when we make decisions independent from Spirit. For many years, I took an array of supplements to defend against the threat of illness. I wasn't ready to stop taking them at first, even after I realized I wanted to live by God's laws instead of the ego's. So I took them *with* Spirit. I offered my mistaken perception to Spirit for correction, then took the supplements consciously, Lovingly and without guilt.

Now, as I release my fear of Love, I find my dependence upon outer idols falling away. I no longer look to worldly strategies or remedies to save me. I realize God's Love is all there is. It is all that sustains me. So whenever I perceive threat, I ask myself: What exactly am I defending myself from? It can only be Love.

Our greatest unconscious fear is Love itself. The Course's introduction tells us removing the blocks to the awareness of Love's presence involves undoing our perception of the body and world. As we undo our beliefs and values, we overcome the body and world. The Holy Self regains awareness of its power and dominion in God's Love.

> "The course does not aim at teaching the meaning of love,
> for that is beyond what can be taught. It does aim, however,
> at removing the blocks to the awareness of love's presence,
> which is your natural inheritance. The opposite of love is
> fear, but what is all-encompassing can have no opposite."
> T-in.2:6-8

Overcoming the body and world means we must learn to be mindful of the instances we perceive threat. These are always opportunities to heal our perception. As the cause of the ego world is healed within our mind, the effects are automatically reinterpreted. Thus are the ego's laws undone in our mind first, and then in our experience.

This is the healing of the dream and all the symbols within it. What was previously made to demonstrate separation and attack, is now used to demonstrate dominion in Christ and to extend Love. This is the body's real and only purpose.

The Happy Dream or Real World is the result of healing our mind, and not of attempts to change the effects, which are only ego projections. We overcome the body and world by healing the mind, not by falling victim to our projections of the body and world. The right mind heals the body, because the body's purpose is no longer dictated by the ego.

Until we renounce our victimhood, recognizing we are never subject to the body and world, we cannot fully embody the power of God as our Holy Self. We remain split between two irreconcilable powers, the ego *and* God. In sickness, the ego witnesses to the world's guilt. When we invite healing of the body as a result of Atonement, we witness to the world's innocence.

"Now in the hands made gentle by His touch, the Holy Spirit lays a picture of a different you. It is a picture of a body still, for what you really are cannot be seen nor pictured. Yet this one has not been used for purpose of attack, and therefore never suffered pain at all. It witnesses to the eternal truth that you cannot be hurt, and points beyond itself to both your innocence and his. Show this unto your brother, who will see that every scar is healed, and every tear is wiped away in laughter and in love. And he will look on his forgiveness there, and with healed eyes will look beyond it to the innocence that he beholds in you. Here is the proof that he has never sinned; that nothing which his madness bid him do was ever done, or ever had

effects of any kind. That no reproach he laid upon his heart was ever justified, and no attack can ever touch him with the poisoned and relentless sting of fear." T-27.I.5.

"Attest his innocence and not his guilt. Your healing is his comfort and his health because it proves illusions are not true." T-27.I.6:1-2

"A major step in the Atonement plan is to undo error at all levels. Sickness or "not-right-mindedness" is the result of level confusion, because it always entails the belief that what is amiss on one level can adversely affect another." T-2.IV.2:1-2

"A miracle of healing proves that separation is without effect." T-27.II.5:2

WHERE IS THE CAUSE
OF YOUR LOSS OF PEACE?

As Jesus says, to undo the ego thought system requires nothing less than the complete reversal of the thinking of the world. Before True healing of any problem's cause can occur, the nucleus of the problem (which is always in the mind) must first be seen and released.

To mindlessly accept the ego's belief that the cause of suffering is outside us, is to make both the threat and the body real in our experience. In doing so, we reject the miracle. We deny healing, by separating the seeming symptom from its real cause within the mind. As long as we believe the cause of suffering is outside us, we reject the undoing of the one True cause of all suffering: Our own unconscious guilt.

I suffered for many years with a gut condition that landed me in the emergency room on two occasions. For more than twenty years, I had placed the cause of my sickness in the body and world, not recognizing the cause resided within my mind. I tried and tried to forgive it, yet nothing really changed. I had no idea that by believing the cause was outside, I was separating the symptom (the effect) from its True cause. And was therefore denying the miracle! No miracle can occur when the cause of suffering is seen outside the mind, whether in the body, the world or in the past.

"The miracle is possible when cause and consequence are brought together, not kept separate."..."Cause and effect are one, not separate." T-26.VII.14:1,13:1

I had attributed the worldly cause of sickness to lactose and gluten. The accepted magical remedy for this condition was to sacrifice all the foods I enjoyed most—which is a typically cruel ego solution to a problem *it* projects. Listening to ego and not to Spirit, I abstained from foods like ice cream, yogurt, cheese and wheat for almost a third of my life. I also believed I would need to take high-dosage probiotics for the rest of my life. The ego's remedies did indeed seem to ease the symptoms, yet relief was inconsistent, with frequent relapses whenever I forgot to take my magical remedies.

As my trust in ego was gradually transferred to Spirit within, I recognized what Jesus means when He speaks of the importance of placing cause and effect in their proper order. And as my trust in God's Love became more certain, so did my ability to sense Spirit's guidance. I identified many areas of my health that were troubling me, and decided to surrender my judgments entirely to Spirit.

I dredged up all my many fears about sickness and medication, and gave them wholeheartedly to Spirit. I gratefully accepted Atonement. I released the outcome, trusting implicitly that the healing of the cause within my mind was now complete. I knew the symptoms (the effects) would eventually come into alignment with their healed cause.

It was during this time that I received the miraculous guidance to keep taking all my supplements, but to take them mindfully with Spirit. Recognizing and suspending all self-judgments whenever they arose, I handed these over to Spirit as well. The result was a great lessening of concern about my health, along with the great relief of knowing I had completely released the issue to Spirit.

The body was no longer my own independent responsibility. I had chosen a greater power within to care for it—safe in the knowledge it would do so, as long as I devoted the body's purpose solely to Spirit. I was told by turning the body over to Spirit's purpose, I could be assured the body would not betray me. I have since learned this to be true.

What a tremendous relief to offload this burden! My job now was only to trust in Spirit's immaculate consistency in healing. Infinite patience yielded immediate results—a paradox indeed! When we trust instead of merely hoping, patience is no longer an issue. We can afford to wait for physical effects to reflect the healed cause, because we know in our hearts it has already been accomplished.

One morning just before leaving home to co-facilitate a retreat, I prepared to take my probiotics as usual, yet felt a strong urge from Spirit to put them aside. The ego responded initially with fear and concern about relapsing while on retreat. But I knew better than to take the ego's advice; dropping deeply into my heart, I listened to Spirit. I heard it was time to release this form of magic.

More than two years have passed since I last took the probiotics, and I have not experienced a single relapse. I eat what I want, and my health is better now than it was when I took supplements and abstained from my favorite foods. For the first time in decades, I am able to eat what I love, without sacrifice, symptoms or any guilt whatsoever. Now I eat mindfully with Love. And because of this, what I eat never betrays me.

I am learning that, like everything else, food is neutral. It has no ability to make me sick or well, fat or thin. The body and the world have no power. My mind is responsible for all I call into my experience; it alone makes the rules. And it attracts either fear or Love, depending upon which messenger I choose to believe.

Unlearning our ego beliefs means we must drop into our heart and rest there, to listen to Spirit. *This business of undoing is not an intellectual pursuit.* We must be very present, moving consciously out of the head and into the heart. The heart alone is where we will feel Spirit's direction.

PRAYER FOR HEALING PERCEPTION OF SICKNESS AND MAGIC

The following is a prayer I use for healing. Feel free to adapt it to your needs:

"I'm scared of this sickness/pain/scarcity, and I recognize my faith in this medicine/magic is temporarily stronger than my faith in God's Love. Therefore, I surrender all of it to you, Spirit. I ask that you take my perception and heal it.

I trust that once the cause in my mind is healed, so must healing transfer to its effects/symptoms. I open my heart, in this instant, to receive your healing. I accept the miracle, the Atonement that heals all. And I surrender the timing of the miracle. Amen."

DO YOU BELIEVE THE BODY IS YOUR IDENTITY? A SELF-INQUIRY EXERCISE

Following are some questions to help to reveal the extent to which you still believe in the body and world. When reviewing these questions, please answer with radical self-honesty. Rather than answering intellectually, try dropping into your heart to allow your real beliefs to be raised to the light of conscious awareness.

Here, they can be seen and forgiven. When you are ready, you can offer each of these beliefs to Spirit and ask to have it healed.

• Can you find specific instances where you believe the cause of pain, sickness, aging, scarcity, conflict or suffering is outside your own mind—in the body, in others, in the past or in the world? Take time to write these beliefs down.

• Do you see sickness and pain as legitimate and inevitable experiences here in the world?

• Which do you believe is the greater error: To be the victim of attack, or to be the perpetrator of attack?

• Do you believe physical death is not only a natural, legitimate part of life, but that it is inevitable? In other words, do you believe life always ends in death?

• Do you believe the body and its state of health sustain your life here in the world?

• Do you believe in the ego's laws of scarcity, attack and loss? And do you see yourself as hostage to these laws?

• Do you often make decisions and plans independently from Spirit?

• Do you attempt to protect yourself, your life or loved ones independently from Spirit?

• Do you believe some foods are good for you, while others are bad for you?

• Do you believe food increases weight, while dieting sheds weight?

• Do you believe cancer (or any sickness) is caused by external influences like diet, heredity, lifestyle, smoking or environmental toxicity?

• Do you place your faith in the world's laws of economics, rather than in Spirit's law of endless supply and abundance?

• Do you believe the laws of nature are immutable?

• Do you believe your body will naturally age and deteriorate?

• Do you believe sacrifice or struggle is legitimate, in order to be happy, loved, healthy and abundant?

• Do you believe you need to earn your right to be both Loved and worthy?

• Do you believe death offers some advantage that life does not—such as escape from the body, the end of ego, the end of conflict, a state of peace, rest, reunion with God or loved ones, or a state of completion?

Much of our independent will is unconscious, until we bring it to the light of Spirit for forgiveness and transformation. If you answered "yes" to most of these questions, your belief in the ego's world and its laws is strong. What you believe is what you unconsciously expect. Because your will is as powerful as God's, your expectations *must* materialize.

As long as we believe we are independently responsible for the body and world, apart from Spirit, not only do we reinforce that the body and world are real, but we abdicate our Holiness. This Holiness reverses all the laws of the world.

What *really* sustains us? Is it the body and world? Or is it God's Love? We cannot know and trust that God's Love will sustain us, if we persist in running our life apart from Spirit. In doing so, we mistakenly deem the body and world are the source of our existence.

All these mistaken beliefs are not bad in themselves. Yet keeping them apart from reinterpretation by Spirit while we independently try to sustain and protect our self, ensures our unconscious guilt remains intact. Jesus is very clear as He assures us it is God alone who sustains us, and that we are under no laws but God's:

> *"I am sustained by the love of God:"*
> *"Here is the answer to every problem that will confront you, today and tomorrow and throughout time. In this world, you believe you are sustained by everything but God. Your faith is placed in the most trivial and insane symbols; pills, money, "protective" clothing, influence, prestige, being liked, knowing the "right" people, and an endless list of forms of nothingness that you endow with magical powers..." " All*

these things are your replacements for the Love of God."
W-50.1,2:1

"The seeming cost of accepting today's idea is this: It means that nothing outside yourself can save you; nothing outside yourself can give you peace. But it also means that nothing outside yourself can hurt you, or disturb your peace or upset you in any way. Today's idea places you in charge of the universe, where you belong because of what you are."
W-70.2:1-3

"I am under no laws but God's:"
"Think of the freedom in the recognition that you are not bound by all the strange and twisted laws you have set up to save you. You really think that you would starve unless you have stacks of green paper strips and piles of metal discs. You really think a small round pellet or some fluid pushed into your veins through a sharpened needle will ward off disease and death. You really think you are alone unless another body is with you." A Course in Miracles, W-76.3.

"It is insanity that thinks these things. You call them laws, and put them under different names in a long catalogue of rituals that have no use and serve no purpose. You think you must obey the "laws" of medicine, of economics and of health. Protect the body, and you will be saved." W-76.4.

"These are not laws, but madness. The body is endangered by the mind that hurts itself. The body suffers just in order that the mind will fail to see it is the victim of itself. The body's suffering is a mask the mind holds up to hide what really suffers. It would not understand it is its own enemy; that it attacks itself and wants to die. It is from this your "laws" would save the body. It is for this you think you are a body." W-76.5.

"There are no laws except the laws of God. This needs repeating, over and over, until you realize it applies to everything that you have made in opposition to God's Will. Your magic has no meaning. What it is meant to save does

not exist. Only what it is meant to hide will save you."
W-76.6.

"We will begin the longer practice periods today with a short review of the different kinds of "laws" we have believed we must obey. These would include, for example, the "laws" of nutrition, of immunization, of medication, and of the body's protection in innumerable ways. Think further; you believe in the "laws" of friendship, of "good" relationships and reciprocity. Perhaps you even think that there are laws which set forth what is God's and what is yours. Many "religions" have been based on this. They would not save but damn in Heaven's name. Yet they are no more strange than other "laws" you hold must be obeyed to make you safe..."
" There are no laws but God's. Dismiss all foolish magical beliefs today, and hold your mind in silent readiness to hear the Voice that speaks the truth to you." W-76.8,9:1-3

PRAYER TO RELEASE BELIEF IN THE BODY AND WORLD

Do you truly wish to release these blocks to the awareness of Love's presence, and free yourself from ego beliefs and values? Go within and ask Spirit which of these limiting beliefs you are ready to release for healing at this time. You may find this prayer helpful:

"I recognize my faith in this body and the world's laws is temporarily stronger than my faith in God's Love. Therefore I surrender my beliefs in_____to you, Spirit. And I ask that you heal my perception. I trust that once the cause of suffering in my mind is healed, so must healing transfer to its effects/symptoms. I open my heart, in this instant, to receive your healing. I accept the miracle, the Atonement that heals all. And I surrender the timing of the miracle. Amen."

Healing means choosing to be mindfully aware of how the ego uses the body and world to bolster its dictatorship. We look *with* Spirit, and we watch this process with neither judgment nor self-judgment. We sincerely turn every block over to Spirit, asking that our perception of the body and world be divinely reinterpreted. This is True forgiveness.

As the *Course* tells us, God's teachers need a body through which to communicate His message. As long as the world is still terrified of Love, fear prevents direct communication with Spirit. The body is therefore extremely valuable to Spirit, as it is the perfect medium to convey the message of Truth in this fearful world.

> *"Only very few can hear God's Voice at all, and even they cannot communicate His messages directly through the Spirit which gave them. They need a medium through which communication becomes possible to those who do not realize that they are spirit. A body they can see. A voice they understand and listen to, without the fear that truth would encounter in them. Do not forget that truth can come only where it is welcomed without fear. So do God's teachers need a body, for their unity could not be recognized directly." M-12.3:3-8*

> *"The teachers of God appear to share the illusion of separation, but because of what they use the body for, they do not believe in the illusion despite appearances." M-12.4:6*

> *"The central lesson is always this; that what you use the body for it will become to you. Use it for sin or for attack, which is the same as sin, and you will see it as sinful. Because it is sinful it is weak, and being weak, it suffers and it dies. Use it to bring the Word of God to those who have it not, and the body becomes holy. Because it is holy it cannot be sick, nor can it die. When its usefulness is done it is laid by, and that is all." M-12.5:1-6*

PUNISHING THE BODY
EXERCISE: HOW DO WE USE OUR BODY LOVELESSLY?

The body is nothing but a projected image, with no ability to change of its own accord. All changes in the body are directed by the mind. As long as we think we're a body, our body is used by the ego. This way, unconscious guilt is projected onto the body so it suffers and dies. This is the ego's extreme deception, orchestrated to hide our true Identity from our awareness.

> *"You have displaced your guilt to your body from your mind. Yet a body cannot be guilty, for it can do nothing of itself. You who think you hate your body deceive yourself. You hate your mind, for guilt has entered into it, and it would remain separate from your brother's, which it cannot do." T-18.VI.2:5-8*

How have you allowed the ego to use the body for unconscious self-attack? You cannot heal until you see it, and willingly join with Spirit to exchange self-attack for miracles. This is a process of discovery. We work with Spirit to raise our awareness of all the ways we have unknowingly abused the body in pursuit of the ego's goals. We may find we have been dishonest with our Holy Self. Perhaps we have abandoned or betrayed our self.

As you realize these betrayals, you may feel sadness or grief at the recognition you have abandoned your self and body. This is good. You may want to sincerely apologize to the body for scapegoating it—after all, you've unfairly blamed it for all the things it never did. It was never the *cause* of pain, illness, appetites, addictions, sabotage, or anything else.

As you come to recognize for yourself that the ego in the mind tells the body what to do, you can consciously withdraw your projections and judgments from the body. Now you can enter a truly Loving agreement with the body. You might choose to express your new dedication of the body's purpose to Spirit, if it feels right. Together with Spirit, write a heartfelt letter to the body. This would act as a symbol of your transfer of the body's purpose to Spirit, Love and healing.

Note: Consider each of the following questions carefully and write your answers. Please do this exercise without guilt or shame. If any guilt, criticism, shame or self-judgment arises, know this is of the ego and not Spirit.

Some questions:
How do I abuse the body? How do I neglect it? How do I deny it? How do I use it to guilt-trip myself? How do I use it to guilt-trip others? How do I use it to get my ego needs met? How do I abandon or betray it? How do I use it pridefully? How do I use it for self-attack through pain/disease/aging/accidents? How do I use it to demonstrate scarcity? How do I use it to defend myself emotionally or physically? How do I use it as a substitute for True Self-Love? How do I make it an idol? How do I assign it power over my own mind? How do I judge it? How do I blame it? How do I shame it? How do I make it my identity?

Taking your Answers to Spirit through the Atonement Process
Take your answers to Spirit by going through the Atonement Process with each one. What are you willing to offer to Spirit, to be healed in your perception? The Atonement Process is found on page 297.

To punish the body is insane—yet that's what we do every time we feel pain or get sick. The body is used to create a gap between our self and the rest of the world. It has no ability to see, hear or feel other than what we tell it to sense. The body is completely neutral.

"Who punishes the body is insane. For here the little gap is seen, and yet it is not here. It has not judged itself, nor made itself to be what it is not. It does not seek to make of pain a joy and look for lasting pleasure in the dust. It does not tell you what its purpose is and cannot understand what it is for. It does not victimize, because it has no will,

no preferences and no doubts. It does not wonder what it is. And so it has no need to be competitive. It can be victimized, but cannot feel itself as victim. It accepts no role, but does what it is told, without attack." T-28.VI.1.

We do believe in a hierarchy of illusions. Every day we make a thousand decisions, and most are made independent from Spirit. We think we know our own best interests, yet nearly all our daily choices are made *between* illusions, instead of overlooking them entirely. As a result, we busily shift the deck chairs on our sinking Titanic. To serve the millions of ego choices we make, is to damn the body to pain, decay and finally, to death. Thus is the body used lovelessly.

To escape suffering, there is but one decision to make: Regardless of appearances, the choice for peace must be prioritized above all else. This means we must recognize the goal is to use every situation as a means to return to peace through forgiveness. In this goal, the body is not used lovelessly.

"Health is the result of relinquishing all attempts to use the body lovelessly." T-8.VIII.9:9

To use the body as an end goal or beneficiary in itself, is to call upon death. The body, if properly understood, is purely a vehicle through which we communicate forgiveness. To attempt to fix the body, or harm it, or satisfy its needs or appetites apart from Spirit, is to increase guilt and call upon disease and death.

When we feel the need to satisfy the physical or emotional needs of our own body or another's, we are deluded. In delusion, we believe we are the body; that the body is our identity. And when we misidentify that we are a body, the body will seem to threaten us.

" My brother, child of our Father, this is a [dream] of death. There is no funeral, no dark altars, no grim commandments nor twisted rituals of condemnation to which the body leads you. Ask not release of [it.] But free it from the merciless

*and unrelenting orders you laid upon it, and forgive it
what you ordered it to do. In its exaltation you commanded
it to die, for only death could conquer life. And what but
insanity could look upon the defeat of God, and think it
real?" T-19.IV.C.8:2-7*

The body was made as a substitute for our Self in God. As long as we
use it as an end in itself, as sole beneficiary, it will appear to victimize
and betray us. Yet when we turn the body's purpose over to Truth, it
will happily reflect the Holy purpose our mind has given it.

*"Today we seek to change our minds about the source of
sickness, for we seek a cure for all illusions, not another shift
among them. We will try today to find the source of healing,
which is in our minds because our Father placed it there for
us. It is not farther from us than ourselves. It is as near to us
as our own thoughts; so close it is impossible to lose. We need
but seek it and it must be found." W-140.8.*

USING THE BODY LOVELESSLY:
MY OWN EXPERIENCE

As we undo the ego's compulsion for self-attack, our secret death
wish (the one we've projected onto the body and world since the
beginning of time) is finally exposed and surrendered. Projection
is withdrawn and erased. The blocks to the awareness of Love's
presence are dissolved, and no illusions obscure the immensity of
the power we share with God. We have reversed everything we
made with the ego. We no longer attack our own True Identity;
we know who we are.

This process is my calling. All other priorities have dropped
away. I experienced an immense heart opening when I did my

own radical self-inquiry about loveless use of the body, using the above exercise. I was overcome with grief when I discovered all I had demanded from this body. I could scarcely believe the degree to which I had unknowingly punished it by projecting my guilt. When I allowed myself to feel deeply into all I had commanded the body to do, and the many ways I had condemned it, I was heartbroken. I had spent a lifetime regarding the body as my enemy, believing it held the power and intention to victimize and betray me. Had I treated my dog the way I treated this body, it would have killed her many times over.

I had never been comfortable in the body, and now saw I had unconsciously looked forward to physical death as a welcome escape from it. This is exactly what the ego wants! At all costs, it wants to keep us from awakening to God's Love while in the body. I wept many tears as I saw my role in this. And yet it was the most liberating experience to see all this at last.

Finally, I could genuinely forgive the body for what it did not do. I used my forgiveness prayer to do this: *"Spirit, help me to forgive myself for using this body to attack myself and to separate from you as my Holy Self."*

With this heartfelt prayer, the body was set free. And with it, so was I. Not only was I now under no laws but God's, but this body was too. The body is no longer my enemy, nor is it my responsibility. It is now used purely as a communication device for Love, and my commitment is that it will no longer be used for fear and attack. I have wholly committed the purpose of this body to God's Loving Will, and I have never felt so free, so utterly boundless.

"Yet is the [body] prisoner, and not the mind. The body thinks no thoughts. It has no power to learn, to pardon, nor enslave. It gives no orders that the mind need serve, nor sets conditions that it must obey. It holds in prison but the willing mind that would abide in it. It sickens at the bidding of the mind that would become its prisoner. And it grows old and dies, because that mind is sick within itself. Learning is all that causes change. And so the body, where no learning can occur, could never change unless the mind

preferred the body change in its appearances, to suit the purpose given by the mind. For mind can learn, and there is all change made." T-31.III.4.

I saw with laser-like clarity how I had mindlessly projected onto the body—and I saw we all do this. We make an independent identity of it. We use the body as a defense against God's Love, a monumental distraction from the Truth of our Holy Self. We do virtually everything for the sake of the emotional or physical body. All our defenses and all our desires are negotiated on its behalf. And all we defend against, we unconsciously attract.

This exercise allowed me to exhume a large mass of unconscious beliefs, values, fears and projections. In fact, as I allowed the body to be forgiven, it felt as if a giant tumor suddenly vanished. Looking back, I recognize this exercise has probably saved me many lifetimes of suffering.

Now as I advance in years, my lesson is to surrender any remaining beliefs about the body and its seeming needs. All fears of pain, aging, disease and death are being reinterpreted by Spirit. This is no longer "my" body. I have surrendered it to Spirit, and am therefore learning it needs no defense. Sure, I look in the mirror sometimes and still see the gray hair, but I'm believing less in what my body's eyes show me. And I am trusting more in the vision that comes from Willing with God.

"There is no world apart from what you wish, and herein lies your ultimate release. Change but your mind on what you want to see, and all the world must change accordingly. Ideas leave not their source." W-132.5:1-3

The healing of my relationship with the body has been miraculous, because in doing so, its purpose was wholly surrendered to God's Love. Now I have a Holy Relationship with the body. I no longer condemn it, nor do I expect it to meet the imagined needs of the ego. As a result, I feel greatly at peace with the body. I recognize the body has no ability to change, get sick or cause pain; it is neutral. The old physical pain, osteoporosis and celiac disease have all fallen away. Because I saw the cause within my mind, I was able to ask for and receive healing.

The Atonement is the key to healing every conceivable problem. It is an immediate tool I use every time I feel fear, pain or doubt. Through it, I release my suffering and in doing so am learning the true purpose of the body.

> "The body is the means by which God's Son returns to sanity. Though it was made to fence him into hell without escape, yet has the goal of Heaven been exchanged for the pursuit of hell. The Son of God extends his hand to reach his brother, and to help him walk along the road with him. Now is the body holy. Now it serves to heal the mind that it was made to kill." W-pll.5.4.

CHAPTER NINE

GUILT: EXPOSING THE SOURCE OF OUR PERSISTENT SENSE OF THREAT

Earlier in my *Course* studies, I was not able to make a direct feeling link between my own suffering and my unconscious guilt. It seemed impossible to connect adversity to its real cause, because I could detect no direct feelings of guilt. Nor could I recognize experientially that whatever seemed to threaten me from outside was a direct byproduct of my concealed belief in my own guilt. I understood intellectually that guilt and suffering were connected, but did not know this in my actual experience.

Yet now in almost every instance that fear, scarcity, doubt or concern arises, I can immediately trace it back to that single core belief. I do this by dropping within to inquire, staying focused there until I reach the core feeling beneath the original loss of peace. Without fail, the nucleus is always the underlying expectation that I will be attacked and/or punished because I must be guilty.

This internal inquiry process helps me recognize more quickly the fear I feel (or the anger, anxiety, sickness, etc.), is never personal. Nor is it caused by the particular trigger the ego thinks is the offender. Only one fundamental unconscious fear drives all our conscious fears. It is the deep-seated fear of God that envelops and conceals the ego's underlying guilt. We believe we are guilty for abandoning God, making for ourselves a wholly independent, autonomous identity and world—all to keep God out.

Our imagined fear of God's punishment is always the root of our persistent sense of threat, and our defense against God's Love. We stay busy with endless seeking and problem-solving to distract our self from this constant sense of impending doom.

Before we get to the nucleus of all fear, the unconscious fear of God, we must first recognize our conscious fear. All fear derives from the ego's conscious projection that we are being stalked by death. Death is the ego's smokescreen, designed to distract us from seeing our true fear. Because, of course, as soon as we identify and heal our real fear of God's Love as Self, the ego thought system is no more.

Remember death appears in many forms, including scarcity, sickness, pain, conflict, loss and sacrifice. These many distractions are all meant to divert us from the ego's real terror. Through these preoccupations it ensures we will never inquire deeply enough to recognize the root of its unconscious projection. All this ego sleight-of-hand is kept from our conscious mind.

When we look deeply, we see death is not the identity of the terrifying stalker that attacks us in so many forms; it isn't death the world tries so hard to escape. It is the ego's projection of god.

Our unconscious mistaken belief is that God is out to get us for what we did at the separation. This is the real source of all our guilt. As long as the guilt remains denied and projected outward, it represents our unconscious attraction to, and manifestation of death in all its forms, including physical death. To the ego, the stark finality of physical death proves God is indeed fearsome, and that trusting in God leads to both sacrifice and death.

"If you identify with the ego, you must perceive yourself as guilty. Whenever you respond to your ego you will experience guilt, and you will fear punishment." T-5.V:3:5-6

"Listening to the ego's voice means that you believe it is possible to attack God, and that a part of Him has been torn away by you. Fear of retaliation from without follows, because the severity of the guilt is so acute that it must be projected." T-5.V:10-11

INNOCENCE AS THE ULTIMATE DEFENSE

I am learning a deeply felt sense of divine innocence is the best, most immediate defense against the ego in my mind. Innocence is the only True defense, because it alone cannot attack. The ego's pseudo-innocence, on the other hand, always attacks because it plays the game of polarization.

Ego innocence needs an opposite, a guilty party to justify its innocence. Divine innocence sees the Truth that only Love is real—therefore attack in any form must be illusion. Divine innocence needs no defense, as neither victim nor perpetrator exist in Truth. It recognizes all seeming attack is really ego self-attack; as such, it simply overlooks the illusion.

Our innocence is God's Will. Nothing can oppose it. The innocence of the Christ Mind is bestowed upon us by God, and cannot be threatened. Only our independent will to experience suffering masks our awareness of it. Yet we reclaim this state of divine innocence in any instant we accept Atonement, an immediate portal through which our eternal Identity is reclaimed. Atonement is an eternal shaft of light piercing the ego dream of suffering and time.

We don't earn innocence. It is already given. Nothing we could do would decrease or increase it. It remains perfect and changeless. Nothing we feel badly about has ever appeared on God's radar.

All our mistakes, judgments, worries, shame and self-criticism do not exist. God does not judge us. So why do we insist on judging our self and others? The ego cannot survive if we remember to accept our divine innocence.

Awareness of this innocence is fiercely defended against. If it were allowed to remain in our awareness, the ego would disappear entirely. The ego feeds on our misperceptions and judgment. It would starve if we steadfastly remembered only innocence.

Guilt is like a darkened room; light is the Love of God. The ego must keep the light of God from entering this room of guilt. As long as we believe ourselves unworthy, we cling to darkness and reject the light.

The darkened room represents our fear of God. When we make the choice to feed this darkness with seeming worldly evidence such as conflict, sickness, depression, pain, scarcity and death, we reject the light of our own innocence.

What would happen to the darkness if the light were switched on? Guilt, like darkness, would simply disappear. And when we see and accept our own innocence, we cannot help but see this state reflected in others as well.

FINDING YOUR ETERNALLY IMMUTABLE INNOCENCE

The quest to remember my own divine innocence began in earnest six months after Tomas left physical form. In May of 2011, I was sitting on a sunlit porch, marveling at the glorious life bursting forth from the garden all around me. I began to wonder: *How could life possibly have an opposite? How could life end in death? If God is Love, and Love is eternal Life without opposite, how could the concept of death be taken seriously?* In that moment, I had an epiphany.

I knew with all my being that death was not real. I had been experiencing waves of similar insight ever since my breakdown/breakthrough experience just after Tomas left physical form. These insights had clearly begun to pierce my ego belief system. Apparently they left an opening big enough for Spirit to enter now and illuminate the remaining blackness of untruth.

During this euphoric time, my heart cracked open further. As it did, I saw and felt Love's all-encompassing Truth. At last I really understood the deeper meaning in the introduction to *A Course in Miracles*:

"This is a course in miracles. It is a required course. Only the time you take it is voluntary. Free will does not mean that you can establish the curriculum. It means only that you can elect what you want to take at a given time. The course does not aim at teaching the meaning of love, for that is beyond what can be taught. It does aim, however, at removing the blocks to the awareness of love's presence, which is your natural inheritance. The opposite of love is fear, but what is all-encompassing can have no opposite." T-in.1.

This course can therefore be summed up very simply in this way: Nothing real can be threatened. Nothing unreal exists. Herein lies the peace of God." T-in.2-4

Before, these had merely seemed beautiful ideas; now I deeply felt their Truth. The opposite of Love is fear. But what is all-encompassing can have no opposite. Love, then, has no opposite. And fear does not exist.

Only Love is real; only Love is all-encompassing. And Love, in its perfect Reality, cannot be threatened. Nothing unreal exists. Fear is unreal, and cannot threaten Love. So what is it we defend our self from, if Love is all there is?

We believe the threat of fear is real. Yet nothing we fear actually exists. What do we really defend against, if fear does not exist? What is left after the illusion of fear falls away?

The ego never wants us to see the truthful answer to that question: Whenever we defend our self, we really defend our self *from Love.* It may look as if we're struggling to sustain and defend our life, yet we are really blocking out Love. We our self made everything we seem to defend against in this world. That's how powerful our will is.

"You make what you defend against, and by your own defense against it is it real and inescapable. Lay down your arms, and only then do you perceive it false." W-170.2:6

At the core of our urge to defend our self, is our defense against Love. Through defense and grievance, we unconsciously project self-attack as sickness, pain, scarcity or conflict, making fear seem a legitimate defense.

Yet all defenses were made to hide the one power of Love as our Holy Self. To become aware of Love's presence is to recognize our innocence is found in the release of all defenses into God's hands—for we no longer desire or need protection from Love. Guilt and fear, along with their defenses, are no longer required because we no longer need to project these obstacles as barriers to Love.

On that sunlit porch as I basked in newfound release, only Love was present. In my own defenselessness and divine innocence, I could not even imagine feeling the sharp sting of fear ever again.

Just then, three large wasps zeroed in on me, and would not leave me alone. Instinctive fear tried to shoot through me, yet I resisted the urge to allow it in. I refused to abandon myself to fear, recognizing guilt had caused this fear, and with it, the automatic urge to defend myself.

If, in that moment, I recognized I was only Love and innocence, everything that appeared outside me must be Love as well. After all, the body and world are in my mind. But which inner teacher would I choose to perceive them with? I asked myself silently, *"Would Love betray me? Could divine innocence attack me?"*

I became one with the Love and innocence I recognized deep within. Remaining absolutely still, I breathed these knowings into the core of my being. I chose not to see the wasps through fear, but through Love. Perceiving them from this deeply embodied innocence and safety, I knew they were harmless.

If all suffering and fear are born from unconscious guilt in my mind, the embodied experience of my own divine innocence, even if for just an instant, *must* return my awareness from fear to Love.

"God's blessing shines upon me from within my heart, where He abides. I need but turn to Him, and every sorrow melts away, as I accept His boundless Love for me."
W-pI.207:2-3

Only Love exists, without opposite. What am I actually fearful of, if fear does not exist? Love. I fear the one power of God's Love. This is my incorruptible, eternal Identity as Love itself. If I defend myself, I'm using fear as a defense against Love, an attack on Love—on the very Self I am. Defending myself, therefore, is self-attack. Yet could divine innocence ever attack itself? Could God's Love ever betray itself?

Our deeply unconscious terror of divine Love as Holy Self is at the heart of every perceived fear or suffering within this ego paradigm. Deep down, we know once we begin to wake up, we will see through the lie. We will recognize we made up this entire paradigm, as an attack on God as our Holy Self.

This recognition will cost us the world as we know it. It is the complete reversal of the thinking of the world, and totally transcends the laws of this world. No ego laws are exempt, not even the laws of nature, which are based in death, not Life. The cycle of birth and death is a lie.

No longer will we defend our self from what we made, to hide from the all-encompassing Love that we are.

"If I defend myself I am attacked. But in defenselessness I will be strong, and I will learn what my defenses hide."
W-135.22:4-5

"Defenses are the plans you undertake to make against the truth. Their aim is to select what you approve, and disregard what you consider incompatible with your beliefs of your reality. Yet what remains is meaningless indeed. For it is your reality that is the "threat" which your defenses would attack, obscure, and take apart and crucify." W-135.17.

False humility, self doubt, fear and concern are burned away in the blazing light of embodied innocence. This divine innocence, when accepted truly, is our infinite safety. Nothing of the ego remains.

Innocence is the direct result of sincerely accepting Atonement. This is True forgiveness. In this, we dare to express our vulnerability and drop our defenses. Real safety and security arise only when we release the desire to hide in darkness. We gently let go with a deep sigh of relief within as we unburden our self. We release the heavy load of fear, guilt and control we've carried for eons.

This has been a gradual process for me over these past two years. More and more, I recognize all my concerns are really reflections of my lack of trust in God's Love. I still feel fears, but now when I look at them with Spirit, I am shown the same root cause again and again. A pattern emerges; every fear shows itself as the one mistake. All seeming external cause is generalized and distilled into this single recognition.

Every one of my fears stems from guilt—from my belief I stand alone, apart from God. If it were true that I did indeed stand alone, apart from God, I would have every reason to be fearful! And every reason to try to control my life independently, defending myself from perceived threat. But however grand my hallucinations of autonomy might be, I could never make them real.

I now know any fear, concern or need to control comes from the mistaken belief I am not worthy of God's Love. This moment is the only one that exists, and my awareness is all I have in Truth. All else is transient. So where am I when I believe in fear? And where am I when I believe in Love?

Whenever I feel fear or desire to protect or defend the body, myself or another, I stop and recognize exactly what my fear is masking. Always, it is my hidden expectation of punishment, due to my remaining belief in guilt. We must learn to mindfully detect this one unconscious desire beneath each of our fears and defenses.

As long as we secretly expect punishment in the form of sickness, pain, conflict, scarcity, loss and death, we will manifest these. The ego's defenses work to unconsciously attract the very fears we attempt to shield our self from. Our will is just as powerful as God's Will, and whatever we expect, God cannot save us from.

When I can locate and release that core feeling of guilt along with my subsequent expectation of punishment, regardless of the particular form of perceived threat, I am immediately returned to peace. In my defenselessness my safety lies.

GUILT OR GUILTLESSNESS: WHICH DO YOU VALUE?

All fear and need to control arise from unconscious fear of God's Love. This single unrecognized fear underlies every fear or concern we appear to experience. The ego dream of the world was made, and is sustained by, our fear of God. This core fear is the profound fear of Love itself. Without this extreme fear of Love, we could experience no suffering, conflict, sickness, scarcity or death.

Our return to Love depends upon how much we desire to undo this fear of God. Are we willing to be constantly vigilant? This means a determination to see and release unconscious guilt wherever it surfaces, refusing any temptation to perceive outer circumstances as the true source of our discomfort.

Guilt alone is responsible for feeding the ego's relentless drive for unconscious self-attack. We must commit to experiencing the embodiment of our own (and others) complete guiltlessness, if we are to remember God's Love.

Our memory of guiltlessness is only returned to our awareness by consistently applying forgiveness to every area of life. This repeated choice for forgiveness looks beyond all we have projected onto our body, others, the past, God and the world.

As we uncover and sincerely surrender our mistaken projections, fear must fall away. And as fear is undone, the memory of our safety and invulnerability is restored. To undo our projections by accepting Atonement is to experience this embodied knowing.

We remember we are God's Self, and thus share in the one power of God's Love. We recognize we already have everything because we already *are* everything. Our divine innocence is reflected everywhere we look, because we have finally forgiven our self for using the world to attack us.

This is not innocence as the world recognizes it. From the ego's perspective, my innocence is always bought at the cost of another's guilt. Yet divine guiltlessness recognizes no one is ever guilty. All guilt I seem to see out there depends on having seen it first within. In denying and attempting to get rid of it, I project it outward and then seem to see it in others, the body, the past and the world. I cannot possibly perceive attack in any form, unless I harbor guilty intent within. Hence all attack is always self-attack, regardless of the circumstance. Divine guiltlessness recognizes this, and perceives it only as a call for Love.

For some of us, guilt seems to manifest most strongly within. We are our own harshest critic, full of self-judgment. But guilt is guilt, whether it is projected outside or within. It is still attack. And where attack is, Love is not. Self-judgment is every bit as lethal an attack as judgment of others. It's the ego's attempt to keep us apart from the source of all Love, our Holy Self. At some point we need to say, "no!" to this incessant inner critic. We may still hear these judgments as they arise, but only we possess the power of choice, not to believe its judgments any longer.

Jesus tells us if we believe we or anyone else is guilty, we must believe He is guilty also, for we are all one. Yet if Jesus conquered guilt and overcame the world, through Him we must have done so as well.

> *"Let me be to you the symbol of the end of guilt, and look upon your brother as you would look on me. Forgive me all the sins you think the Son of God committed. And in the light of your forgiveness he will remember who he is, and forget what never was. I ask for your forgiveness, for if you are guilty, so must I be. But if I surmounted guilt and overcame the world, you were with me." T-19.IV.B.6:1-5*

As long as I harbor guilt, I will always project this self-attack outward onto my body, others or the world. I not only get to keep this guilt, I actually *increase* it by projecting it outward. And what I give, I receive.

The body and world are not out there, but within our mind. Everything we share, we give to ourselves. Projection of guilt is the way we keep it. This is why it's so important to practice observation whenever our buttons are pushed. Stop and notice what you're doing when you catch yourself blaming the body, your self, another or the world for your seeming distress.

Believing the cause of suffering to be outside the mind is an immediate signal we have rejected the real source of our discomfort; we have refused to recognize the hidden guilt within. And as a result, we will continue to place the blame everywhere but within our own mind.

"As long as you believe that guilt is justified in any way, in anyone, whatever he may do, you will not look within, where you would always find Atonement. The end of guilt will never come as long as you believe there is a reason for it." T-13.X.6:1-2

We mistakenly believe we will not be whole or happy if we must choose between guilt and guiltlessness. Our distorted perception thrives on valuing both. Yet only guiltlessness, the total relinquishment of judgment, will restore our wholeness and happiness.

"You do not want either [guilt or guiltlessness] alone, for without both you do not see yourself as whole and therefore happy. Yet you are whole only in your guiltlessness, and only in your guiltlessness can you be happy. There is no conflict here. To wish for guilt in any way, in any form, will lose appreciation of the value of your guiltlessness, and push it from your sight." T-14.III.2:3-6

When we're tempted to see guilt outside the mind instead of within, we must remember if we blame the body, another or the world, it means we unconsciously expect punishment. And because we expect it, we will manifest it.

"Whenever the pain of guilt seems to attract you, remember that if you yield to it, you are deciding against

happiness, and will not learn how to be happy. Say therefore, to yourself, gently, but with the conviction born of the Love of God and of His Son: What I experience I will make manifest. If I am guiltless, I have nothing to fear. I choose to testify to my acceptance of the Atonement, not to its rejection. I would accept my guiltlessness by making it manifest and sharing it. Let me bring peace to God's Son from his Father." T-14.III.3:3-9

The ego cannot fathom Spirit's interpretation of guiltlessness. Fear is the ego's means of sustaining its world. It cannot imagine True innocence. Fear is the direct by-product of guilt—it can't exist without guilt to spawn it. This is why True guiltlessness is invulnerability. In guiltlessness there can be no fear, and therefore no attack.

Much of our guilt and subsequent self-attack stems from the habit of making decisions alone, without consulting Spirit. These decisions are judgments designed to get the ego's needs met. But anything we do to meet the ego's needs will cause suffering.

A prayer to help me choose guiltlessness:

"Spirit, please reveal to me my guiltlessness. Show me there is nothing to fear. Increase my trust in you, and help me embrace your miraculous perception. In which ways do I unconsciously defend myself from Love? In which areas of my life do I compartmentalize apart from you? Please help undo my perception of attack/judgment, and let me rest in certain knowing that my perfect safety lies only in my defenselessness. Amen."

FINDING THE GREATEST LOVE OF ALL: YOUR HOLY SELF

You can only be truly helpful to Self, God, others and the world, if you are prepared to Love and *be* your Self—the Holy Self. Few of us were raised to be our true Self. Thanks to the painstaking efforts of parents, schools and cultural norms, we have mistakenly grown up believing we are separate identities, incomplete and fundamentally lacking. As a result, the Holy Self as Truth within has rarely been seen, let alone acknowledged or encouraged.

Most of us were taught not to trust our self. We were not encouraged to seek out the still, small Voice within. Instead, we were trained to seek outside for approval and completion. At the time, none of us realized the high cost of learning to distrust our Self. To lack Holy Self-trust is to be incapable of trusting others and the world. Because we don't trust our Self, we project that distrust onto others and the world—and they, in turn, respond as we request: They will abandon and betray us.

The un-relinquished ego uses others to attack us. This is why in True forgiveness, we are never forgiving another. Instead, we forgive our self for using another to attack us. No one could hurt us, had we not unconsciously asked him to. In our encounters with others and the world, we will perceive out there only the reflection of our own inner feeling state.

"What would you see? The choice is given you. But learn and do not let your mind forget this law of seeing: You will look upon that which you feel within." W-189.5:1-3

Our True desire, our ever-present underlying longing is for Love. Yet through the ego, we only chase our tail in search of it, because the ego's mantra is *seek but do not find.* So the necessary prerequisite for experiencing Love is the undoing of all our ego blocks to awareness of its presence. Love, the one Holy Self, is the center of our being.

We must learn to initiate an authentically Loving relationship with our Self, before real Love can be experienced. With Spirit, we forgive our self for using others, the body and the world to attack us. In forgiveness we reunite with our True Identity, gradually coming to recognize, accept and trust our Holy Self.

"By supplying your Identity wherever It is not recognized, you will recognize It." T-14.X.12:7

Our world and all our relationships are mirrors of our own Self-Love, or lack thereof. We cannot be abandoned or betrayed, unless we have first unconsciously abandoned or betrayed our Self. We must learn to be our own best friend. But we cannot do this while also giving authority to the ego in our mind, for the ego's weapons are fear and guilt. We must be willing to show up for our self; to remain present *especially* when we feel threatened or triggered by self-judgment, by others or by circumstances.

How do we abandon our self? We do it in lots of different ways. Some of us may typically go on the defensive when triggered; others more often on the attack. Or we may retreat and scramble to people-please instead, in a desperate attempt to restore seeming harmony. All these responses represent our own methods of self-attack. Not one is Loving. Not one is more guilty or innocent than another. The Loving thing is to steadfastly stand by your Self, staying present and asking Spirit to help you perceive this situation differently.

How on Earth could you ever be Loving, trusting and faithful to others, if you can't extend these qualities to yourself? And how can you receive the Love you desire, if you're not willing to receive it from your Holy Self? Are you able to be True to your Self? Are you honest, patient, supportive, encouraging, unconditional, nurturing and trusting of your Self?

The ego will always fill your mind with criticism, but you can choose to disbelieve it. Are you willing to drop all guilt trips, shame and self-punishment? Are you willing to relinquish judgments against others, since you cannot judge them without incurring self-attack?

What about worry—are you willing to let that go? When you take on the responsibility of worry, you unknowingly reject Spirit's help. At first glance, worry may not seem in the same category of self-abandonment as the others, yet it indicates your choice to let the ego substitute for divine trust in Spirit as your Holy Self.

Are you comfortable spending time alone with your Self? If you feel alone or lonely, it's because you don't yet know and trust your Self—for if you did, you could never feel alone. Can you drop within, to the quiet inner space of your Holy Self? And do you feel safe enough to reveal your deepest, darkest fears here?

What is your inner dialogue like? As long as you listen to the ego's voice of fear and doubt, you will not hear Spirit's Voice within. The voices of both ego and Spirit are always present within our mind. We can learn to discern between them, but we really must learn to firmly say "no" to the ego. It offers a continual stream of unhelpful thoughts and beliefs based in fear and deprivation. Although the ego's arguments can be seductive at times, we do have the power to decide which of these voices to believe.

TRUE DESIRE

True desire is God's Will flowing effortlessly from within. How can you tell if this desire is truly of God? There is no guilt behind it. It does not emerge from fear or doubt. It arises from Love and trust, and calls to itself within the world. In its extension it returns to us as Love, often in forms we recognize. Because True desire wells forth from our divinity within, Holiness is its sole intent.

True desire is an expression of Love. It is this essence of Love we seek, but it cannot be discovered and fulfilled while it remains concealed beneath the ego's substitutes for Love and trust.

True desire is an intrinsic part of God's Will, expressing itself through us here in the dream. Without it, we could not undo the fear that precedes awakening to our Holy Self. The more we get to know and trust our Holy Self, the more our desire seems to shift and morph to reflect ever-greater trust in Spirit.

At first our desires are clouded by the ego's obsession with deprivation. Seeing us as incomplete and unworthy, it searches endlessly for relationships, experiences and accomplishments to fill the bottomless pit it believes we are. Desires that emerge from this sense of deprivation are propelled by fear, not by Love.

As fear and doubt fall away and trust in Spirit deepens within, a palpable sense of inner security and Love bubbles up inside us. While it may wane from time to time, once we've experienced this inner strength we will never fully believe the ego again. From this growing sense of peace and Love springs an unmistakable joy welling up from within. Often it is this joy that sparks True desire.

In this joy, we can securely sense our desire is in sync with God's. There is no sense of lack beneath it. Unlike ego desire, we feel no need to hoard, or attempt to fulfill our guilty desires apart from God. True desire is guiltless. We sense it is an extension of God's Will flowing through us. As such, True desire is never dependent upon an outcome. Because no guilt is attached to it, we feel confident our desire and God's Will are one. They are not in conflict. And from this inner security, we can afford to wait for our desire's fulfillment without anxiety. Patience is natural, when we know without a doubt our happiness is God's Will.

As an expression of God's Love through us, True desire is unselfish. It wishes only to extend, to share. As fear falls away, we grow increasingly aware of our Holy Self, embodying its Truth more and more. Here we discover all our needs are met effortlessly. When we know with confidence that our needs are always met, we rest in gratitude. And from this deep sense of inner appreciation, the desire to be of service grows ever stronger.

Of their own accord, our desires shift from getting to giving. The Love within cannot be contained; it must be shared. In this awareness, we deeply understand Jesus' teaching that giving is receiving. What we give, we keep. The way to keep something is to give it away.

Spirit already knows our deepest desire is for the Love of our Holy Self. Yet through the ego, we are afraid of it. Most of us do not yet know or trust our Holy Self—for if we did, we would have to recognize the same Holy Self in every other human being. The Holy Self is the one light within us all that illuminates the world.

Spirit knows our greatest desire, and is eager to help us embrace it. Spirit's only desire is to help us return to the awareness of our pristine innocence, the memory of our majesty. To the one Holy Self as Love. We believe we irrevocably lost this Self, but it is here and now, in any instant we truly desire to join with Love.

Perhaps you might set aside a few moments to contemplate this deeper desire to unite as your Holy Self. If Love is all there is, and Love is all you desire, are you willing to receive it with every fiber of your being? Remember in this world, God's Love is most often expressed as healing through forgiveness and joining. Following is a short prayer that is especially powerful when you feel relaxed and receptive:

"I join wholeheartedly with all God Lovingly wills for me. And I accept wholeheartedly all God Lovingly wills for me. This is God's Will. Amen."

" I am the light of the world. That is my only function. That is why I am here." W-61.5:3-5

"Who is the light of the world except God's Son? This, then, is merely a statement of the truth about yourself. It is the opposite of a statement of pride, of arrogance, or of self-deception. It does not describe the self-concept you have made. It does not refer to any of the characteristics with which you have endowed your idols. It refers to you as you were created by God. It simply states the truth." W-61.1.

"To the ego, today's idea is the epitome of self-glorification. But the ego does not understand humility, mistaking it for self-debasement. Humility consists of accepting your role in salvation and in taking no other. It is not humility to insist you cannot be the light of the world if that is the function God assigned to you. It is only arrogance that would assert this function cannot be for you, and arrogance is always of the ego." W-61.2.

"True humility requires that you accept today's idea because it is God's Voice which tells you it is true. This is a beginning step in accepting your real function on earth.

*It is a giant stride toward taking your rightful place in
salvation. It is a positive assertion of your right to be saved,
and an acknowledgment of the power that is given you to
save others." W-61.3.*

*"Today we will claim the miracles which are your right,
since they belong to you. You have been promised full release
from the world you made. You have been assured that the
Kingdom of God is within you, and can never be lost.
We ask no more than what belongs to us in truth. Today,
however, we will also make sure that we will not content
ourselves with less." W-77.3.*

HEALING THE ROOT
OF ALL EMOTIONAL PAIN

Through the ego, we believe our state of being is defined by the
emotions we feel in any given moment. For instance, when we're
sad we say, "*I am* sad," as if sadness is my identity. Emotional
states that come and go are often mistakenly assumed to be part
of our identity. But we are not our emotions.

Imagine you are the sky itself: Open, vast and eternal. Now
picture a dark cloud flitting across the sky. A negative emotion is
like this cloud. It's temporary. It is not *who* you are. What can this
cloud do to you, the sky? If your Identity is as great as the sky, the
passing of a cloud is just that—a passing emotion and not your
Self. Mistaking an emotion for who you are is an ego trick meant
to distract you from the Truth of your invulnerability in Spirit.

When we're angry or sad, we usually want to find the ego cause
outside us, so we can problem solve it and avoid the feeling again.
Likewise when we're happy, we attribute the cause to something
or somebody, and try to attract more of this pleasurable emotion.
We believe pleasurable emotions are good—signs that everything

is on the right track. And we believe negative emotions are bad, indicating something needs to be fixed.

It's important to recognize the real value of emotions, especially negative emotions. They are signposts pointing out remaining areas that require forgiveness. In themselves, they are neither good nor bad. They are part of the ego's construct, just as the body is. And as with the body, the question to ask is: What purpose do our emotions serve? Are they used on behalf of forgiveness, healing and Love? Or do they reinforce the ego's illusions of pain, attack and separation?

When we believe what the emotion tells us is true, we separate it from being healed. If I experience a negative emotion and link it to a cause outside me, such as my childhood abuse, I have misplaced the real cause, which is my unconscious guilt. Because I see the cause in the past (or in another, in my body or the world), I unknowingly deny healing of the true cause of my emotion. Genuine healing occurs when I recognize my emotional response is a symptom of my unhealed guilt. The cause is guilt and the effect is my emotion.

Real healing is available to me now, because I have placed the cause and effect together where they can both be healed. I have recognized they are both in my mind. If I place the cause of my distress in my childhood, I separate cause and effect. When cause and effect are kept apart, they cannot be healed.

This is how the ego attempts to heal. It first tells us the cause is somewhere outside us. While we're busily trying to heal these mistaken external causes, the real and only cause of all suffering is left unrecognized and un-remedied.

To heal, we must place cause and effect in their proper order. The one cause of my negative emotions is always unconscious guilt. And my emotional response is purely an effect. The real purpose of emotional healing is to recognize the one cause—guilt as unconscious self-attack—and offer it to Spirit in exchange for a miraculous perceptual shift.

In my earlier years of *Course* study I did what many do: I separated emotional pain from physical pain, not realizing they are both the same error, and are thus healed in the same manner. Both require forgiveness and acceptance of Atonement. Through the ego, the emotional body and the physical body share the same purpose. Pain, whether physical or emotional in nature, serves to convince us the body is real. The ego wants us to believe we are a fragile and corruptible body, not immortal Spirit.

> *"Pain demonstrates the body must be real. It is a loud, obscuring voice whose shrieks would silence what the Holy Spirit says, and keep His words from your awareness. Pain compels attention, drawing it away from Him and focusing upon itself. Its purpose is the same as pleasure, for they both are means to make the body real. What shares a common purpose is the same."..."Sin shifts from pain to pleasure, and again to pain. For either witness is the same, and carries but one message: "You are here, within this body, and you can be hurt." T-27.VI.1:1-5,2:1-2*

Fear is the one emotion that lies beneath all upsetting emotions. All fear is spawned by the unconscious belief we are guilty of separating from our divine Source. To trace it back even further, guilt is the single cause of all destructive emotions. If guilt is the one cause, then surely guiltlessness must be the one cure. Guiltlessness is achieved through forgiveness.

To begin, we must desire the peace of forgiveness *more than* we want to keep our anger, sadness, fear or pain. We offer up our wrong-minded perception, and instead invite an instant in which we willingly suspend doubt and judgment. In that instant, the Atonement occurs, and the miracle heals our perception. It may or may not be recognized immediately, yet a healing has occurred. And the results of this perceptual shift will eventually make themselves known.

All emotions not supremely joyous stem from the ego in our mind. As such, they are effects of our unconscious belief we are guilty and deserving of punishment. Jesus makes it clear the correction of fear is *our* responsibility. We can't expect Spirit to take away our fear. That would be totally disempowering, a breach of our own independent will.

We made fear. God did not. We chose fear, therefore it can't be taken away from us. We can, however, choose differently. We can consciously recognize any sense of suffering is an immediate sign we have fallen into wrong-mindedness. When in this state we feel separate from Love, from our one Holy Self. And we can ask for right-mindedness and removal of fear.

If we are willing to acknowledge our wrong perception is where the problem lies, and not in someone else, the body, the past or the world, we unite with God's Will in that instant. We wholeheartedly acknowledge both cause (our guilt), and effect (destructive emotion), are together in our mind. Now Spirit can heal both the cause and the effect.

But when we still believe the source of the problem is outside our mind, we remain unforgiving. Then Spirit cannot help us, because we have separated cause from effect. We have tried to make the effect (whether pain, disease, emotion, problem or person) something real and independent from our mind.

> "The correction of fear [is] your responsibility. When you ask for release from fear, you are implying that it is not. You should ask, instead, for help in the conditions that have brought the fear about. These conditions always entail a willingness to be separate. At that level you [can] help it. You are much too tolerant of mind wandering, and are passively condoning your mind's miscreations. The particular result does not matter, but the fundamental error does. The correction is always the same. Before you choose to do anything, ask me if your choice is in accord with mine. If you are sure that it is, there will be no fear." T-2.VI.4.

Only the ego can be hurt, or suffer emotional pain. You, the Holy Self, are invulnerable. So if you feel emotional pain, ask yourself this: Which self do you want to be? If you choose to reclaim awareness of your Holy Self, you must be prepared to give up all emotional pain— including all the stories and memories it evokes. Emotional pain and your Holy Self are irreconcilable. The presence of one in your awareness negates the other.

One can use many valuable techniques for emotional healing, yet the most important point is always to remember the real cause of the emotional pain or trauma. While you still believe the cause is outside you in another, the body, the past or the world, it cannot be healed truly. All healing techniques are magic, including methods for emotional release. They are useful tools, to the degree we use them to help us forgive our self for having used someone, something, or the past, to attack our self.

How do *you* use others, self, past or world to attack yourself? Are you willing to bring in the light of Spirit to look upon this with you? I used my childhood abuse to justify many years of emotional and physical pain. It became my story, and was a major part of my false identity. I used it to blame my mother, and to separate myself from feeling Loved, cherished and supported.

My emotional and physical healing occurred once I reassigned the true cause of my suffering. I recognized the ego in my mind had used my mother to abuse me. There was no other cause. And when I saw this Truth, I was able to exchange it for authentic forgiveness. And as I did, the miracle healed my perception. All emotional pain, and the memories attached to this suffering fell away. At the same time, my old self-destructive patterns quickly faded. Miraculous, indeed.

That's my example. In your areas of perceived pain, where are *you* ready to withdraw your belief the cause is outside you?

CHAPTER TEN

THE AIM OF FORGIVENESS

What is the aim of forgiveness? It is to restore awareness of our natural state of guiltlessness. Guiltlessness is real invulnerability, for in guiltlessness we are undefended against God's Love. By harboring fear or guilt, we reject God's Love, help and healing. The ego floods us with a multitude of seeming needs, yet there is really only one real need. There is only one True answer to the countless problems of the world, and that answer is forgiveness through Atonement.

> *"A sense of separation from God is the only lack you really need correct."* T-1.VI.2:1 *"To give up all problems to one Answer is to reverse the thinking of the world entirely."* M-4.IX.1:6

Through the miracle, Spirit returns our awareness to guiltlessness. The miracle undoes the fear and guilt that caused us to perceive attack. Guilt always triggers fear, yet fear wears countless masks, many of which are not recognized as fearful. The masks of fear include anger, frustration, conflict (inner and outer), the need to control, jealousy, fatigue, worry, scarcity, sadness, pain, disease, depression and feelings of being victimized, among others.

> *"I am never upset for the reason I think because I am constantly trying to justify my thoughts. I am constantly trying to make them true. I make all things my enemies,*

*so that my anger is justified and my attacks are warranted.
I have not realized how much I have misused everything I
see by assigning this role to it. I have done this to defend
a thought system that has hurt me, and that I no longer
want. I am willing to let it go." W-51.5.(5)*

Fear is a master of disguise. The ego uses these disguises as decoys, diverting our attention from the one cause of all our upsets. This one cause is always unconscious guilt. Fear, regardless of its form, must be recognized and surrendered to Spirit, so the miracle of True forgiveness can occur. For Atonement is the undoing of fear, and thus the undoing of guilt.

Every seeming attack we perceive arises from our unconscious guilt. Without guilt to spawn them, neither fear nor attack could exist. Conflict, abuse, betrayal, sickness, physical and emotional pain, financial scarcity, accidents, loss and death all stem from un-relinquished unconscious guilt. All guilt manifests as self-attack or self-sabotage.

But we cannot overcome this unconscious self-attack until we see it first. And we can't see it until we are willing to discover its only source of origin. No perceived attack ever finds its cause externally in the body, in others or the world. To believe the cause of our upset is outside is to fall into the ego's delusional trap. By not placing the cause where it really is, we will therefore be unable to heal it.

"Spirit, help me forgive myself for using (another, pain, sickness, the past, scarcity, etc.,) to attack myself, and to separate from your Love as my Holy Self. Amen."

Unconscious guilt is the core of all our imagined needs and frustrated desires. Everything we think we need, and everything we defend against is prompted by unconscious fear of attack— of being alone, unloved, betrayed, abandoned, unworthy, unsupported, unheard and unseen.

We spend our life seeking substitutes for the forgotten, invulnerable God Self that we are. Perhaps we have a long list of pleasurable dreams we hope to experience before we die. But every instant in which we feel anguish or pain, is a direct unconscious result of our anticipation of attack or loss. That's what guilt is: The expectation of punishment in the form of attack—and the subsequent manifestation of it.

Our vague memory is that we abandoned God, by making this false self and world in which to hide from Love. And this is the nucleus of all guilt. We can't experience fear without a deep sense of guilt to trigger it.

There's nothing wrong with having dreams and goals, but let's look clearly at the motivation behind them: We want to seize every morsel of pleasure, approval, happiness, health and wealth in life, because we expect it could be cut off by suffering or death at any moment. The ego says, *"It's a short life, enjoy it while you can."* We greedily snatch every opportunity to get our needs met, before death takes us. Because of un-relinquished guilt, this is our expectation.

Let's look at the idea of retirement. Retirement from what? Many compromise themselves throughout their working lives to feed the family, fund education, buy a home and the adult toys that help make life's regular bouts of bitterness taste just a bit sweeter.

So the ego says, *"With only a few short years left before we die, let's make up for a life of sacrifice by cramming these remaining years with a taste of freedom. We deserve it, after all we have sacrificed!"* Yet the cost of compromising our self is pain. It is never freedom, as the ego would have us believe.

Whenever we sacrifice, we unconsciously demand payment. The outcome is we end up paying. Why is this? Because in Truth, only one self exists. The payment exacted is most often attack on the body through aging and illness, followed by death. The joke is on us.

There would be no need for retirement or deferred freedom if there were no separate self to believe in scarcity and sacrifice. Only a separate self fears being attacked, alone, cheated, unloved, unworthy, unsupported, broke, sick, unheard or unseen. The Holy Self does not experience any of these states.

Can you imagine what it would be like to live out from a wholly healed Self? As the ego's projections of self-attack are withdrawn through genuine forgiveness, nothing would remain to defend against. No false goals to strive for, as there would be no needs not already met. And nothing would remain as a threat to be resisted. Can you imagine the freedom—the total liberation from suffering and responsibility?

If we could only see how much we stand to gain by wholeheartedly forgiving the world! Every idol we place our faith in will betray us. This is the nature of ego idols. Once attained, these cherished idols invariably leave us with a sense of incompletion, or worse. Our special relationships, whether romantic or otherwise, all fall into this category.

Yet these relationships can only seem to betray us, because we betrayed our self first. We chose to abandon our Holy Self to find someone or something out there to complete us instead.

What is a relationship *for*? This question pertains to all our relationships, including those with children, parents, siblings, partners, friends and colleagues. They have but one purpose—what is it? Is it to fulfill the ego's assigned role of parent, lover, spouse, child, friend or colleague? Is the purpose to get our emotional needs met? Or perhaps to get our physical needs met, through financial security or sex? Do we use our relationships to fulfill our inherent sense of incompletion?

The answers to these questions must be courageously exhumed and released to Spirit. If you wholeheartedly will to know your own invulnerability and guiltlessness, your unassailable security, happiness and joy, you must examine your motives with complete honesty. Only by doing so can you engage in any real relationships—ones that cannot be threatened by anyone or anything.

The sole purpose of all relationships is forgiveness. How else can you unearth your own unconscious self-hatred and guilt, except by being shown them? How else will you heal the only need you have, the sense of separation from your beloved Holy Self?

Like I did for so many years, some still choose to carry the scars of childhood. Our parents or others may or may not have behaved monstrously; that is not the point. The deeper Truth is we chose to enter this life for one reason only. We wanted to learn to forgive our self for using others and situations to attack us. My forgiveness was not so much of my mother, but in learning to forgive myself for using her for my own self-attack. This is quantum forgiveness, and as it was accomplished, my unconscious guilt magnet for attracting self-sabotage was undone.

Forgiveness undoes our unconscious desire for self-sabotage. If we knew and trusted the guiltlessness that lies undisturbed within our Holy Self, we would be unable to feel fear in any form. This includes all of fear's disguises, as stated earlier: Anger, frustration, conflict, the need to control, jealousy, fatigue, worry, scarcity, sadness, pain, disease, depression and feelings of victimhood.

I now feel great gratitude for all the uncomfortable challenges I've encountered in my life. Without them, I would never have recognized the source of all attack is within my own mind. I now know I have the power to overcome any attack, because it's always self-attack. I have cultivated great appreciation for forgiveness opportunities as they arise, as I recognize they form the breadcrumb trail leading me out of the dark dream of terror. In fact, they carry me gently Home to the one Holy Self.

Ask Spirit to reveal where you still judge others, yourself, the past or God. Ask to see where you have abandoned or betrayed yourself through self-dishonesty. When we betray or abandon our self, we unconsciously sacrifice our Truth in exchange for illusion. This illusion might come in the form of special love, security, money or approval, to name but a few. And whenever we sacrifice, we pay the price.

Invite Spirit to help you forgive yourself for using these people or experiences to separate from your Holy Self. These grievances are always self-accusations that induce guilt, thereby denying you access to the safety of your own indestructible innocence. Following is a powerful prayer to do just this:

"Spirit, please reveal to me my guiltlessness. Show me my complete invulnerability in your Love. And let me rest safely in the shelter of my innocence that I share within the oneness of all. Thank you. Amen."

THE ATONEMENT: AN IMMEDIATE BRIDGE FROM SUFFERING TO PEACE

Our Holy Self rests within the one Mind of God. Yet as long as we think we're in this body and world, we are split-minded between ego and Spirit. Both appear to have reality. And while we value both, we will experience the suffering wrought by this intolerable state of mind.

Atonement is the undoing of the split mind. It is the return of awareness to our divine innocence, eternal safety and security. Atonement gradually restores our one-minded or non-dual state, by helping us become increasingly right-minded.

While the split mind could be undone and returned to our original one mind in an instant if we truly desired *only* that, it seems to take time because of the fear and doubt we still harbor. We are free to choose between illusions and Truth, therefore we must freely choose only God's Will, if we are to see complete results instantly. Yet if our free will is still unconsciously driven by fear to some degree, we won't willingly dredge up that fear in its entirety, nor surrender it to Spirit for healing.

The Atonement is a divine gift offered us in any Holy Instant we sincerely desire peace more than suffering. This gift is always available, yet through the ego we often feel great resistance to it. No matter what symptoms our suffering may present, there is always only one cause: Our belief we're separate from God. The effect of this cause is a deep sense of unworthiness and guilt. Just as there is only one cause for the many ego problems we face, there is also just one solution: To accept the Atonement.

Atonement is a miracle. This, the world's most powerful and under-valued tool, is much misunderstood. Tomas and I did not recognize its power; only recently have I seen and accepted the infinite healing it delivers. Until I experienced it for myself, I did not realize the immensity of its scope and impact. *Accepting Atonement is the single most important practice when undoing the concepts of separation and suffering.*

Atonement is a miracle available to us in every single now-moment. It is an immediate portal to the right-minded state. No matter what kind of agony we think we're in, Atonement is the undoing of the underlying cause of any manifestation of attack.

The suffering we experience through the ego is illusion—and it takes no effort to undo illusion. Once recognized as an illusion we no longer want, we simply let it go. Is there any effort, loss or sacrifice in letting go of something we don't want? Something that has caused us only suffering?

A few things require acknowledgment, if we are to embrace this particularly speedy means of undoing the ego. First is the subject of trust. Our trust rests with the ego and world more than with Spirit. Therefore, we may doubt the Atonement actually works. Why? Because it is so simple and requires so little of us. The ego is insulted by its simplicity.

In Atonement, we don't actually *do* anything; the ego and its effects are made obsolete. Atonement exists to undo what the ego appeared to manifest. It brings unholy illusion to Holiness, correcting our mistaken beliefs for the purpose of True healing.

> *"The Atonement does not make holy. You were created holy. It merely brings unholiness to holiness; or what you made to what you are. Bringing illusion to truth, or the ego to God, is the Holy Spirit's only function." T-14.IX.1:1-4*

The ego is rendered powerless in Atonement. Our part is to allow its undoing by surrendering our wrong perception. We admit we need help; we recognize our own faulty judgment and perception have resulted in scarcity, conflict or emotional/physical pain.

These are the warning signs we have perceived wrong-mindedly. We don't need to understand or analyze our ego misperceptions—we just have to be willing to exchange them for right-minded perception. The ego is completely cast aside in favor of Atonement. In an authentic Holy Instant, ego is thoroughly discarded. In that instant of perfect Atonement, we choose to remember our dependence remains exclusively on God, and never on the ego. The ego falls away in our awareness, perfectly eclipsed by God's Love.

> "It is this that makes the holy instant so easy and so natural. You make it difficult, because you insist there must be more that you need do. You find it difficult to accept the idea that you need give so little, to receive so much. And it is very hard for you to realize it is not personally insulting that your contribution and the Holy Spirit's are so extremely disproportionate." T-18.IV.7:1-4

> "Forget not that it has been your decision to make everything that is natural and easy for you impossible. If you believe the holy instant is difficult for you, it is because you have become the arbiter of what is possible, and remain unwilling to give place to One Who knows. The whole belief in orders of difficulty in miracles is centered on this. Everything God wills is not only possible, but has already happened." T-18.IV.8:1-4

The healing has already happened! Nothing more is required. This is the foundation of the Atonement. We must not waver or doubt the Atonement's immense power, even if it does not yet appear to us that healing has occurred. What we see and feel with the body's senses is not real. The ego sends our senses out to the body or world, to report back what *it* projected. It wants us to react to these phenomena as if they were real. Its existence depends on our belief in its phenomena and our reactions to it. We must not fall into its trap.

Accepting Atonement affords us right-minded vision. We remember the body's eyes see only what the ego chooses. We look beyond the appearance of suffering, and ask to see only the Truth beneath it.

THE MOST HATEFUL RELATIONSHIP: THE BODY

My longest and most hate-filled relationship has been with the body. More than any human relationship, the body has appeared to betray me repeatedly. Despite this, as I review all my life relationships, I see this was the last one to be turned over to Spirit for healing. (I am not alone in this. Our relationship with the body is the final special relationship we all willingly surrender to Spirit.)

The body was the last repository for my belief in sin, guilt and attack. Although my human relationships had been miraculously transformed through forgiveness over the years, my relationship with the body remained unhealed. It was not until Tomas was diagnosed with cancer that I seriously offered True prayer and surrender, concerning the body.

Although we know intellectually the body is an illusion, this fact cannot be known in experience until the body itself is fully surrendered to Love instead of fear. And I didn't realize we must work *with* the body, using it as a vehicle for unearthing unconscious guilt, before we can transcend the body itself. If we avoid doing this, we will unconsciously invite guilt to punish the body through pain, decay or disease, ending the cycle once again in physical death.

I did not surrender the body to Love until recently. I had allowed the ego to use the body to convince me it was both my sustenance and my identity. To some, the body is a revered identity used for pleasure or pride; to others like myself in the past, it is largely used for pain. I wanted very badly to escape the body. Little did I realize this desire to escape the body always leads to separation and death.

There is no hierarchy of illusions. Using the body for pleasure, pride, shame or pain—it's all the same. They all share the same purpose, which is to convince us our identity is the body and not perfect Spirit. The ego uses the body to make something out of nothing. The body becomes an idol to be either revered or resented. All these beliefs attract separation, suffering and death.

In my first twenty years of *Course* study, I was confused about the body. I unknowingly used my favorite quote, *"I am not a body, I am free,"* to justify my refusal to use the body as Jesus asks. In a different quote, we are asked to do as Jesus did, and more. He overcame the body because He knew without a doubt His Identity was before and beyond the body. The body, when correctly perceived, is just a projected image whose only purpose is to communicate the Truth that Love cannot be overcome by fear.

Jesus used His body to demonstrate the power of God totally reverses all ego laws. He was a living expression of divine indestructibility. Through His resurrection, He overcame death itself, and urges us to do the same. We are not asked to suffer, we're only asked to reject the ego's interpretation of the body's purpose, as well as the ego's laws. We will not, cannot see the glory of God's laws, as long as we maintain allegiance to the ego's laws. Only one set of laws can be embraced at any one time. And we cannot reverse the ego's laws if we refuse to use the body as Jesus asks.

My own learning was greatly tested and accelerated by Tomas' journey through cancer and physical death. I didn't see then that Tomas and I, despite our two decades of *Course* study, still had a foot in each camp, so to speak. We had not exhumed all our hidden dependencies on the ego and world. Many unconscious beliefs had been exposed and surrendered, yet there were others we were unprepared to look at or release.

I now recognize I lacked the single-mindedness required to help someone heal completely. To heal means we must prioritize peace over the desire to have the body healed. I was simply unwilling to hold such an unwavering priority at that time. Peace arises from our unflinching desire for healed perception above all other concerns. To have peace above all else, we must truly yearn for it by choosing only peace, despite appearances. And to desire peace as our sole priority requires great trust in Spirit, along with an unwavering certainty we are absolutely worthy of healing.

Peace is an essential component of healing through the miracle. The miracle is blocked by the presence of fear, so healing cannot come about through fear. Fear signals illusion is believed to be real. And while we still believe illusion is real, it cannot be healed. I believed, at least partly, in the illusion of Tomas' illness. And therefore the miracle could not be complete.

My trust in Spirit is so much greater now than it was when Tomas passed. I still have a ways to go before my trust is complete, but I am aware of this. I remain vigilant only for God, offering to Spirit every sign of resistance that surfaces in my mind. My current classroom is once again the body. It's time to heal the last of my special relationships. I am enjoying the process. To transcend the body it must first be seen, accepted, excavated with Spirit for the unconscious secrets it holds, and forgiven.

The ego tells me this is an impossible task. It says I am not advanced enough in faith, and will therefore fail miserably. But that's the ego's belief, not mine. Jesus' deeper teachings involve a radical perceptual shift. They are opposite to the world's mistaken beliefs in disease, conflict, scarcity and death. Through the Atonement, all mistaken beliefs can be healed in an instant—any instant—regardless of the seeming lack of mastery possessed by the student. Only willingness is required.

SAFETY IS THE COMPLETE RELINQUISHMENT OF ATTACK: SICKNESS AS ATTACK

Disease, scarcity, conflict and pain are not God's Will. Therefore, they are not part of our True Identity. Throughout my years of *Course* study, I thought I knew what Jesus meant by "attack." He often tells us our safety comes from complete relinquishment of attack. This means forgiving others for what they did not do. So I learned to forgive myself for using others to attack myself. That's True forgiveness. But now, as I am shown more deeply the intent behind Jesus' teachings, I see He is asking us for nothing less than *complete* relinquishment of attack. I recognize there's quite a bit more to it than I previously thought.

Yes, it's necessary to forgive others for what they did not do, yet we must also learn to identify how we use the body for attack. In doing so, we learn to forgive our self for using the body as a weapon to prove attack is real. Whenever we use sickness, lack or pain to attack our self, we demonstrate to the world that we are indeed separate from God's Love, and from each other.

Sickness, scarcity and pain are very common forms of self-attack. When we exhibit any of these symptoms, we unknowingly demonstrate to our self and others that attack is real—and that we can be attacked. If we believe in these symptoms, we cannot forgive what we still believe is real.

While we believe any form of attack is real, God's Love is *not*. As Jesus explains, all forms of sickness are signs the mind is split. In sickness, we do not accept the unified purpose of God's Loving and healing Will. We must choose only one purpose, either the ego's or Spirit's. To believe in these mutually exclusive purposes simultaneously, is to split the mind in extremely painful fashion. This is the cause and continuation of all separation and suffering.

> *"Yet sickness is not of the body, but of the mind. All forms of sickness are signs that the mind is split, and does not accept a unified purpose." T-8.IX.8:6-7 "Safety is the complete relinquishment of attack. No compromise is possible in this. Teach attack in any form and you have learned it, and it will hurt you. Yet this learning is not immortal, and you can unlearn it by not teaching it" T-6.III.3:7-10*

There is no hierarchy of illusion. The body seems to be the final hiding place for the ego; its very last stronghold against God. Physical death is the goal of its final defense against Love. All unconscious attack thoughts must be relinquished, in order to restore the body's purpose to God.

> " A sick body does not make any sense. It could not make sense because sickness is not what the body is for. Sickness is meaningful only if the two basic premises on which the ego's interpretation of the body rests are true; that the body is for attack, and that you are a body. Without these premises sickness is inconceivable." T-8.VIII.6:5-8

> "Sickness is a way of demonstrating that you can be hurt. It is a witness to your frailty, your vulnerability, and your extreme need to depend on external guidance. The ego uses this as its best argument for your need for [its] guidance. It dictates endless prescriptions for avoiding catastrophic outcomes." T-8.VIII.6:1-4

HOW IS HEALING ACCOMPLISHED THROUGH ATONEMENT?

Remember the body is purely an effect of a cause that occurs within our mind. The cause of the body's state of health is always in the mind, no matter what the ego believes to the contrary. The body is never a cause in itself, no matter how hard the ego tries to convince us otherwise.

True healing transpires as a result of our joined Will with God. This is the *only* cause of healing. Atonement is the recognition we are not the ego. In the Holy Instant of Atonement, the ego does not exist in our awareness. And by withdrawing our belief in ego in that instant, the Reality of perfect healing is then free to replace the ego's unreality. This is how True healing occurs.

NOUK SANCHEZ   269

God's Love is the only True cause. Love, joy, peace and health are its effects. But through the ego, we seem to experience suffering. No effect can exist without a legitimate cause, yet the ego does not exist in Truth. Therefore it cannot be a legitimate cause. If it does not exist, how could it cause pain, scarcity, conflict or sickness? If it does not exist in Reality as a cause of suffering, how can the effects of sickness, conflict, scarcity or pain be real? They can only be real if we want them to. If we choose to cling to the belief they are real, we endow them with seeming reality.

Pause a moment, and ask Spirit to help you see this monumental Truth. Once you have fully recognized this, you will never believe consistently in the ego again.

> "Fatherhood [is] creation. Love must be extended. Purity is not confined. It is the nature of the innocent to be forever uncontained, without a barrier or limitation. Thus is purity not of the body. Nor can it be found where limitation is. The body can be healed by its effects, which are as limitless as is itself. Yet must all healing come about because the mind is recognized as not within the body, and its innocence is quite apart from it, and where all healing is. Where, then, is healing? Only where its cause is given its effects. For sickness is a meaningless attempt to give effects to causelessness, and make it be a cause." T-28.II.2.

> "Always in sickness does the Son of God attempt to make himself his cause, and not allow himself to be his Father's Son. For this impossible desire, he does not believe that he is Love's Effect, and must be cause because of what he is. The cause of healing is the only Cause of everything. It has but [one] Effect. And in that recognition, causelessness is given no effects and none is seen." T-28.II.3:1-5

In the Holy Instant, we willingly accept Atonement and the ego disappears for the duration of that instant. It vanishes as the single cause of suffering. So what happens to physical symptoms, once their cause has vanished? Without a cause to uphold them, the effects or symptoms *must* disappear. This is how Jesus healed the sick, and performed so many healing miracles. He had surrendered His belief in a hierarchy of illusions, and thus reversed effect and cause. He knew and demonstrated this:

> *"There is no order of difficulty in miracles. One is not "harder" or "bigger" than another. They are all the same."* T-1.I.1:1-3

Jesus knew there is no ego in Truth. He knew all physical effects of the ego are mere hallucinations. The ego's laws, including the laws of nature, held no influence over His right-minded dominion in God's Love.

The ego uses the body against the mind. It does this because it is extremely fearful we will discover the mind's limitless power. In the acceptance of this power, it knows we could end the reign of the ego and body in an instant.

> *"The ego uses the body to conspire against your mind, and because the ego realizes that its "enemy" can end them both merely by recognizing they are not part of you, they join in the attack together. This is perhaps the strangest perception of all, if you consider what it really involves. The ego, which is not real, attempts to persuade the mind, which [is] real, that the mind is the ego's learning device; and further, that the body is more real than the mind is. No one in his right mind could possibly believe this, and no one in his right mind does believe it."* T-6.IV.5.

A prerequisite to True healing is the withdrawal of belief that our suffering is caused by anything other than the ego mind itself. We must review our own hierarchy of illusions, including the laws we believe sustain and attack us. We look at them with Spirit, asking sincerely that our perception of these be healed.

Food does not make you fat, and disease does not make you sick. Unconscious guilt is the sole cause of all suffering. Our return to the awareness of Love as our Holy Self is the end of all suffering. In every moment we choose Atonement, we return to this awareness of Love. Each return we make to this Holy Instant strengthens our trust in Love, and weakens our belief in fear.

Accepting Atonement is the healing of both cause and effect. Cause and effect are always together in our mind and are never separate. Heal the cause Truly, and the effects must follow.

> *"Healing might thus be called a counter-dream, which cancels out the dream of sickness in the name of truth, but not in truth itself. Just as forgiveness overlooks all sins that never were accomplished, healing but removes illusions that have not occurred."* W-137.5:1-2

Atonement heals with gentle certainty, and cures all sickness— because it heals the mind itself that causes sickness. We may still see symptoms of disease, scarcity or pain, yet because we've accepted the Atonement, we trust in God's Love. We choose to look past these symptoms, and onto the shining face of Christ beyond them. We no longer choose to believe the effects of mis-thought. We know without a doubt we have already surrendered our miscreation to Spirit, and are therefore no longer burdened with the responsibility of trying to heal the ailment our self.

We have placed this responsibility with Spirit, not with the ego. We may still choose to use magic remedies, but we take them consciously *with* Spirit, asking sincerely that our perception be healed. The guilt that caused the problem has been wholly surrendered to Spirit, and the remedy has been accepted. Therefore, with guilt removed, sickness has no basis to continue, nor to return. Atonement heals the single cause of all adversity, and demonstrates that the right mind holds dominion over the ego's misuse of the body.

> *"Atonement heals with certainty, and cures all sickness. For the mind which understands that sickness can be nothing but a dream is not deceived by forms the dream may take.*

Sickness where guilt is absent cannot come, for it is but another form of guilt. Atonement does not heal the sick, for that is not a cure. It takes away the guilt that makes the sickness possible. And that is cure indeed. For sickness now is gone, with nothing left to which it can return." W-140.4.

"Healing is the one ability everyone can develop and must develop if he is to be healed." T-7.V.3:1

"The Holy Spirit does not work by chance, and healing that is of Him [always] works." T-7.V.5:1

WHAT ARE WE SECRETLY TERRIFIED OF? AND WHY DO WE REJECT HEALING?

A Course in Miracles often refers to the split in our mind. What is the nature of this split? The ego needs guilt to survive—yet we find guilt intolerable, because it blocks our experience of the infinite security, joy and peace found only in God's Love. This push-pull concerning guilt represents the deepest split within our mind. We are torn between the heartfelt yearning to return to Love, and the ego's extremely convincing threats.

Our greatest desire is to reunite with our perfectly innocent essence, the Holy Self. Yet if we retain guilt as the ego demands, we cannot be our Self. Only by letting our self be convinced the ego is our identity, can we possibly be compelled to keep projecting guilt, thereby hanging onto it. As we have seen, holding onto guilt is sure to manifest as ongoing unconscious self-attack. This is why we are secretly attracted to pain, aging, sickness and death. They are among our most cherished symbols of guilt.

Can you see how the ego works? Our guilt is projected as attack onto the body in the forms of pain, illness, aging and death. As a result of our belief in their reality, we keep the guilt in our mind. While suffering of any kind is evident, it witnesses to the guilt yet to be healed within the mind.

Guilt is also projected, and thus kept as self-attack through judgment of others, self and world. Yet guilt cannot be part of our Real Identity, because guilt is antithetical to God's all-encompassing, Loving innocence. We can only suffer if we believe we are guilty. If we continue to judge independently, apart from Spirit, it means we have rejected our Holy Self in favor of guilt.

> "The ultimate purpose of projection is always to get rid of guilt. Yet, characteristically, the ego attempts to get rid of guilt from its viewpoint only, for much as the ego wants to retain guilt [you] find it intolerable, since guilt stands in the way of your remembering God, Whose pull is so strong that you cannot resist it. On this issue, then, the deepest split of all occurs, for if you are to retain guilt, as the ego insists, [you cannot be you.] Only by persuading you that it is you could the ego possibly induce you to project guilt, and thereby keep it in your mind." T-13.II.1.

The ego projects guilt in an attempt to get rid of it, yet we end up amassing it. Then, we feel even more guilty or fearful, but have no idea why. This feeling may not come in the form of recognizable guilt, but rather a sense of impending threat: Guilt demands and expects punishment.

The guilt we carry makes us feel inadequate and unworthy, yet the deeper belief is kept at bay. We might uneasily believe we have somehow "failed," yet we don't realize it is our Holy Self we are failing, because we persist in hanging onto guilt. And in this unintentional Self-betrayal, we carry a deep sense of grief.

> "Yet consider how strange a solution the ego's arrangement is. You project guilt to get rid of it, but you are actually merely concealing it. You do experience the guilt, but you have no idea why. On the contrary, you associate it with a

*weird assortment of "ego ideals," which the ego claims you
have failed. Yet you have no idea that you are failing the
Son of God by seeing him as guilty. Believing you are no
longer you, you do not realize that you are failing yourself."*
T-13.II.2.

To carry guilt or judgment of any kind separates us from the
Love that dwells within as our Holy Self. Carrying guilt is akin to
abandoning the greatest Love of our life; it is heart-breaking and
tragic. This Self-betrayal is deeply unconscious, and represents
the dreadful belief we have indeed betrayed the Son of God.

Lurking very deep within the darkened recesses of the ego mind
lies a stark terror: We believe we killed the Son of God. Hence our
persistent sense of threat, the hallmark of the ego's attraction to
self-attack. This self-attack is seen as justifiable punishment for
the seeming sin we never committed. This secret terror and its
consequences are kept tightly bound and hidden from awareness.

The murder of the Son of God never happened. This seeming
sin is only a symbol that reenacts the betrayal of our Holy
Self—for it is our Self we abandoned. And in this one act, we
condemned our self to death, for we have willingly made our self
subject to the ego's cycle of birth and death.

Through the ego, we continue to project our guilt onto the
body, others and the world, in the forms of sickness, pain, loss,
conflict, scarcity, and physical death itself. The ego seeks guilt
through condemnation, perceiving guiltlessness as the ultimate
blasphemy. This is contrived to shield from our awareness that we
abandoned our most deeply cherished, eternally guiltless Holy Self.

*"The darkest of your hidden cornerstones holds your belief
in guilt from your awareness. For in that dark and secret
place is the realization that you have betrayed God's Son
by condemning him to death. You do not even suspect
this murderous but insane idea lies hidden there, for the
ego's destructive urge is so intense that nothing short of the
crucifixion of God's Son can ultimately satisfy it. It does not*

know who the Son of God is because it is blind. Yet let it perceive guiltlessness anywhere, and it will try to destroy it because it is afraid." T-13.II.3.

In the crucifixion of Jesus, we can find an exceptionally relevant depiction of our own carefully hidden secret. This terrible secret, when witnessed with the gentle Love of Spirit, will give way to our own resurrection into endless joy.

The crucifixion of Jesus is a symbol of the ego's ongoing attempts to kill our one Holy Self. The ego attempted to annihilate its greatest enemy. It thought it could kill the sacred, inviolate innocence of Love's one Self. Through the crucifixion, the ego continues to project guilt onto us all, in its effort to eradicate forever the memory of our guiltless invulnerability in God's Love.

Our Holy Self *is* the Kingdom of Heaven. By harboring self-attack through judgment and guilt, we unknowingly exile our self from the uninterrupted joy of Heaven's Kingdom within. Instead we fall for the ego's preposterous idea that Heaven is accessed through physical death! Yet death is an idea apart from God, who is infinite Life. Endless Life is our nature in God.

Guilt beckons us to the illusion of death, to save us from awakening to the glorious Life that lies within our own Holy innocence. This Holy Self, the very heart of Love itself, is our greatest terror. It is the reason we continue to value guilt.

If we are resistant to undoing the ego's beliefs, values, laws and idols, we must be equally resistant to embodying our Holy Self. This must mean we still cherish guilt and self-attack as our strongest defense against the memory of the Love we are—because within the recovery of this memory, all guilt must fall away.

The joyful resurrection of Jesus is a powerful symbol of how our dream will unfold. As we courageously forgive everyone and everything the ego made to attack us, we will witness the resurrection of our own eternally innocent Holy Self. And the holiness of this sanctified Self will indeed reverse all the laws of this world. It will return us to a state of all-encompassing Love with no opposite. This state is the Real World.

ACCEPT YOUR HEALING
IS ALREADY ACCOMPLISHED

If you have forgiven yourself for unknowingly using someone, yourself or a situation to attack yourself, *and* you have already accepted the Atonement's correction of your perception, it is important to let it go. You must trust your misperception has been healed, regardless of appearances at the level of form.

If you still feel loss of peace, it means the ego has made yet another judgment. Do not believe it. Once you allow a Holy Instant where judgment is genuinely surrendered and Atonement has been accepted, it is done. To doubt it has been healed is self-doubt. This healing has been brought about by Holy Spirit, not by your mistaken identity. Any doubt arising comes only from the ego. Trust is necessary now, as Love without trust is impossible. Doubt *and* Love cannot co-exist. Choose one, and the other must fall away.

Atonement means to accept the healing of our faulty perception, which is the one cause of all suffering. It is not our role to hang onto that which is atoned for; our part in it is finished. Once it is given to Spirit, forgiveness takes place. It is not the ego's responsibility to retain it. To hold onto concern, conflict, guilt or doubt allows the ego to perpetuate guilt and suffering. It acts as a block to receiving and witnessing the certainty and consistency of God's healing through the miracle. Our responsibility is to offer Spirit whatever upsets us, to be reinterpreted on our behalf. And then to trust implicitly that God's perfect healing is done.

> "If the sole responsibility of the miracle worker is to accept the Atonement for himself, and I assure you that it is, then the responsibility for [what] is atoned for cannot be yours."..."If you accept the remedy for disordered thought, a remedy whose efficacy is beyond doubt, how can its symptoms remain?" T-5.V.7:8,12

You are not responsible for the problem itself. The ego is. You are responsible for choosing to perceive through the ego, thereby believing in the problem's reality. There is no problem, apart from your erroneous perception of it.

The ego is an impersonal suggestion of sin or evil. It is not real. No one has a personal ego, for the ego is not a specific entity, but a thought system. The ego is only an impersonal projection. You are neither personally responsible for causing the ego in your mind, nor for fixing its illusory problems. In any case, you are not capable of accomplishing either. You are however, responsible for releasing your mistaken perception and accepting the miracle of Atonement instead.

The ego is a thought system we either choose to believe or reject; it is an impersonal stream of thought based on guilt and fear. This thought stream runs like a non-stop looping movie. It doesn't belong to anyone, it just streams its projections over and over, because that's what it was made to do.

We are created by God as His one Child, the Holy Self. In our creation, we knew we were one. We knew our Identity was indestructible, because it was—and is—Love without opposite. We knew we were an expression of God's eternally Loving Will, the Kingdom of Heaven itself. This remains the Truth of who we are, but we have temporarily forgotten. We've gotten lost in the ego's endlessly looping movie of birth and death.

Caught up in the ego's hypnotic amnesia, we have each mistaken this impersonal, fear-filled movie for our own personal identity. As if it's *my* life, my body, my partner, my family and so on. Even in the idea of *my* birth and *my* death, we seize a fragment of the ego's impersonal movie and make it our own. By grasping so tightly onto this impersonal thought system, we unknowingly abdicate our power in God. We forfeit it entirely, preferring to submit our self instead to the ego's illusory laws of suffering, separation and death.

A common and unrecognized trap: The idea of a personal ego
In one of our tele-classes, one participant whom I will call Penny (not her real name) courageously shared a recent traumatic

incident, one that seemed extremely difficult to forgive within the ego's hierarchy of illusions. She witnessed an animal being beaten to death.

We all felt the shock waves of this horrifying act as she recounted the story. Penny was still feeling traumatized two weeks after the event, and although she had attempted forgiveness many times, she was having great difficulty seeing it with Holy Spirit's right-minded vision.

Penny felt overwhelming guilt, believing she was personally responsible for having projected this terribly disturbing scene. Because she had witnessed it, she mistakenly believed this abuse had been manifested personally *by her*, believing it to be caused by her own unhealed guilt—her own personal ego. But there is no personal ego! Whatever we make personal will be hijacked by the ego to increase our guilt and suffering. The ego is an impersonal thought system that is streaming all the time. Penny did not play a part in the cause of the incident, just because she witnessed it. Let me explain.

The ego's impersonal movie will show us all kinds of horrendous phenomena, thereby inviting us to stay engaged within its endless cycle of guilt, fear and death. This is precisely where we must learn to choose again. *Everything* that occurs is neutral. Our only responsibility is to remain aware of our triggers—the times we feel threat of any kind, to any degree. And then to exchange these misperceptions for the Atonement's miraculous forgiveness.

If I am triggered by something, it's not me personally who is triggered. It is the filter I have chosen to look through, which is generating wrong-minded fearfulness. Only fear can seem to be personal. If I am triggered, I am choosing to see with the ego's thought system. I view the event through the ego's lens of guilt and fear. *The event itself is always neutral.* No matter how shocking, unfair or cruel it may appear, the event always remains perfectly neutral in Truth.

In God's Truth, suffering, cruelty or unfairness is impossible. Therefore it is always *my interpretation* of the event that either reinforces my guilt (because I have identified with the ego's interpretation) or frees me from it (because I have chosen Truth instead). If I perceive suffering then I do not perceive with God.

To invoke authentic healing through the miracle, I must, if only for an instant, be willing to join with Spirit in my right mind. If I feel triggered, I am in the wrong mind, and cannot offer True healing to self or others. I must choose to look past the ego's appearances, and bring *myself* through the forgiveness/ Atonement process.

As I forgive by accepting Atonement, my world will heal because it exists only in my mind. As my world heals, the seeming perpetrators, along with the so-called victims are shown their own innocence, thereby receiving True healing along with me.

The ego's movie of pain and suffering and the Holy Spirit's movie of the Happy Dream exist simultaneously within my mind. Without fail, I will witness the world I presently value. Do I choose for innocence and Love, or continued guilt and pain for all? As I learn to look past disturbing appearances with Spirit, the Real World or Happy Dream is revealed to me. But I will not be able to see, or live out from the glory of the Real World, until I choose to systematically reject and undo the ego's filter of wrong-mindedness.

I mention Penny's story here, because it illustrates clearly a common ego trap fallen into by students of the *Course*. We withdraw our projected guilt from outside, others and the world, as Penny did, yet instead of wholeheartedly giving it to Spirit, we inadvertently project that guilt onto our self. Guilt is guilt, whether we see it outside or within; it's all the same attack on our Holy Self.

Judgment, self-judgment and guilt are all immediate signals we are rejecting God's Love. Judgment and guilt are our greatest blocks to the awareness of Love's presence. Whenever they show up, we need to ask Spirit to heal our perception.

The Atonement is the undoing of fear. It is accomplished in any now-moment in which we choose to wholeheartedly surrender our perception to Spirit's Love for healing. But we must sincerely *accept* the Atonement for it to be effective.

In Atonement, we receive the miracle of true and complete forgiveness. It is the miraculous remedy for the ego and all its seeming effects.

"Forgiveness that is learned of me does not use fear to undo fear. Nor does it make real the unreal and then destroy it. Forgiveness through the Holy Spirit lies simply in looking beyond error from the beginning, and thus keeping it unreal for you. Do not let any belief in its realness enter your mind, or you will also believe that you must undo what you have made in order to be forgiven. What has no effect does not exist, and to the Holy Spirit the effects of error are nonexistent. By steadily and consistently cancelling out all its effects, everywhere and in all respects, He teaches that the ego does not exist and proves it." T-9.IV.5.

Remember this: We cannot forgive what we still believe is real.

The ego's plan is to have you see error clearly first, and then overlook it. Yet how can you overlook what you have made real? By seeing it clearly, you have made it real and [cannot] overlook it. T-9.IV.4:4-6

"Give Him your thoughts, and He will give them back as miracles which joyously proclaim the wholeness and the happiness God wills His Son, as proof of His eternal Love. And as each thought is thus transformed, it takes on healing power from the Mind which saw the truth in it, and failed to be deceived by what was falsely added. All the threads of fantasy are gone. And what remains is unified into a perfect Thought that offers its perfection everywhere." W-151.14.

THE UNDOING OF FEAR

"If you want peace, you must give up the idea of conflict entirely and for all time." T-7.VI.8:9

The purpose of accepting Atonement is the undoing of fear and thus, the undoing of unconscious guilt. Everything we think, believe or do while not in a state of unconditional Love and peace, is accomplished through fear. It is a product of the ego.

This includes most of our seemingly caring and loving acts. Before we begin to reverse the ego belief system, we act almost entirely from special love. This version of love, no matter how appealing it sometimes seems, is always based on fear and separation. Therefore, it is really hate in disguise.

If love provokes a sense of threat or loss, a sense of obligation, a desire to limit or control another, or a need to compromise our self in order to be loved, it cannot be real Love. Concern or worry about another's physical or emotional wellbeing is a symptom of fear, not of Love. All anxiety or concern is propelled by fear, never by Love. Real Love necessitates trust in only God's Loving Will. Real Love without trust is impossible. In total trust, Love looks past the seductive appearances projected by the ego, and fixes its unwavering intent only on the Truth of Love beneath the upsetting form of the problem.

Whenever we try to problem solve apart from Spirit, we do it with the ego. And the ego will sabotage our effort, because that's its job. Fear comes in thousands of different disguises; the form doesn't matter. What *does* matter is recognizing the unconscious guilt fueling all fear.

Every desire to control, heal or problem solve independently from Spirit, is propelled by a deeply hidden fear of punishment. This fear of punishment is our unknown, and therefore un-relinquished fear of God. If we experience fear or any of its byproducts, it is a sure sign we are trusting in the ego. There is no compromise in this.

When we accept Atonement, we recognize the problem is no longer our responsibility. We remove it from the ego's to-do list, exchanging our erroneous perception for healed perception—which occurs the instant we wholeheartedly give it to Spirit. The Atonement undoes guilt and fear, the moment we agree to let our self be restored to sanity.

> *"The presence of fear is a sure sign that you are trusting in your own strength." W-48.3:1*

Atonement is crucial to authentic healing, because it undoes the guilt and fear responsible for every seeming problem we experience.

TRUE DENIAL
AS A POWERFUL PROTECTIVE DEVICE

One of the most crucial components of the forgiveness process is the conscious decision to deny any illusion can cause harm. In the *Course*, this is referred to as *true denial*. True denial is a powerful protective device, because in denying illusions the power to hurt us, we are declaring only God's Will is Real. And in this declaration, we call forth God's Loving Reality.

We are then able to invoke miracles by calling only on His Will. This is how Jesus healed the sick and raised the dead. True denial protects us from belief in the illusion that suffering is real. It protects us from temptation to believe in a will apart from God. Right-mindedness depends upon making this essential correction.

> *"True denial is a powerful protective device. You can and should deny any belief that error can hurt you. This kind of denial is not a concealment but a correction. Your right mind depends on it. Denial of error is a strong defense*

of truth, but denial of truth results in miscreation, the projections of the ego." T-2.II.2:1-5

"Can pain be part of peace, or grief of joy? Can fear and sickness enter in a mind where love and perfect holiness abide? Truth must be all-inclusive, if it be the truth at all. Accept no opposites and no exceptions, for to do so is to contradict the truth entirely." W-152.2:4-7

To accept Atonement is the most powerful act there is. In the Holy Instant of Atonement, the ego and its hallucination cease to exist. Instead, we consciously invoke and join with God's Loving Will, which is unlimited in its power.

To successfully transfer trust from the ego's reality to God's Reality, we must first redefine for our self the nature of God's True Will. If we still believe (whether consciously or unconsciously) that God gives painful lessons, or that we must make decisions and plans independent from Spirit in order to be safe, it means we unconsciously fear God.

While we still believe death or suffering are natural and inevitable parts of life, we will not know God and will therefore fear Him. We will fear our one Holy Self. But once we've recognized all forms of suffering and adversity are brought about not by God, but by our belief in the ego's projection of *its* god, we can breathe a huge sigh of relief! This recognition is crucial to invoking the power of the miracle. We cannot genuinely accept the extraordinary healing brought about by the miracle, unless we have begun to authentically recognize any form is suffering is never God's Will.

We vacillate between the ego and God, and no wonder. When we are unclear what is of God, and what is not of God, how can we be confident enough to make this distinction? How can we employ True denial, if we aren't sure whether True denial is true?

We can't invoke the miracle consistently until we learn to definitively say "no" to the ego. And we will lack this single-minded ability to say no, if we are still unsure of the nature of God's Will. Until we are clear on this, we will remain split.

"What is of God is His forever, and you are of God. Would He allow Himself to suffer? And would He offer His Son anything that is not acceptable to Him?" T-10.V.9:2-4

Therefore, in every instant you feel pain, conflict or threat, consciously ask yourself: *Is this God's Will for me? Is this joyful and Loving? Does this elicit warm feelings of wellbeing, a deep sense of inner security and healing?* If not, you can be sure your perception needs healing.

The problem, as you see it, does not exist. It never has. Only your perception of the problem requires healing, because it's only in your perception that the problem exists. While you still entertain the ego's suffering, choosing to believe the illusion's form requires healing, you immediately deny the miracle. For the moment you make a problem real, you separate effect from cause. And by doing so, you prevent the cause from being healed. Instead of denying the illusion, you deny the miracle—and this is exactly what the ego wants.

"Do not perceive anything God did not create or you are denying Him." T-10.V.13:1

The miracle's prerequisite is that we must accept the problem *does not exist* regardless of appearances. The problem is not, and never was God's Will. Yet nothing exists *but* God's infinitely Loving Will. Therefore, the primary task at hand is to clearly learn and know for our self the True attributes of God's Will. In making this effort, we can then confidently deny the reality of all that is not God's Will.

THE CAUSE IS NOT IN OTHERS, THE BODY, THE PAST OR THE WORLD

The ego sees the cause of suffering anywhere except where it really is: The mind. The cause for disease, loss, pain, scarcity or conflict is always believed to be in the body, or the world. Yet the cause can never be outside our mind. Our own misperception is always the sole cause of suffering.

As long as we continue to displace the cause of our problems by seeing it out there, True healing of our perception cannot take place. To invoke the miracle, we must acknowledge the only cause, so the only cure can be received. The body and world only exist as effects of their cause within our mind, so it matters a great deal which inner teacher we choose to trust. We manifest and perceive them from either the right mind or wrong mind.

The Atonement is mandatory to heal the one cause of suffering. We need it to correct our insane perception there is a real problem requiring a real solution. There are no problems in God's Love. God's Love is the remedy.

Yet we can't accept the remedy while we still choose to believe in the reality of what our body's senses tell us. We must choose which teacher to trust—belief in the reality of the problem and in the reality of God's remedy are mutually exclusive propositions.

We must release one in order to have the other. Will we forfeit God's remedy, the Atonement, and keep the problem by judging or trying to solve it independently from Spirit? Or will we offer our perception of suffering to Spirit for healing, and accept God's Loving remedy instead?

If we relinquish our belief in the problem's reality, we can invoke the miracle. Having made this crucial choice, we can willingly hand over our painful perception to Spirit. In any instant we choose corrected perception instead of ego belief, we can accept (and therefore receive) the miracle of healed perception through Atonement. This is the Holy Instant; no preparation for it is necessary.

Your natural state is perfect innocence. No matter what the ego may tempt you to believe about yourself, your True being is without sin or stain. God only knows you as the Love you are. Are you prepared to accept *only* this?

Acceptance of Atonement is the simplest, yet most profound accomplishment we could ever achieve in this world. Yet it's the hardest for the ego, because in the instant of Atonement, the ego ceases to exist in our awareness. Accepting Atonement is to accept our original pristine state of innocence and Love. It only takes an instant to wholeheartedly release our perception in exchange for the miracle.

> *"Atonement heals with certainty, and cures all sickness."* W-140.4:1

> *"Accept Atonement and you are healed. Atonement is the Word of God. Accept His Word and what remains to make sickness possible? Accept His Word and every miracle has been accomplished. To forgive is to heal. The teacher of God has taken accepting the Atonement for himself as his only function. What is there, then, he cannot heal? What miracle can be withheld from him?"* M-22.1:5-12

The miracle can be accepted for yourself, or on behalf of another; the other may still be in a body or not. Remember if you wish to help heal another, you must accept Atonement for *yourself*. The final step in the Atonement process is trust. Trust that healing has already been accomplished, regardless of any continuing appearances to the contrary.

> *"Yet love without trust is impossible, and doubt and trust cannot coexist."* M-7.4:6

> *"The real basis for doubt about the outcome of any problem that has been given to God's Teacher for resolution is always self-doubt. And that necessarily implies that trust has been placed in an illusory self, for only such a self can be doubted."* M-7.5:1-2

CHAPTER ELEVEN

THE SEVEN ESSENTIAL PRINCIPLES OF QUANTUM FORGIVENESS (ATONEMENT)

We're about to delve deeply into the principles and process of Atonement. This is the forgiveness process, the means through which we exchange our perception of suffering for miracles instead. The Atonement brings about the gradual reversal of all our ego beliefs, values and laws. In short, it is a monumental un-learning accomplishment, because it thoroughly reverses the ego's cause and effect. This is the undoing of the ego's world of suffering.

Only three years ago did I discover the critical principles involved in forgiveness, as Jesus teaches it. Like most *Course* students, I thought forgiveness would take place automatically when I set my good intentions to forgive. Yet I was clearly missing something. Countless futile attempts at forgiveness over the years proved there must be some error or omission on my part. With all my heart, I asked Jesus to teach me—to show me what he really means by forgiveness and Atonement.

According to Jesus, we spent millions of years teaching our self to separate from God's Love—and now we need to un-learn or reverse, via the miracle, the destructive illusions we have brought into being. For forgiveness and miracles to take place, seven critical principles must first be accepted. These seven principles contain reality-reversal properties in themselves, but when combined together, they act to bring in the mighty power of God's Love and healing.

A word of warning: Don't presume you already know these principles, just because they may sound familiar. Believe me, these are principles that must be learned through consistent application. It's only in their consistent application that undeniable miracles will unfold. This is how unswerving trust is developed in the power of God's Love and healing.

You've undoubtedly noticed I often repeat certain themes and principles, especially regarding Atonement. It's because I'm aware of the way our minds work: We understand a concept fully, which might lead us to think we've mastered this process. Yet when we are hit with a special challenge, fear or issue that renders us temporarily insane, we tend to completely forget these principles—no matter how thorough our comprehension. In the frequent repetition of this material, my aim is to allow these concepts to sink in deeply, beyond the surface understanding of the intellect.

For until these Truths become our natural default, we must be vigilant in our practice. These thought-reversal principles appear so often precisely because we need reminding over and over until they become second nature. Until this happens, please do book mark these pages on the Atonement/forgiveness process. Better still—print them out and keep them handy.

The seven basic principles of forgiveness/Atonement are:

1) **Apply true denial.**
Recall there is only one Power, and it is God's Loving Will. Therefore, steadfastly deny anything not of God's Love the power to hurt you or anyone else.

2) **Place cause and effect in their proper sequence.**
No matter the form of problem, all cause is in your mind and nowhere else. If you believe the cause is anywhere but in your mind, you will be unable to heal the cause or its seeming symptoms. Recall unconscious guilt is self-attack projected outward. There is no one to forgive except yourself, for unconsciously using others, the body, the past or the world to attack you.

3) **Make healing of your mistaken perception your priority over all else.** You must desire to have your perception of the

illness or problem healed, *more* than you want a physical healing, a physical miracle.

4) Look past appearances.
Look beyond what your physical senses tell you of reality. The ego sends these senses out to report back exactly what it wants us to see; they will always confirm "proof" of separation and suffering.

5) Remember there is no hierarchy of illusions.
One illusion is never truer or bigger than another. They're all equally illusory. As we accept and practice this principle, we also learn and demonstrate there is no order of difficulty in miracles. One miracle is not harder or more impossible to achieve than any other. By accepting and demonstrating the illusory nature of illusions, and the maximal power of miracles, we undo everything the ego made to attack us.

6) Accept the Atonement.
In accepting Atonement, we immediately join with and receive God's Will for healing. This unequivocally cancels out the ego's wish to be unfairly treated. This is the miracle! No matter where we see suffering, we must accept the Atonement, the miracle, for our self. If we perceive suffering in another, the past, the body or the world, healing must be accepted in our own mind first. This is the divine undoing of fear and guilt in our perception.

7) Trust in God's Love and healing!
It is already done. Doubt and trust are mutually exclusive. If we doubt, we cannot accept healing.

A helpful acronym for remembering these seven steps:

> **A***pply true denial*
> **W***atch cause and effect*
> **A***ccept healing of perception above all*
> **K***now Truth beyond appearances*
> **E***qualize all illusions*
> **N***egate fear, accept Atonement*
> **S***ee it done*

DISBELIEVING THE EGO'S POLARITIES

Working miracles is not about positive thinking. Only the ego tries to escape its own conflict through positive thinking. Forgiveness and Atonement look past the ego's obsessive polarities of sickness versus health, depression versus happiness, scarcity versus abundance, and life versus death. Instead, Atonement fixes its vision on the changelessness of God's Love, healing and joy.

When it becomes our consistent priority to seek the Kingdom of Heaven as our Holy Self, then all else will be given to us. Really, there is nothing other than this to seek. Every need we attempt to meet through our own will is a distraction from our one True need. Our only True need is to return our awareness to God.

If we desire True healing for our self or another, we must resist the urge to visualize physical healing. This form of manifestation only serves the ego, as it makes the body and the problem real. Visualizing a healthy body (or other positive outcome) merely keeps the problem within the ego's fixed polarities of sickness versus health, or scarcity versus abundance. Yes, the problem may appear to go away as a result. But in doing this, we have merely traded a dream of sickness for a dream of health. A dream of lack for a dream of abundance. This is not real healing, but one more form of the ego's pseudo-healing.

This cannot be repeated often enough: There is no sickness, no pain, no scarcity, no conflict, no loss and no death to heal— *because there are no problems in God's Love.* All problems we seem to encounter remain in our mind, and are reinforced through our fear and defense against them. Defense attests to their ongoing reality in our mind, and therefore in our experience.

When we desire to help another heal, we must recognize and have confidence in the holographic nature of the miracle. The miracle's divine effectiveness is totally inclusive. It defies all ego laws, working entirely outside them. The Atonement, in other words, is the complete transcendence of the ego's fixed polarities. The miracle transcends time and matter, because it is not subject to the laws we made. In fact it was created to undo these laws.

In all cases of suffering, whether a deeply personal trauma or something upsetting we witness on the news, the focal point for healing is found exclusively within our own mind. We cannot heal it out there, no matter how hard we try. The single source of healing for all the ills of the world is always within our own mind, and nowhere else.

Are we willing to surrender our mistaken fears and beliefs about the problem in exchange for Atonement, the miracle that heals all? As we accept this profound healing, we call forth Truth to replace what the ego has sent our body's senses to find. Thus we learn to trust in inner vision, instead of the ego's capricious vacillations between illusions of sickness versus health, scarcity versus abundance, or life versus death.

> *"The real world can actually be perceived. All that is necessary is a willingness to perceive nothing else. For if you perceive both good and evil, you are accepting both the false and the true and making no distinction between them."* T-11.VII.2:6-8

> *"You who fear salvation are choosing death. Life and death, light and darkness, knowledge and perception, are irreconcilable. To believe that they can be reconciled is to believe that God and His Son can [not.]."* T-3.VII.6:5-7

OUR PART IN THE ATONEMENT

Jesus was the first within the Sonship to fully awaken from the ego's dream of death. He undid all our karma, all our disease and all our conflict. He was the first to wholly embody the Christ, as the Holy Self. And He was the first to complete the Atonement.

Because He has already undone the ego's dream of death, we don't need to do it again. We were with Jesus as the one Holy

Self when He accomplished the end of suffering. It has been accomplished for all of us. The only part of us that disagrees with this Truth is the imposter-self, the ego.

All we are asked is to forgive and accept the Atonement for our self, trusting implicitly that in the instant we accept Atonement, it is done. As it is already done, the only remaining decision is whether we choose to receive what is already complete. We don't need to earn Atonement. It is our inheritance. The memory of our absolute guiltlessness and invulnerability will return as we trust in the power of the Atonement.

There is only one prerequisite for undoing all our suffering: We must *accept and receive* the healing that has already been given us. This is the divine undoing of fear and guilt in our mind.

In any Holy Instant, we can choose to surrender our guilt and judgment of the situation—that's really all it takes. Jesus already accomplished the undoing of all our suffering. The question is, will we accept it?

> "You were in darkness until God's Will was done completely by any part of the Sonship. When this was done, it was perfectly accomplished by all. How else could it be perfectly accomplished? My mission was simply to unite the will of the Sonship with the Will of the Father by being aware of the Father's Will myself. This is the awareness I came to give you, and your problem in accepting it is the problem of this world. Dispelling it is salvation, and in this sense I [am] the salvation of the world..."..."As God sent me to you so will I send you to others. And I will go to them with you, so we can teach them peace and union." T-8.IV.3:1-6,10-11

> "You have no problems that He cannot solve by offering you a miracle. Miracles are for you. And every fear or pain or trial you have has been undone. He has brought all of them to light, having accepted them instead of you, and recognized they never were. There are no dark lessons He has not already lightened for you." T-14.XI.9:2-6

FORGIVENESS SUMMARY

• **Accept yourself *now*, even while caught up in loss of peace.**
No matter how upset you might be, remember you are not your thoughts or physical/emotional feelings. You are the quiet witness, choosing to allow your mistaken perception to be healed in this instant.

• **There is only one power, and it is God's Loving Will.**
Employ True denial by denying anything not of God's Love the power to harm. God's Love is the only power. Everything other than God's Love is unreal and doesn't exist.

• **Identify where you believe the cause of the problem lies.**
Remember the real cause is always guilt in your mind. If you remain convinced the cause of any problem lies in an external ego cause, whether in the body, another, the world or the past, you will deny healing of the one cause of every perceived problem.

If you believe the cause is outside, you are separating cause and effect in your mind. To heal the one cause, you must be willing to suspend doubt—even if for only an instant. The miracle occurs in the instant you withdraw your belief in what the ego tells you is real.

Cause and effect are always together in your mind. Even though the seeming symptoms appear so convincingly real out there, they are not. Cause and effect can never be separate in your mind, although the ego makes it appear they are. The ego wishes you to depend on its own guidance instead of your Holy Self.

Because cause and effect are never separate in your mind, the healing of every effect is readily available anytime you prioritize the healing of your perception, above all other concerns and appearances.

You must desire to have your perception healed more than you want a particular physical outcome—for the problem only exists in your own faulty perception of it. Let go of your belief in what your ego-body's senses tell you, and surrender your mistake to Spirit. Look past appearances!

You may still decide to take action to alleviate the seeming problem. You may elect to choose medication, surgery, quitting your job, helping victims of disaster, or any other "solution." But you will have prioritized peace first, by forgiving and accepting Atonement for yourself. In other words, you will have surrendered the single cause of the problem to God within. And because you have done this, genuine healing can occur.

• **Atonement is the undoing of fear, by Spirit.**
You cannot heal or be healed while you are fearful. Yet if you can surrender fear for just one Holy Instant, the miracle can take place. Remember you alone are responsible for fear, therefore you must be willing to surrender it fully. Spirit cannot help you while you willingly cling to fear and doubt.

• **Notice honestly: Is the problem or issue still real for you?**
If you still believe in its reality, you cannot forgive it. True healing, and True forgiveness only take place when you're willing to recognize your own unhealed perception is the sole reason you see a problem. In giving the problem reality, you invest in an imaginary power other than God's Love and healing.

In false forgiveness, the ego sees a problem and wants to either solve it or deny it. Neither action can heal the fundamental cause. In fact, they exacerbate it! To heal, we must agree to join with Holy Spirit to look beyond the error. If we can't honestly look beyond it, we will believe we—the ego—must undo the problem before we can accept the miracle through forgiveness.

> *"The ego's plan is to have you see error clearly first, and then overlook it. Yet how can you overlook what you have made real? By seeing it clearly, you have made it real and [cannot] overlook it." T-9.IV.4:4-6*

> *"Forgiveness through the Holy Spirit lies simply in looking beyond error from the beginning, and thus keeping it unreal for you. Do not let any belief in its realness enter your mind, or you will also believe that you must undo what you have made in order to be forgiven. What has no effect*

does not exist, and to the Holy Spirit the effects of error are nonexistent. By steadily and consistently cancelling out all its effects, everywhere and in all respects, He teaches that the ego does not exist and proves it." T-9.IV.5:3-6

• Ask for and trust *only* in God's Will to be done.
Invoke God's Will to heal all suffering.

• Remember there is no hierarchy of illusions.
Therefore, there is no order of difficulty in miracles.

• Remember all pain, sickness, upsetting people or situations share the sacred purpose of bringing your unconscious guilt, self-hatred and self-attack into your conscious awareness.
This gives you the opportunity to be healed via forgiveness. For this, you can be grateful.

• Forgiveness is remembering the person or problem you perceive is not really there.
The imagined cause (guilt) *must* be in your own mind. Now real healing can occur as you release the guilt from its source, which is always your own mind.

• You have one altar within.
You cannot honor two mutually exclusive devotions on your altar at any one time. If a person or problem upsets you, *the person or problem is your devotion.* And Spirit cannot help you. But when you place your wrong perception on the altar and ask sincerely for healing, Spirit is free to heal your perception.

• You must accept Atonement if you truly want to undo error and heal.
Atonement is the divine correction of your perception. It undoes the guilt and fear that caused the problem. You don't need to understand the problem, you only need to accept the remedy of Atonement in order for miracles of healing to occur.

THE ATONEMENT PROCESS

1) I acknowledge I am not at peace, so I must be wrong-minded. And I want to be at peace, so I ask Spirit now to help me look at my mind.

2) I remember any sign of threat, pain, sickness, conflict, or scarcity is not God's Will. I acknowledge this loss of peace is the work of the ego in my mind. I remember I must deny the ego's appearances, and focus on the Love that is Truth, beyond all appearances.

3) I invite You, Spirit, to look at these fears and judgments with me. I will not judge myself or another while we do this. I will leave a space of total non-judgment, so you can fill it with Love and healing.

4) We look at these fears and judgments together. I say to myself with sincerity: *Even while this appears as a problem, and DESPITE feeling fear, pain, anxiety, unworthiness, anger, guilt, or doubt—I open myself, in this instant, to receive healing through the miracle.*

5) There is only one power; there cannot be two. The ego's suffering is not of God. Trust only in the one power of God's Love. God is in everything I see, because God is in my mind. Together we look past ego appearances, as they represent unconscious wishing with the ego. In looking past appearances, I join with God in asking to perceive only what is true, beyond ego appearances. God is in everything I see, because God is in my mind—*and what God sees through my mind is therefore healed!* Do not doubt this. This is forgiveness. Trust and doubt cannot co-exist, and Love without trust is impossible.

6) A Prayer to Spirit within: *"Spirit, I accept your Atonement. I accept your divine correction of error in my mind, and I allow your healing to flow through my mind. I accept you have already healed both the cause and symptoms/effects of this problem. If the problem's appearance continues, or if continuing symptoms cause me to doubt, I offer these doubts to you as well, for correction in my mind. I remember that any Holy Instant in which I sincerely accept Atonement, it is done! To remain concerned after I have forgiven* and accepted Atonement, is to doubt your Love and prolong the illusion of time and suffering. I remember Love without trust is impossible—doubt and trust cannot coexist. I remember this, and I am grateful Spirit has already healed my mind. I accept the healing of all symptoms/effects. It is done!"

Note: If you are still too fearful to trust *only* in God's Love, you will find comfort in alternatives for now, and this is perfectly okay. For example, you may take medication, see a physician, etc. The most important point to remember is to do these things with conscious awareness of Spirit. Although you might take medication, you no longer take it alone (with guilt). You ask Spirit to heal your perception, while you take or use a temporary alternative. In this way, you are gently led out of fear and into Love. Remember, if you experience any sign of judgment or guilt, exchange this, too, for the miracle.

Atonement Short Cut:
1) **Acknowledge** your perception needs to be healed. Express willingness to surrender it.

2) **Surrender** your wrong-minded perception.

3) **Accept** the Atonement, the miracle. Trust it is done!

THE QUICK FORGIVENESS PRAYER

Place the name of the person, illness or issue that upsets you in the following prayer:

"Holy Spirit, please help me to forgive myself for using _____ to attack myself and to separate from your Love as my Holy Self. Amen."

HEALING AND ATONEMENT

Healing and Atonement are one and the same. Atonement is the divine undoing of guilt and fear in our mind. It is the undoing of the single cause of all suffering. As explained earlier, Jesus has already accomplished the Atonement principle. He undid all errors for everyone, for all time.

The sole reason we don't experience complete healing of the ego dream, is because we still fear God's Love. We don't believe Atonement/forgiveness will heal all. And if we don't believe it, how can we honestly accept the Atonement? Acceptance requires a degree of trust, which can only come about as we willingly surrender our faulty ego beliefs, values, laws and stories. (Please review *"Are you fearful of God? exercise,"* on page 93.)

> *"It is this that makes the holy instant so easy and so natural. You make it difficult, because you insist there must be more that you need do. You find it difficult to accept the idea that you need give so little, to receive so much. And it is very hard for you to realize it is not personally insulting that your contribution and the Holy Spirit's are so extremely disproportionate. You are still convinced that your understanding is a powerful contribution to the truth, and makes it what it is. Yet we have emphasized that you need understand nothing. Salvation is easy just [because] it asks nothing you cannot give right now."* T-18.IV.7.

INVOKING THE MIRACLE:
THE ATONEMENT PRAYER

Let's look at what true forgiveness is, and what it really means to accept the Atonement. What, exactly, do we receive in that

Holy Instant of healing? Atonement is the complete forgiveness of what never was. It is the undoing of the sole cause of whatever form of suffering the ego appeared to make. It matters not what form it might be. Pain, disease, conflict, loss, scarcity or even death are all equally illusory ego appearances. When we accept Atonement for our mistaken perception of these, we accept healing and forgiveness of the single cause of them all. It is our guilt, manifesting as unconscious self-attack, that is healed (along with its seeming symptom).

"The offer of Atonement is universal. It is equally applicable to all individuals in all circumstances. And in it is the power to heal all individuals of all forms of sickness. Not to believe this is to be unfair to God, and thus unfaithful to Him." M-22.6:1-4

The Atonement has already happened. No matter what your physical senses tell you, the world is already healed and so are you. It takes no time for this to occur, because perfect healing is already here. Yet it *does* take time for you to learn to transfer your trust from the ego and its physical senses, to your inner vision and your Holy Self.

You will only value what you trust, and what you value you will see and experience. As your trust in the miracle accelerates, you will value it. As a result, you will witness what you value. You will increasingly see and experience the miracle at work in your own life.

The Atonement requires so very little of you. Yet it returns to you more than you can possibly imagine. When you sincerely accept the miraculous exchange of wrong-minded perception for right-minded perception, your mind is brought back to God in that instant. This is the miraculous forgiveness process—and it really works. Below is a prayer process meant to be practiced with deep conviction and devotion, anytime you feel threatened by fear or death in any of their many illusory forms.

If an issue or person, present or past, is causing you suffering, take this person or situation through the following process:
Get comfortable and take a few deep, relaxing breaths. Make

a conscious decision to accept yourself fully in this instant, no matter what sort of turmoil you might feel. Just deeply accept yourself with each breath, overlooking any judgments or self-judgments that may arise.

Center yourself and drop within to your heart area, gently allowing your breath to open this area for receiving God's healing Love. With each breath, let yourself begin to release the issue that has caused suffering. It may be your own pain or another's. If you are concerned about another, you can heal for them through this process, by accepting the Atonement on their behalf. This will help to heal both of you.

Move through this process and take in its powerful healing. As you do so, you will invoke the miracle. When you accept the Atonement, this is what you wholeheartedly agree to and accept:

• I perceive_____is causing me to suffer. I recognize this suffering is not God's Will, and that I have been mistaken in choosing to believe it. I don't want to believe this suffering any longer. I ask you, Spirit, to heal my perception in this instant.

• As much as I want the form of suffering to cease, I accept that I must desire to have my perception healed *MORE* than I want the seeming form of the problem to be healed.

• I accept the only problem is my perception of it as a problem. No matter if the suffering is great or small, this is always the case.

• I deny anything not of God's Will the power to hurt me or others. God's Loving Will is the only power. The ego has no power unless I choose to believe it does.

• I accept the divine undoing of fear and guilt, which is always the sole cause of my issue.

• I accept the Loving and healing Will of God, allowing it to replace the ego's desire for suffering.

• I claim my eternal guiltlessness, which is the Will of God. Fear and attack fall away as I claim this divine guiltlessness.

• I accept miracles as my inheritance.

• I accept my will is now joined as one with God's Loving Will.

• I surrender my personal responsibility for the seeming problem, as I hand it over to Spirit.

• I accept my Holiness reverses all the laws of the world.

• I accept God's laws always overrule the ego's laws of this world. Sickness, pain, scarcity, conflict and death have no power and no meaning in God.

• I accept healing in God is always certain, and that it has already taken place. I acknowledge healing is always God's Will for me.

• I accept my perception is healed, so the effects/symptoms must heal as well. I recognize the timing of this healing of symptom/effect depends only on my degree of trust in the miracle; the miracle itself is instantaneous.

• I accept my only responsibility now is to trust implicitly that God's Loving Will has already healed the cause of the problem, regardless of any continuing appearances to the contrary. Appearances are just that—appearances only. They are not real. I choose to trust implicitly in God's Loving Will *and nothing else.* Thy Will be done...and so it is. Amen.

EXERCISE: FINDING THE PROBLEM'S SOURCE AND SOLUTION IN THE SAME PLACE

1) Find an issue, person or problem you'd like to resolve. Look at the problem as it currently appears. Notice it is seen as a problem because it threatens the illusory idea that your identity is the body (emotional or physical).

Examples of these threats include:

- self criticism
- anxiety, depression
- anger at another or self (past or present)
- fear for self or another
- emotional or physical pain
- disease (physical or mental); yours or another's
- any form of loss, scarcity or deprivation
(lack of approval, love, money, opportunities, etc.)
- body image, weight issues, etc.
- grief
- death

2) Consciously identify the cause of your problem. It may seem to be in the body, in another, in the past or in the world, but the real and only cause is unconscious guilt. If you feel any lack of peace, you can be certain the cause is in your mind and not external in any form. Anything upsetting you is always the effect of its cause within your own mind. Be willing to acknowledge this.

> "God's Son needs no defense against his dreams. His idols do not threaten him at all. His one mistake is that he [thinks] them real. What can the power of illusions do?"
> T-30.IV.5:12-15

3) Review the issue, no matter how convincing the problem appears, and acknowledge you have been mistaken. You have believed the problem is real, and that it is separate from the answer (which is Spirit in your mind). Make healing your goal. Do not look at the problem as a problem, first making it real, and only afterward attempt to forgive and heal it.

As long as you maintain there is a problem, you won't be open to seeing its cause and remedy rest together in your mind. You must accept cause and effect are both found within your mind, and not out there as the ego insists. Sit quietly with this insight. Allow Holy Spirit to show you the Truth. Perhaps you could journal, and allow Spirit to write to you about this. There are no problems in God's Love. And if you see one, you are deluded. There is no compromise in this. Please recognize your confusion, without any self-judgment. This act of non-judging recognition opens you to the miracle.

The very belief there is a threat, is the immediate alarm that signals the onset of delusion. Our body's eyes do not see Truth, nor do our emotions sense reality. Through the ego, we never recognize Truth, nor the actual purpose beneath our unease. To heal, we must be willing to detect that alarm signal and respond accordingly.

Refuse to analyze the perceived problem, and instead openly confess *you don't know what this is for*. Admit there is a perceptual error in your mind. In this defenseless state, a state of non-resistance, ask for and accept the Atonement, the supreme correction of the one cause of all suffering. All errors emanate from guilt and the unconscious self-attack it projects. The miracle is extended by the Christed Holy Self, as it heals through us.

THE ATONEMENT:
ACCEPTING WHAT IS ALREADY HERE

Atonement is the divine correction of our misperception. All we seem to experience in this world exists only within the mind. As we interact with these mind-made experiences, we either extend Love from our Holy Self, or we indulge in miscreation, projecting unconscious guilt from the ego. In our natural state, we are without guilt and fear. All we are, and all we perceive is Love. In this state, there cannot be an opposite to Love, so no threat can exist, nor any unconscious fear of punishment.

In choosing to perceive from the split mind, we have forgotten who we really are. We have dissociated from the memory of our inherent invulnerability in God's Love as Self.

We have dissociated, because we fear our Self as God's indestructible Will. Once the guilt is removed, this Holy Self is all that exists. No other self and no other laws can threaten this Holy Self, once it is recognized and accepted without opposite.

The cost of embodying the Holy Self is complete relinquishment of all conflicting beliefs, values, goals and defenses—for we made all these sources of suffering through the ego. In letting go of all these, we recognize we really *are* everything good. And because we are everything good, we *have* everything good. In this knowing, there can be no unmet needs, nor any threats requiring defense.

Our terrible fear of awakening to our Holy Self is caused by our dissociation of the ancient memory of our Holy Self's state in God. We have rejected our True Reality. Our inheritance, after it was dissociated, was immediately replaced by the ego's world and its insane laws. Consequently, our dependence on the ego world has made us exceptionally fearful of, and defensive against Truth.

"Yet to give up the dissociation of reality brings more than merely lack of fear. In this decision lie joy and peace and the glory of creation. Offer the Holy Spirit only your willingness to remember, for He retains the knowledge of God and of yourself for you, waiting for your acceptance. Give up gladly everything that would stand in the way of your remembering, for God is in your memory. His Voice will tell you that you are part of Him when you are willing to remember Him and know your own reality again. Let nothing in this world delay your remembering of Him, for in this remembering is the knowledge of yourself." T-10.II.2.

To recall the Truth requires that we gladly give up everything standing in the way of our memory of God's Love as our Identity. Accepting Atonement is accepting the Truth of who we are, and we do it in any Holy Instant. As we do this, we reclaim the memory of our perfect guiltlessness. Our eternal state of perfect innocence already exists. It can never change. Nothing we ever did, or didn't do here in the dream can affect it. But our guilt blinds us to the Truth, making it monumentally difficult to recognize and accept.

We cannot accept Atonement while we still prefer to judge another, a situation or our self. It's our responsibility to renounce our delusional judgments—to admit that although they seem terribly real, we now choose not to believe them any longer.

Acceptance of the Atonement clears illusory distortion from our mind. This removes the barrier that keeps us from seeing and living out from our Holy Self. The ego acts as a convincing smoke screen, making its illusions seem oh-so-real, so we won't open our self to acceptance of the miracle instead.

If we believe we are seeing or feeling anything that is not total Love and joy, we are delusional. And that is our cue: "I *must* be delusional because I perceive pain, loss, sadness, depression, grief, anger, jealousy or scarcity. If I perceive any of these, it's always a sign I've fallen for the ego's unconscious wish to be unfairly treated. I've allowed this ego wish to temporarily hypnotize me."

The sincere choice for forgiveness gives us immediate access to our Holy Self's state of being. The Atonement is our acceptance of what is already here—our natural inheritance. Our inheritance reveals itself in the absence of the ego's deception tactics. We don't need to earn the Atonement. We just need to decide we don't want our present perception, and we do want True perception.

> "To remember is merely to restore to your mind [what is already there]. You do not make what you remember; you merely accept again what is already there, but was rejected. The ability to accept truth in this world is the perceptual counterpart of creating in the Kingdom. God will do His part if you will do yours, and His return in exchange for yours is the exchange of knowledge for perception. Nothing is beyond His Will for you. But signify your will to remember Him, and behold! He will give you everything but for the asking." T-10.II.3.

RELEASING ALL FORMS OF SUFFERING

Any form of suffering is an attack and is authored by the ego, never by God's Loving Will. As long as we accept that even one form of attack is real, we will believe we can be attacked. If we can be attacked, we are not invulnerable—therefore we must not know who we are in Truth.

Nothing can harm us. We are the Holy Self, the Kingdom of Heaven. There are no degrees of insanity in adherence to the ego; one form of attack carries the entire ego thought system of attack.

While we attack our body with pain or sickness, our self or another with judgment, or indulge in depression, worry, anxiety or a host of other symptoms of ego insanity, we deny our healing.

Through attack, we teach our self we are not the Holy Self, but the ego. We can only cherish one devotion on our inner altar at any given time. When we perceive attack, this is the idol we place on our altar. When we release our perception of attack through forgiveness, Love is restored to its central place on our inner altar. We cannot keep both the perception of attack and Love together; the presence of one excludes the other.

When we believe in the ego's appearances, we deny our Holy Self. And when we deny our Self, we attack it. So whenever we perceive our self as unfairly treated, we are denying our True Self as God's perfect Will. No matter who or what upsets us, we always attack our Self first! When we believe suffering is possible, we deny our Self as God created us. No perception of attack occurs without first attacking our Self. The invulnerable Holy Self is wholly incapable of attack, or even of perceiving attack. Only the ego perceives attack, and only the ego can appear to be hurt.

"All attack is Self attack. It cannot be anything else. Arising from your own decision not to be what you are, it is an attack on your identification. Attack is thus the way in which your identification is lost, because when you attack, you must have forgotten what you are. And if your reality is God's, when you attack you are not remembering Him.

*This is not because He is gone, but because you are actively
choosing not to remember Him." T-10.II.5.*

When we are upset, it is because we choose to be unfairly treated.
It is a decision (conscious or not), and it occurs so quickly we
think we did not make it. Therefore we believe it occurred
independent of us.

If we set peace of mind as our one True goal, our peace
could never be threatened again. Peace of mind is an internal
decision, a disciplined commitment that every situation becomes
a means to reach the goal of peace. Armed with the powerful tool
of forgiveness, we can achieve this goal in every circumstance,
provided we do not value a separate ego agenda instead of, or in
addition to peace.

Peace arises from within and does not depend on anything
external. Safety then, is the complete relinquishment of attack.

*"If you realized the complete havoc this makes of your peace
of mind you could not make such an insane decision. You
make it only because you still believe it can get you something
you want. It follows, then, that you want something other
than peace of mind, but you have not considered what it
must be. Yet the logical outcome of your decision is perfectly
clear, if you will only look at it. By deciding against your
reality, you have made yourself vigilant [against] God and
His Kingdom. And it is this vigilance that makes you afraid
to remember Him." T-10.II.6.*

It is this vigilance against God's Love as our Holy Self that
invites untold suffering. We prefer to suffer the consequences of
rejecting Truth, rather than drop our defenses against it. When
we perceive we have been unfairly treated or victimized by
anyone or anything, we choose to defend against Truth. And it is
for precisely this the power of the Atonement was given us. True
correction of our perception offers us complete healing in any
moment we choose differently.

THE ATONEMENT: WILLING WITH GOD

Everything we do through the ego is idle wishing, and it's all done from fear. We join with illusion. In reality, nothing happens except suffering. Yes, we see many things and experience a vast range of emotions, yet nothing real occurs. Unknowingly, in our choice to believe and live out from the ego's perception, we have abandoned our Self. All betrayal and abandonment arises first from this desertion of our true Self. No one and nothing could harm us in Truth, if we stayed present in awareness of our Holy Self.

We can return to our Self in any instant we desire that our perception be healed. The Atonement, True healing, occurs in our willingness to join with Love. This can take place in any instant fear is absent. For that instant to occur, we must surrender the ego. Any moment we choose to exchange fear for God's Love, we release the ego's will and join in Love to Will with God. We choose God in that instant. Perhaps one instant is all we can manage, but one is all it takes. In consciously choosing Love, we join with God's Will, thereby strengthening it in our awareness and experience.

God Will is our perfect joy, Love, abundance and healing. God's Will is our own True Will, because it is our Holy Self's Will. In Reality only God's Will exists, yet we seem to see and experience something very different here in the ego's dream. Yet we always see exactly what we want to see and experience. And as we have learned, most of what we ask to see is unconscious guilt and self-attack, until we exhume the ego's thought system. Although it doesn't always feel like it, we suffer because we choose to. Suffering still has value for us.

"When you want only love you will see nothing else." T-12. VII.8:8

It's a bit like tuning into a TV station: the Doom and Gloom Channel. When you're watching it 24 hours a day, every day, even as you sleep, you will believe in it completely. By choosing the ego, we are glued to that one station. We have no idea there is a big beautiful world out there, magnificently safe, forgiven and forgiving. In Truth, this lovely world is part of our inner landscape. The *Course* calls it the Real World. It's already here within our right mind, existing simultaneously with the ego's world. And this Real World becomes our experience by systematically taking every judgment and suffering to Spirit in exchange for forgiveness and the miracle.

God's reality is all there is. Perfection already exists. Healing has already happened. The Real World is already here. Jesus already overcame all our suffering and karma. He even overcame death through His resurrection. God's Will is already complete— we do not have to wait for it. It is already done. Rest deeply in this Truth! Your only responsibility is to wholeheartedly accept and receive this healing.

The only reason we seem to see and experience suffering, is the same reason we don't see immediate miracles: We don't yet believe in God's Love as our Self. We perceive our self apart from perfect Love and innocence. We still trust the ego's self-evaluation more than God's, so our own self-doubt delays the miracle's perfect immediacy.

God's Will for us is perfect joy without interruption or opposition. And God's Will is already done! If we see anything apart from this perfect Love, we are delusional. And we further our delusion when we believe and attempt to problem solve independent from Spirit.

When we do this, we place a veil of terror over the Truth of God's Loving Reality. This ego veil is the world we seem to see. Whenever we perceive something upsetting within the veil, the choice of response is always ours. Do we remember it's just a veil, and look beyond it to join with the brilliant light of God's Love and healing? Or do we join with the darkened images in the veil, trying to heal or fix them by using other images found within the same veil of terror?

God's Reality is all that exists. All else is illusion. In any present moment we can invoke the miracle effortlessly. No preparation is necessary, except heartfelt desire to exchange fearful perception for Love. In fact, there is nothing more we *can* do! Anything more than this will come exclusively from the ego. The ego thrives on action and control; it dies in surrender to Love.

The Atonement is an instant of deep, trusting surrender into Love. In this instant, fear and guilt do not exist, so the problem falls away. God's Reality is now free to be revealed in our awareness.

We join with God's reality in this instant, and what was previously perceived as separate, now becomes one. For in this instant, the false self falls away and we embody the God Self. God's perfect Will is recognized as *our* perfect Will. In this instant, our defense against God's Love and healing is put aside, as we join with our own True Will. This is the miracle, and within it all True healing occurs. The miracle transcends the laws of time. All miracles are already here, waiting for us to receive them. The miracle heals all, because it undoes the guilt that is the one cause of all suffering.

> *"Atonement heals with certainty, and cures all sickness."*
> *W-140.4:1*

In the Holy Instant, we release ourselves into the Atonement. As we do, we open to receive what is already here in God's Reality. The veil of terror is pierced, for our willingness to accept and receive Atonement disarms the ego's defense against God's Love.

A MEDITATION: WILLING WITH GOD

Please note: To download the audio version of this meditation, go to www.EndOfDeath.com

In the Atonement, we Will with God. There is nothing in the universe more powerful than this act. How do we Will with God instead of wishing with the ego? Let's do a little exercise to help bring this teaching out of the intellectual realm, and into the heart of your being.

For this meditation exercise, think of something you truly desire. It might be something you think you desperately need right now, or it could be something you've yearned for deeply over a period of years. Please be radically honest. Whatever it is, search your mind and heart to bring this desire into our meditation exercise. We'll take a look at your desire from two very different perspectives.

Wishing with the Ego

Get comfortable, and find a place where you won't be disturbed for 15 minutes or so. As you settle in, close your eyes and take a few deep, slow breaths. With each breath, feel your body relaxing more and more. Let yourself melt. Let all of your muscles relax into deep peace and safety. Find a place of deep tranquility within your body, and drop slowly down into it. When you have reached this place of rest and stillness, call to your heart's desire. Ask it to meet you there. Now really look closely at this thing you yearn so deeply for.

As you look upon it, notice this thing you yearn for stands apart from you. You want it. But you don't yet have it. It may be in the past. Or in the future—or maybe it is just out of reach. You want to join with it, but you can't. There is a gap between you and this object of desire.

Feel deeply into this sense of lack, this gap. This sense of separation from what you love. How does it pray? How does this sense of separation and lack attempt to bring you what you want? At best, it may say, *"I hope Spirit hears my call. I hope Spirit will answer my call."* What does this feel like, this state of need, this state of helpless desire and lack? Where do you feel it in your body?

Now...take some deep, slow breaths. Gradually remove your focus from this experience and become aware of your entire body. Very slowly and gently, release your focus and just relax. Leave this exercise, and open your heart and mind to experience something very different.

Willing with God

Now we'll slowly move back into a quiet, restful place within. Breathing slowly and deeply, hold the same object of greatest desire. Don't let it go. Breathe with it; let it breathe with you. See it clearly as being here with you, right now.

Joining your heart with God's Love, drop deeply into this knowing: "I trust completely that Spirit knows exactly what I need. Spirit has *already* answered my call. I openheartedly accept the essence of what I yearn for, is deeply yearning for me. I rest in total trust that Spirit has already healed my perception of lack, separation and scarcity.

I trust completely that my needs are already met; that Spirit wants only joy, Love and peace for me. I remember any form of lack, separation, pain, loss or sickness is not God's Will—and I want only God's Will. I now join with God's Loving Will as I trust, accept and receive my joyful inheritance. To accept and receive is all that is asked of me. It is already done."

Now gently breathe in your acceptance of the knowing that all your needs are met. Breathe this in throughout your body. Bring it down into your heart. Bring it into your abdomen. Breathe it into your pelvic region, and all the way down to your feet. Keep breathing your acceptance all the way down into the Earth, and let it take root there. Feel every cell of your body fill with gentle acceptance of God's Loving Will.

Can you sense that you have already received the essence of what you thought was separate from you? Can you rest in a sense of gratitude that this is so? Feel this newfound sense of peace, this release from hunger and lack.

Now...gently return your awareness to your body. Become aware of your surroundings, and slowly come back into the room. When you are ready, open your eyes.

Conclusion

What was your experience with each of these extremely different ways of perceiving? Which of these two raised a sense of separation and lack? And which brought about a sense of joining and peace?

As you have seen, wishing with the ego is very different from Willing with God. Perhaps you will be inspired to take a good look at all the areas of your life where you've been unconsciously wishing with the ego. Review them with Spirit, and consciously decide to Will them with God instead.

Wishing with the ego means you project from fear. As such, it is an unconscious joining with the ego in self-sabotage. It is separation in disguise. Wishing with the ego is a prayer arising from lack. But there is no lack in God, therefore God cannot respond to that which does not exist. He cannot fulfill a prayer requesting to remedy any sense of deprivation. Praying to fulfill a desire born of a sense of lack ensures we attract more deprivation from the ego.

Willing with God is willing with Love. It is extending from Love. It is True union. Therefore it is a conscious joining with our Holy Self to bring about limitless healing and joy. When we align with Gods' Love within, we will know there is no lack in God. Therefore there can be no lack in our self. Only guilt causes a sense of lack. All our needs are met. And True prayer declares that we trust God's abundance with absolute certainty. This prayer is one of gratitude to God, declaring we joyfully accept that God's Will be done.

AN EXERCISE: WHAT DO YOU DESIRE MORE THAN PEACE AND FORGIVENESS?

Bringing our illusions to Truth is a necessary first step in spiritual awakening. What we think we want, and what we want to avoid, represent our current blocks to the awareness of Love's presence.

1) What do you desire *more* than the peace of God?
Is there anything, anyone, or a situation that you desire more than you want to have your perception healed?

Exercise: Name something (or someone) you think you want more than peace.

I want _____ more than peace because I believe it would bring me _____.

• Now, look at this statement and ask, "Is this really true?"

• What do you think this thing will give you that your healed perception (forgiveness) will not?

2) What do you resist?
When we try to resist or avoid something, this thing is what we actually desire more than Truth. Why is this? Anything we fear or try to control without Spirit, will act as an unconscious magnet. It draws the feared thing to us, and blocks our ability to trust in God's Love. What we fear and resist become unconscious idols that the ego holds apart from Spirit in our mind. Because they are not surrendered to Spirit, we will attract them into our experience. For example, if I fear betrayal or abandonment, I will attract these.

3) Is there anything, anyone or any circumstance that is causing you concern or suffering?
Is there anything you feel you need to control?

4) Is there anything, or anyone from your past or present that still upsets you now?

5) Review your answers.
Which of these are you now prepared to surrender to Spirit for forgiveness and acceptance of the Atonement? Make sure to take these through the Atonement/forgiveness process (on page 297).

WHAT DO YOU DESIRE MORE
THAN FORGIVENESS?

When we desire healing for our self or someone else more than we want to undo our own mistaken perception, we unknowingly add to the very problem we seek to cure. We make the sickness or problem an idol above and apart from God's Love within. While we still fear something and have not yet forgiven it by surrendering it in exchange for the miracle, we will unconsciously continue to attract it. This is ego manifestation at work. And while everybody is subject to this cycle of ego manifestation, it can be a particular challenge for those in the healing profession.

A patient appears to require healing, psychologically, emotionally or physically. Yet as the practitioner, it is always *my own perception* in need of healing. If I perceive suffering, it's my mind that calls for healing. I learn to accept Atonement and the miracle for myself—and only then am I free to share it. Until I do, I cannot help heal the guilt that caused the perceived problem.

Tomas and I learned a lot about healing in 2009 and 2010, but not quite enough to trust only in God's Love. Neither one of us yet possessed the conviction necessary to heal completely. As a result, Tomas awakened though his experience with illness, and it was a joy to behold. But he awakened in the dream, as did many masters before him. And awakening in the ego dream is very different than awakening from the ego's dream of birth and death altogether.

I have learned many things since Tomas left the body. And my trust in God's Love has grown immensely since then. Perhaps this story will tell you just how much:

At one of our *Power of Power* retreats this year, a participant leaned forward with great determination and said, "I want to experience a literal miracle." A minute later, he suffered a heart attack and "died!"

Looking firmly past appearances, we refused to be swayed by the emergency before us. As one person continuously administered CPR, the rest of the group held this man's Holy perfection in our right minds, each of us unwaveringly accepting Atonement for our self and therefore for him.

The result? Although he was "dead" for nearly half an hour with no oxygen to the brain, he is now very much alive and anything but brain-dead. Doctors can find no explanation for this miracle, but I know without a doubt exactly what happened.

There is nothing, in short, that I desire more than forgiveness. Will you join with me in this?

EPILOGUE

Although Tomas Vieira has seemingly passed, he is living the undoing of fear along with me. The evidence is undeniable. He is very present, and this book could not have been written without his participation. Just before he passed he told us, "There is no death, and through the Christ in me, I pledge to demonstrate this is true."

This book unites with *A Course in Miracles* in the one message: The end of guilt is the end of death. This is the closing of a dream of fear, and our joyful return to Love and innocence with no opposite. You are God's treasure. No one and nothing is more valuable to God than you.

If this book has helped undo your fear of God's Love as your Holy Self, I am genuinely overjoyed. Thank you for joining with me, joining with "us." In your healing we all heal. And for this I thank you with all my heart.

~ Nouk

ABSOLUTE CERTAINTY

The DEATH of DEATH

ABOUT EMBODIMENT

Editor's note: The teachings within the *End Of Death* series are undeniably powerful on their own. Yet in the *Power of Power: Know ThySelf* retreat workshops, embodiment is given equal priority. For it is this embodiment process of moving from intellect alone to heart-based knowing, that enables participants to truly absorb these deeper teachings of *A Course in Miracles*.

In the retreat workshops, Stacy Sully's daily embodiment meditations, exercises and one-to-one sessions have allowed participants to heal and transform individually and together as a group. It is our wish to allow readers of this book to experience some of this vitally important embodiment process for themselves.

Following is a text that explains the embodiment process. Stacy has also recorded a thirty-two minute guided embodiment meditation expressly for readers of *The End Of Death*. The meditation can be downloaded at *www.EndOfDeath.com*. To learn more about embodiment, go to *www.stacysully.com*.

THE KINGDOM OF HEAVEN IS WITHIN: EMBODIMENT OF THE LIVING CHRIST

By Stacy Sully

To *Know thySelf* requires that we allow Spirit to show us all aspects of our self, the conscious and unconscious, so we may come to know the Truth of our innocent and radiant nature. In the knowing of this Truth, we become it, and embody it. The Truth in the words *I am not a body, I am free* can be claimed only through the heart, and lived through direct experience as the Christ.

To *Know thySelf* asks that we liberate the unconscious, by bringing the Light that we are to all the hidden places inside that are begging for illumination. In Jesus' words: *"to love yourselves as I love you."*

By doing this, we come to recognize self-love and Divine Love are One Love. We set free our deep hidden judgments, guilt and fear from the illusion of separation—this means we rest within and stand unconditionally available and accepting, as the Way, the Truth and the Light that we are. This is the ultimate in forgiveness.

Our physical form has become the storehouse of the unconscious. So many people remain disconnected from their bodies, deep down inside harboring a hatred of their form. In this hatred/denial/judgment, the perfect value of the form is disregarded and lost—and also lost is the deeper direct experience of Truth, as well as the invulnerably anchored connection to Heaven that can be found through the body. Our birthright of Divinely intimate communion with our Holy Self remains untapped, because we fear exploration of something that is not "real."

Our resistance to looking squarely at our shadow is the very refuge denial hides in, persuading us to ignore the body on our spiritual journey. Yet, when we deny nothing, we welcome genuine intimacy with God. We lay our self open before the Divine, freely giving access to every inch of the unconscious that has concealed itself within the form.

As we release our fear of inhabiting the body in full acceptance of the Light that we are, we begin the deep descent inward. We move into the heart and out of the head; as we do this, we bring Heaven to Earth. We anchor the Christ through the form. Surrendering all and denying nothing, we experience fearless embodiment of the Christ Self.

The deeply sleeping unconscious mind experiences its own revelations, and its own liberation as the call for Love is answered. We bring our awareness within, and the heart's capacity expands. Consciousness shifts into a deeper, more universal knowing of itself. This expanded consciousness is like the sun penetrating the leaves and branches of the mighty oak tree. It does not rest until it has permeated all the way down to the very deepest roots. Imagine being available to clear the unconscious at these levels, welcoming the wisdom and expansion that follows in the wake of this clearing.

"The body, if properly understood, shares the invulnerability of the Atonement to two-edged application. This is not because the body is a miracle, but because it is not inherently open to misinterpretation. The body is merely part of your experience in the physical world. Its abilities can be and frequently are overevaluated. However, it is almost impossible to deny its existence in this world. Those who do so are engaging in a particularly unworthy form of denial. The term "unworthy" here implies only that it is not necessary to protect the mind by denying the unmindful. If one denies this unfortunate aspect of the mind's power, one is also denying the power itself." T-2.IV.3:6-13

Our bodies are actually *designed* to hold the radiance of the Divine mind. The movement of our Light into our form is the essence of Love: to *Know thySelf.* Even beneath the most extreme appearances of polarity, Love enfolds us at our core. This embodiment of the Light, and of our True essence, is the healing of the mind. This is the True healing of humanity.

We can use our physical form to help enlarge our perception. The goal in this is to achieve real vision, of which the physical eye is incapable. Learning to do this is the body's True usefulness.

The greatest response one can offer to a call for Love, is to be available within. Every call for Love originates from here. Our willingness to access our inner Being ensures we are aligned with *cause* in the mind—not the illusory effects on the horizontal plane.

Our alignment with the Christ is the vertical path. This is where True healing occurs. Within each of us is a central column of primordial essence/Light. This vertical column of living Light is the bridge between Heaven and Earth. This vertical axis is what Jesus referred to when He said, *"No man cometh unto the Father but by me."* He is referring to our alignment with Source, as it appears in this world. Jesus goes on to say:

"this does not mean that I am in any way separate or different from you except in time, and time does not really exist. The statement is more meaningful in terms of a vertical rather than horizontal axis. You stand below me and I stand below God. In the process of "rising

up" I am higher because without me the distance between God and man would be too great for you to encompass. I bridge the distance as an elder brother to you on the one hand and as a Son of God on another."T-1.II.4:1-5

This deep union with Truth cannot be achieved through the intellect. Only the heart knows how to birth consciousness, and when we choose the heart instead of the head, we fulfill our pure potential.

When Jesus says, *"the Kingdom is within,"* He means our True access point is the heart, in natural alignment with the vertical channel. When we our self know this, we automatically orient our awareness within, and away from the illusory horizontal world. In this way, we begin to use our body to enlarge our perception. Christ vision deepens, as we ground our self in the present moment.

As you begin to experience this vertical alignment within the body, you will also notice a natural centering that takes place. Stand with arms outstretched and notice the center of your chest; close your eyes and breathe. You'll find an intuitive knowing of what Jesus refers to when He says, *"You stand below me and I stand below God."*

In this position, the mind obeys and the heart surrenders. It is the position Jesus took on the cross. Heart surrendered and arms outstretched, He embraced the world and collapsed all time within His heart. Embodied within Him was a love of humanity this deep and vast: *"I and my Father are One."*

When Jesus said, *"Forgive them Father, for they know not what they do,"* He could have just as easily said, "Forgive them Father, for they know not who they are."

Utilizing the body, we begin to use this vertical axis consciously with Spirit. In doing so, we access some of the deepest layers of the unconscious, bringing unprecedented healing to the mind. In the process, we come to know our Self Truly, as the infinite radiance we are. We embody as the Living Christ.

The body becomes a temple to God—but only when we willingly abdicate the ego along with all its seeming needs. Ego uses the body as an "end" in itself, while Holy Spirit uses the body purely as a "means" to communicate our invulnerability (our infinite Love) in God.

As the ground of Being becomes directly experienced through the body, fear can be met by Spirit viscerally and cellularly. This meeting allows Light to live and breathe in the very marrow of our bones. Through this healing journey, consciousness transcends the body to realize its GodSelf again and again, infinitely extending.

By offering the body as a "means" to Holy Spirit, we begin to rest within Life, rather than resisting it. In Truth, Life is within. When we know this for our self, we look out upon the world with new eyes. Christ vision becomes anchored through the heart, and we become deeply known to our Self. And with this inner mastery, perception is refined, as wisdom becomes Knowledge.

As we heal, we *become* the living Truth, the ground of Being. We anchor and embody this Truth, this Beingness, wholly and completely. Human/Divine......Divine/human. Self-love and Divine Love—we discover for our self they are the same One Love, the same One Truth.

"When you know yourselves then you will be known, and you will understand that you are children of the living father." (Thomas 3:4)

What happens when a spontaneous glimpse of this reality dawns? If you manage to authentically integrate it, this experience becomes embodied, or grounded, as part of your permanent awareness. If it has *not* become grounded in the body, this glimpse remains in the conceptual intellectual realm. Although it may have become a deeper understanding, it doesn't yet "live" within you as a stable realization.

The vertical column of light is a valuable tool in the embodiment process. We use it consciously to unearth the unconscious, and to directly experience the Love that is the substance beneath everything that is.

The deep healing of the mind that occurs when we consciously practice this way is far beyond what the ego can witness. The body becomes a conscious vehicle of Light and Love. A True communication device.

"You are not limited by the body, and thought cannot be made flesh. Yet mind can be manifested through the body if it goes beyond it and does not interpret it as limitation." T-8-VII.14:1-2

The Holy purpose has a name: Love. Embodied, grounded, present. Immersed and resting in quiet stillness of deep ground and open truth. This is the ultimate expression of Love.

About *The End of Death, Volume Two:*

Jesus' teachings within *A Course in Miracles* herald the end of our unconscious attraction to suffering and self-attack. We need no longer relive the crucifixion over and over. The resurrection is now upon us! We consciously claim this sacred rebirth in every instant we forgive and accept the Atonement, the miracle that collapses all time, suffering and death. There is no death. Only life, joy and Love await us now...

> *"The end of the world is not its destruction, but its translation into Heaven." T-11.VIII.1:8*
>
> *"Very simply, the resurrection is the overcoming or surmounting of death. It is a reawakening or a rebirth; a change of mind about the meaning of the world. It is the acceptance of the Holy Spirit's interpretation of the world's purpose; the acceptance of the Atonement for oneself. It is the end of dreams of misery, and the glad awareness of the Holy Spirit's final dream. It is the recognition of the gifts of God. It is the dream in which the body functions perfectly, having no function except communication." M-28.1:1-6*

The End of Death, Volume Two is subtitled *How to Work Miracles.* It is a practical exploration of this resurrection experience, as we learn to embrace the Real World and live out from it. We become *literal* miracle workers who demonstrate the power of the risen Holy Self.

A large section of Volume Two redefines the body's sacred purpose, restoring it to its rightful function as a vehicle used exclusively for communicating the peace, healing and Love of God. With this as its sole purpose, it can no longer teach attack through disease, pain, aging, scarcity, conflict or death.

PRACTICAL SUPPORT ON THE JOURNEY

If you feel strongly drawn to this spiritual path, please consider reaching out for some mutual support while courageously working to undo the ego thought system. This process is made much easier and less fearful when we join with like-minded others who are genuinely committed to the same path. We all need mighty companions to help illuminate the darkest parts of our journey, especially when confusion and doubt appear to overshadow our ability to trust in Holy Spirit.

We have founded a nonprofit organization dedicated to sharing these deeper teachings of *A Course in Miracles*. *Take Me to Truth, Inc.* is its name, and our website is www.Undoing-the-Ego.org

On our website, go to the HELPFUL RESOURCES link, where we offer support in the form of the following:

• *Power of Power: Know ThySelf* retreats:
Note: A limited number of scholarships are available for these retreats.

• Teleclasses

• Phone mentoring with Sparo Vigil

• An e-newsletter to keep you up to date with new material and resources as they become available. Please do sign up.

Other resources:

• Facebook support group: on Facebook, search *Take Me to Truth; Undoing the Ego*, and ask to join.

• One-on-one embodiment Sessions with Stacy Sully by phone: StacySully.com

• For more practical exercises and diagrams, some of which are not included in this book, go to www.EndOfDeath.com

As our fledgling nonprofit grows, we trust we will be able to offer many more helpful resources. Eventually, our dream is to secure our own retreat center. If you feel guided to support and join our mission through financial donation or in other ways, we would be immensely grateful: Undoing-the-Ego.org/donate

As you embrace and embody these deeper teachings of the *Course*, you will undoubtedly experience many miracles for yourself. You may wish to provide encouragement to others by sharing these experiences. If so, please visit our MIRACLES BLOG to contribute your miracle experiences at www.EndOfDeath.com

ABOUT the book *Take Me to Truth; Undoing the Ego*

This book, *The End of Death*, is the result of Nouk's own continuing journey on the path of awakening from the ego. She also co-authored a hugely popular best-selling book, *Take Me to Truth; Undoing the Ego* in 2007 with Tomas Vieira.

Take Me to Truth was written as an introduction to the principles of *A Course in Miracles*. It is a practical book that describes in-depth the ego thought system. It is also the first book to expand in detail the *Course's* section on *The Development of Trust* (Manual for Teachers), which describes the typical stages one might experience on the path of undoing the ego.

Together with that broader explanation of the six stages of the development of trust, a large portion of the book is dedicated to Holy Relationships—the healing of relationships, through transformation from the conditional, special relationship to the unconditional, miraculous Unified Relationship, or Holy Relationship.

Take Me To Truth; Undoing the Ego is widely available online, or ask for it wherever books are sold.

CPSIA information can be obtained at www.ICGtesting.com
Printed in the USA
LVOW11s1149160214

373870LV00001B/55/P